THE
ECLECTIC
ENCYCLOPEDIA
OF
ENGLISH

NATHAN BIERMA

William, James & Co. • Sherwood, Oregon • www.wmjasco.com

Publisher   Jim Leisy (james_leisy@wmjasco.com)
Editor   Tom Sumner
Publicity   Dan Eichler

Printed in the U.S.A.

Rights and Permissions
William, James & Co.
22462 SW Washington St.
Sherwood, Oregon 97140

William, James & Co. is an imprint of Franklin, Beedle & Assoc., Inc.

Library of Congress Cataloging-in-Publication data

Bierma, Nathan L. K.
  The eclectic encyclopedia of English / Nathan Bierma.
      p. cm.
  Includes index.
  ISBN 978-1-59028-209-0 (alk. paper)
  1. English language--Etymology--Dictionaries. I. Title.

PE1580.B54 2009
422.03--dc22

                                2008051200

CONTENTS

INTRODUCTION

Five Strange Twists and Turns in the History of English

I USED TO BE picky—really picky—about English grammar and usage. By the time I was in high school, at the dinner table I was correcting sentences that ended in a preposition. I was shaking my head scornfully when someone confused "lay" and "lie." I was trying to right the course of the English language, one error at a time.

All that changed when I took my favorite course in college, "The History of the English Language" with language genius Jim Vanden Bosch at Calvin College. That's when I learned the truth: English, over its long history, has changed so much and so drastically, and has added words from so many different languages, that by now it is nearly unrecognizable from its Beowulf days, and any notion of overall logic or purity in the language can be exposed as laughable.

Each new century, it seems, gives English an extreme makeover. An introductory look at just five of these makeovers should be enough to prove two points: first, that language change is inevitable and often inexplicable, and second, any perception you or I have of an "error" in the language is just a function of historical perspective. Just as no one raises any complaints anymore about these five changes, so no one will notice or care about, centuries hence, most of what picky purists notice and care about today. That's why, as you'll notice throughout this book, I'm constantly trying to calm furious readers down with some simple historical perspective.

So here are five quick history lessons that show the futility of trying to get the English language to stand still or trying to keep others from budging it—five strange twists and turns in the history of the English language.

1. **THE COLLAPSE OF CASE ENDINGS IN MIDDLE ENGLISH.**
   In Old English, a millennium ago, the same word had different endings depending on how it was being used—as most of the

world's major languages still do today. So, for example, "tham waetere" meant "to the water," while "thaes wateres" meant "of the water," as Guy Deutscher explains in *The Unfolding of Language.*

It's true that English seems simpler now without these case endings. But this change created its own headaches. For one thing, it made English reliant on word order for meaning—"You ate the fish" is much different than "the fish ate you." Other languages just change the endings and don't have to worry about where the word has to stand in the sentence. We have to make sure to put every word in the right place.

This change also meant that English has gotten cluttered with helping verbs—like "has" and "gotten" in the phrase "has gotten cluttered." New words had to take on the work that the old endings used to do. That gave English what I call a "clunky modality"—a cumbersome system of auxiliaries and modals, like "has" and "gotten." What Old English achieved—and most world languages still can achieve—with endings, Modern English has to achieve by piling on modals, as in "going to be helped" or "might have been being helped." By comparison, other languages seem more efficient. What appears to be a simplification—from an elaborate word-ending system to a lean one—instead gives English a clunky modality.

2. **THE MERGER OF THE FOUR FORMS OF THE SECOND-PERSON PRONOUN INTO ONE.**
This is the biggest scandal in the history of English grammar. English used to have four words for "you"—the singular "thou" and "thee," and the plural "ye" and "you." Each word had a different function, depending on whether it was singular or plural, and subject or object. It was a useful setup.

But in the 1500s, people started using "ye" and "you" in place of "thou" and "thee," and before long, "you" took over for "ye." Eventually, only "you" was left. Ever since, English has lacked a distinction between the singular and plural "you." Ask a group of people, "Did you see that movie?" and someone can say, "You mean all of us, or just him?"

Before this change happened, if you wanted to tell a group of people to eat their vegetables—and then reiterate the point to a particular person—you would say, "Ye know they're good for you. And thou knows they're good for thee." Today that's "You know they're good for you. And you know they're good for you."

Imagine if the same merger happened among first-person pronouns. Instead of saying, "We know they're good for us. At least, I know they're good for me," you'd be stuck saying, "Us know they're good for us. At least, us know they're good for us."

Ironically, people consider the informal plural pronouns "you guys" and "y'all" (in Southern dialects) to be ignorant or lazy, when in fact those words are very smart attempts to rescue the helpful distinction between singular and plural second-person pronouns in English. We'd be smart to adopt them in Standard English, but stubborn snobbishness has so far prevented it.

3. THE GREAT VOWEL SHIFT.

The 1500s were a turbulent time for English. Around the same time that "thou" and "thee" were being evicted from English, the so-called "Great Vowel Shift" was wreaking havoc on English pronunciation.

Up until this time, English spelling was more predictable: the "ea" vowel combination was always pronounced "ay," so "meat" and "threat" rhymed with "great." Now those three words have three different sounds.

The letter "a" was always pronounced "ah," as in "father," until the Great Vowel Shift. Now it has a different sound in "apple," and a different sound in "favor." English learners are left to sort out when to use which pronunciation.

As Melinda Menzer points out in her website on the Great Vowel Shift (at www.furman.edu/~mmenzer), knowing some of these pronunciation changes is the key to getting some of Shakespeare's puns. In *Henry IV*, Shakespeare plays on the fact that the word "reason" rhymed with "raisin" (they were both pronounced "ray-sin"). Falstaff says, "If Reasons were as plenty as Blackberries, / I would give no man a Reason upon compulsion, I." "Reasons" sounds like "raisins," so it sounds like Falstaff is saying, "If Raisins were as plenty as Blackberries . . ."

The Great Vowel Shift is one of the main reasons schools have spelling tests. If the Shift had never happened, spelling would be more straightforward (*see* **spelling**). As Deutscher writes in *The Unfolding of Language*, "So really, it is unfair to say that English spelling is not an accurate rendering of speech. It is—it's only that it renders the speech of the sixteenth century."

4. **THE LOSS OF CAPITALIZED ABSTRACT COMMON NOUNS.** English writers used to capitalize words on a whim. Now, only proper names are capitalized in a sentence after the first word.

Jonathan Swift, for example, once wrote in a letter, "Your Lordship hardly leaves us room to offer our good Wishes, removing all our Difficulties, and supplying all our Wants, faster than the most visionary Projector can adjust his Schemes." (The letter, by the way, was titled "Proposal for Correcting, Improving and Ascertaining the English Tongue"—proving that dissatisfaction with language, and attempts to "improve" it, are both very old and very unlikely to make much difference.)

Swift's capitalization lends some appropriate weight and grandeur to the words "Wishes," "Difficulties," and "Schemes." When I teach English 101, my students often capitalize words like "honor," "faith," and "capitalism." I always mark them wrong, but deep down I know that they're just trying to do those words justice, as Swift did.

Capitalizing distinguished common nouns also acknowledges that these are abstract concepts, not concrete objects. A "chair" is just a chair, but "Honor" is obtuse and elusive, an ideal, in need of definitions and examples to grasp it. I probably won't stop putting red marks by capitalized mid-sentence common nouns in my students' papers, but I'll always try to appreciate them.

5. **THE BIRTH OF THE DUMMY "DO."** Linguists call the word "do" a "dummy" word when it stands in for another word. We say, "Do you know her?" instead of "Know you her?"—with "do" standing in for "know" at the beginning of the sentence. It's just a mannequin, a place-holder. In the same way, to negate a statement, instead of saying "I want not to go," we say, "I do not want to go," with "do" again taking up space

and shoving its referent to the back of the sentence.

"Know you her?" and "I want not to go" used to be Standard English, but not anymore. And now English is cluttered with these dummy "do"'s. In fact, some linguists estimate that "do" is one of the most common words in English, other than function words like "the" and "and." That's a lot of airtime for a word that just stands idle most of the time—too much fame and recognition for a worker that sleeps on the job.

This dummy "do"—this redundant auxiliary—has made English more cumbersome, mucking up most of our questions and negations. You could argue that starting to scrub all this do-do out of English would be an important—and far-reaching—way to improve the language. But nobody seems to notice, or care.

So if these five changes in the history of English—the first three massive and obvious, the second two quiet and obscure—can fall like plagues upon the language and then, a few centuries after wreaking their havoc, go almost completely unnoticed by most native speakers—well, simply put, I find it harder to believe that your pet peeve is "ruining the language." Complaining about "lay" and "lie" but not uttering a peep about the scandalous, tragic death of the singular second person pronoun "thou" is as shortsighted as it is uninformed. It's like prescribing hair care products to a recovering triple-bypass patient—there's a lack of perspective, a lack of properly weighed risk factors leading to poorly corresponding treatments.

My new approach to language can be called joyous bewilderment. Rather than fretting about oddities, trends, and variations, I delight in them. The variation and change is exactly what makes language so interesting. I'm a work in progress, but gradually I'm learning to see quirks and changes in English and rather than respond with "How dangerous," to reply instead, "How cool!" or at least, "How interesting!" What follows is an initial report from the field, some strange species and behaviors I've noticed or someone else has noticed for me. Like a zoologist in the Amazon, I pause briefly to write them down, point them out to others, and then quickly go on, eagerly looking for more.

Acknowledgments

Lilah Lohr has edited my column for the *Tribune* from the beginning and has always improved it. Tim Bannon and James Warren have supported me ever since I was a summer intern in the Tribune Tower. Tom Sumner and Jim Leisy of William, James & Co. have been enjoyable co-dreamers of this book, and I'm grateful to them for making it a reality.

Everyone I've quoted in my columns has been gracious with their time and help, and they've rescued me from countless errors and ignorances (and are not responsible for those that remain). I've always said one of the best parts of journalism is asking smart people interesting questions, and they've proven me right. In particular, some of my go-to experts—Grant Barrett, Laura Dickey, Carmen Fought, Anatoly Liberman, Erin McKean, Geoff Pullum, Bill Walsh, and Arnold Zwicky—field more than their share of e-mail from me, in part because their answers are always so knowledgeable and interesting.

Countless readers who have written or talked to me with questions and observations about language have brought words and trends to my attention, and shown me the inadequacy of listening to English with only my own pair of ears.

Jim Vanden Bosch, my linguistics teacher in college, changed the entire trajectory of my linguistic interests, and deepened the joy I take in language. John Wilson and John Witvliet have been supportive editors and colleagues throughout the four years of work represented here.

My dad, Lyle, was the first to teach me an appreciation for the intricacies of language. My son Benjamin, one-year-old at the time of this writing, is quickly becoming my favorite linguistics teacher. My wife Andrea directly inspired at least one column (*see* **Andrea-ese**) and indirectly inspired many more, and I dedicate this book to her.

THE
ECLECTIC
ENCYCLOPEDIA
OF
ENGLISH

alphabet

WHAT WOULD you say was the most influential invention in human history? The wheel? The light bulb?

How about the alphabet?

We tend to take it for granted, but the alphabet was a human invention.

Without it, we wouldn't read books and newspapers or write shopping lists and e-mails. We would have to rely on recitations and recordings to transmit language. But as vital and visible as the letters of the alphabet are, they usually go unappreciated.

David Sacks changes that in his fascinating overview of the alphabet's history, *Letter Perfect: The Marvelous History of our Alphabet from A to Z* (paperback: Broadway Books; the hardcover was called *Language Visible*). Sacks' dissection of the alphabet is thoroughly informative and generously illustrated, but not snoozingly detailed.

The invention of the alphabet—a system that used symbols to represent individual sounds rather than things or ideas—revolutionized human language. Before the alphabet was invented, only scholars could write, since hieroglyphics used hundreds of symbols for words and syllables that took years of training to master.

Today our 26 letters do all the work of representing the approximately 45 phonemes (individual sounds) and 500,000 words of English.

"With the alphabet's invention, the farmer, shopkeeper, the laborer have been able to read and write," Sacks writes.

The roots of the alphabet reach to about 2000 B.C. in ancient Egypt. But the great-grandmother of modern alphabets, according to Sacks, was the 22-letter Phoenician alphabet of about 1000 B.C.

Based in what is now Lebanon, the Phoenicians distributed their alphabet to the many nations they traded with, including ancient Greece. The alphabet was adapted for Greek, then for Latin and eventually for other languages, including English.

Letters began as pictures. "A" was a picture of an ox's head; it was written sideways, with its point as the head and two horns sticking out. "A" signified the first sound of the Phoenician word "aleph" for "ox." "K" stood for "kaph," the word for hand, and K's extremities still look like fingers today. "M" was for "mem," meaning "water," its bumps resembling the waves of the sea. "O" was for "ayin," the word for "eye."

"The system meant that once a Phoenician child had memorized a list of 22 common nouns, he or she had a handle on each letter's sound (the same as the name's opening sound) and on each letter's shape (typically a rough sketch of the object named)," Sacks explains.

Sacks takes the alphabet letter by letter. The longest histories belong to the letters that made the most roundabout journeys to their current jobs.

The letter "F" originally looked like "Y" and sounded like "W," before the Romans changed it to look like "E" (minus its bottom branch) and sound as it does today.

The letters "J" and "V" were latecomers. For centuries, "J" was considered merely a variant of "I," and "V" was a variant of "U." Not until Noah Webster published *An American Dictionary of the English Language* in 1828, and devoted separate sections to "J" and "V," did the two letters gain individual recognition and respect, and only then did we officially have a 26-letter alphabet.

Sacks also tells stories of jealousy and betrayal. G's place and prominence in the alphabet were stolen by the letter "C." The caper started when the Etruscans, who didn't use the hard-G sound in their language, changed the Greek letter gamma (which looks like "Y") to the letter "C" and gave it a "K" sound.

When the Romans adopted the alphabet from the Etruscans, they needed a letter for their hard-G sound, so they designed a "G" and gave it the seventh slot in the alphabet. (The soft-G sound wouldn't enter English for another millennium, when English mingled with French after the Norman Conquest in 1066)

And so children learn their ABC's instead of their ABG's. And "G" watches "C" enjoy its former spotlight, even though "C" contributes no unique English sound except when it combines with "H"; it steals most of its work from "K" and "S."

Sacks also shows how different letters call for different tricks of the tongue, feats we perform regularly without thinking. To say "L," you press the tip of your tongue against the top of your mouth and let the sound slide around both sides of it. Drop your tongue down, and you have "R."

We like our letters so much, we make them words and names unto themselves: a, I, oh, Dubya. We wear T-shirts, make U-turns, go to Plan B and watch "The X-Files."

Centuries after hieroglyphics died out, the alphabet's triumph is clear. "The alphabet," Sacks writes, "was an invention to change the world."

alternative

Growing up in Egypt, my English teacher was very strict on when to use "alternate" and "alternative" as adjectives. The former means "every other," i.e. when things succeed each other by turns, whereas the latter means either one would do. I have noticed widespread use of "alternate" in this latter sense, as in "alternate routes." I can feel my English teacher from 50 years ago turning in his grave every time I hear this. Is this now considered standard English?

—*Shamel Shawki, Naperville, Illinois*

YES, OR nearly, according to *The New Fowler's Modern English Usage* (third edition), which says that in 20th century American English, the word "alternate," as an adjective, "usurped some of the territory of 'alternative' in its ordinary sense '(of one or more things) available in place of another.'"

As for "alternative," Fowler's says, "The traditional view that there can only be one of two (not more) alternatives because [the Latin] 'alter' means 'other (of two)' can no longer be maintained."

American English

TO GET a feel for the variety of what Robert MacNeil calls "the great family of North American Englishes," start with the opening sequence of MacNeil's engrossing 2005 three-hour documentary *Do You Speak American?* for PBS.

In the opening montage, Americans from Malibu to Maine speak the program's title in their own dialect. A Californian says, "Do you, like, speak American?" A woman from Cajun country in Louisiana asks in French, "Tu parles Americain?" Hip-hop artists chime in, "Do you speak American, dawg?" Southern comedian Jeff Foxworthy asks, "Do y'all speak American?" A Spanglish-speaking TV host says, "Estas hablando American?"

MacNeil also hosted the landmark 1986 documentary *The Story of English.* "I'm curious to see how the language has moved on since then," he says as he signs on for *Do You Speak American?* "So I'm setting out on a journey now to see what's happening to English in the United States."

Do You Speak American? spends a little too much time showing MacNeil driving from place to place and not enough time actually listening to the everyday speech of Americans—and it uses the terms "language," "dialect," "accent," and "slang" too loosely and interchangeably. But the program provides some wonderful snapshots of American English today, and it proves MacNeil's point that our language is "restless, slangy, constantly changing and ever more informal."

MacNeil begins in New England, where "R's" disappear from the end of such words as "car" and "store." When the British started dropping their "R's" in the early 19th century and developing what we think of as the BBC accent, East Coast cities, through travel and trade, adopted some of its features—though the resulting accent turned out sounding less like Alistair Cooke and more like John F. Kennedy.

MacNeil continues through Times Square in New York City, with its flashing advertisements and news and stock market messages rolling by on electronic "zippers." The city's financial, publishing, and media might, MacNeil says, make it "the global capital of the English language."

Language "wars" get special attention, especially the intense rivalry between prescriptivists and descriptivists. The first group insists the role of English teachers and writers is to prescribe language, instructing people to follow the rules of Standard English at all times. Descriptivists say English isn't static, so all anyone can do is describe the language as it changes and adapts to different settings and time periods.

New York magazine critic John Simon is solidly in the prescriptivist camp. The failure of today's speakers of American English to follow traditional rules means the language "has gotten worse," he laments to MacNeil. "It's been my experience that there is no bottom, one can always sink lower, and that the language can always disintegrate further."

Jesse Sheidlower, North American editor of *The Oxford English Dictionary* and an avowed descriptivist, doesn't buy it. American English, in all its variety and flavor, he says, "has always taken great pleasure in its slang. You can find even Walt Whitman writing in praise of slang in the 19th century, about how wonderful it is and how poetic it is, and how this is the American spirit distilled into language." (Simon retorts that Sheidlower and his lot are "a curse upon their race.")

Anxiety about language change is nothing new, says Dennis Preston, linguist at Michigan State University. He tells MacNeil, "There's a kind of American linguistic insecurity which is very, very old." On the one hand, we consider British English to be more elegant than ours. "On the other hand, there's American populism and a desire not to be stuffy, not to be too correct," Preston says.

What *is* considered correct, Preston says, is the Midwest

5

accent. Linguists refer to that region as the "inland North," and it sets the standard for the "normal" pronunciation of American English.

Allan Metcalf explains how this came to be in his superb overview *How We Talk: American Regional English Today* (Houghton Mifflin). In that book, he credits English professor John Samuel Kenyon with helping to shift the perception of standard pronunciation away from the East Coast and closer to Kenyon's native Ohio. In his 1924 book *American Pronunciation*, Kenyon, not so modestly, divided American accents into "Southern," "Eastern" and, for his own region, "General American."

However, that influential Midwestern pronunciation is showing signs of recent change. In a fascinating segment, linguist Bill Labov plays audio clips to demonstrate a phenomenon he calls the Northern Cities Shift: Short vowels have started to become longer in the mouths of many Midwestern speakers. The word "block" has begun to sound like "black"; "bit" resembles "but"; and "Ann" can sound like "Ian" (*see* **Northern Cities Shift**).

"Is it fair to say," MacNeil asks, "that North Americans are, in different regions, growing further apart from each other linguistically?"

"I think so," Labov replies. "It's hard to believe. Everyone says to us, we all watch the same radio and television—how can that be? It's a very surprising finding."

Americans also maintain a remarkable ambivalence toward accents—the Southern accent (or accents) in particular. On the one hand, Americans tend to admire the emotion and sincerity they associate with the Southern accent. On the other hand, they often hear it as a sign of inferior intelligence.

Foxworthy, the comedian who popularized "You might be a redneck" jokes in the 1990s, doesn't mind being a punch line. "I think Southerners really don't care that Northern people think that [the accent sounds unintelligent]," he tells MacNeil. "Some of the most intelligent people I've ever known talk like I do."

But Foxworthy has some fun with the stereotype. "Nobody wants to hear their brain surgeon say, 'Al'ight now, what we're gonna do is saw the top of your head off, root around in there with a stick and see if we can't find that dadburn clot.'"

Today, American English increasingly takes cues from California ("I'm all, like, 'As if!'") (*see also* **Clueless, linguistic legacy of; I'm all;** and **like totally**) and Latino dialects such as Spanglish and Chicano. In particular, the linguistic melting pot of Los Angeles is a cause for alarm to prescriptivists and other purists who fear Spanish will displace English as America's common tongue, but linguist Carmen Fought assuages these fears.

As with European and Asian immigration, "It's still the classic pattern that the first generation born in the United States often will retain the home language, but by the second generation born here, the home language is very often lost," Fought tells MacNeil. "If anything, it's Spanish that's in danger."

"I think there's variations of speaking American," TV and radio personality Steve Harvey tells MacNeil. "You have to be bilingual in this country. And that means you can be very, very adept at slang, but you have to be adept at getting through a job interview."

See also **Canadian English, Northern Cities Shift**.

American Indian vs. Native American

See **Indian country**.

American Midland

THERE'S A book on American English in the Midwest that makes Chicago seem exotic.

It's certainly not the title: *Language Variation and Change in the American Midland: A New Look at "Heartland" English* (John Benjamins Publishing Co.), edited by Thomas Murray and Beth Lee Simon. And it's not the picture on the cover, which shows a Brown Line "L" stop with the Sears Tower in the background.

It's the label at the top of the cover, identifying the book as the 36th volume in a series called "Varieties of English Around the World." Other books in the series include *Dublin English* and *Singapore English*. Midwesterners may find it jarring to be considered just another "variety of English" among company like this, just another cage in the zoo.

But the book makes it clear: Despite its reputation for plain pronunciation and featureless vocabulary, the American Midland has an English all its own, even though linguists don't always give the region its due. "There has been significantly less research, and in particular, less follow-up research, on Midland dialect . . . or Midland linguistics culture than, say, on the South or on such sub-regional Midland areas such as Pittsburgh or Appalachia," Simon writes in her introduction.

But where, exactly, is the American Midland? Linguists disagree. Dialectologists in the mid-20th century mapped the Midland as extending roughly from Pennsylvania to Nebraska, Illinois to Arkansas, based largely on distinct vocabulary in that region. The monumental *Atlas of North American English*, published in 2006 by the eminent sociolinguist William Labov and colleagues, has a clearly defined Midland reaching from central Ohio to eastern Nebraska. But as recently as the 1980s, one linguist argued that the Midland dialect was "nonexistent"; there was only the "Lower North" and "Upper South."

Chicago actually lies just north of the Midland on most maps, in a region called "the Inland North," which makes you wonder why that picture of Chicago is on the cover of a book about the "American Midland." While most Americans lump the Midland

ANDREA-ESE

When you live with someone, one of the things you learn is that person's unique vocabulary. On my third wedding anniversary I made a list of some of the words and phrases I first heard from my wife, Andrea. Given this level of inventiveness displayed by one person, is it any wonder that language as a whole changes and evolves as much as it does?

analyzation: combination of "analysis" and "rationalization," connoting excess, as in, "Don't ruin the movie with your analyzations."

Of my three favorite dictionaries, *Merriam-Webster's Collegiate Dictionary* (*MWC*) and *The American Heritage Dictionary* (*AHD*) list "analyzation" as a variant of "analysis," while the second edition

and Inland North together as "the Midwest," linguists usually try to keep them apart.

Chicagoans would recognize few of the 17 language features of the Midland that Murray and Simon list in their opening chapter, based on a stack of available linguistic atlases and some of their own research.

They begin with the phrases "all the far," "all the farther" and "all the one." Midland speakers might say, "That's all the far they can go," or, "Is this all the one you have?" Another Midland oddity is using the word "anymore" with what is called "positive polarity," as in, "We always use coupons anymore when we shop." In Standard English, "anymore" has negative polarity, appearing in negative statements such as "She doesn't work here anymore."

The closer you get to the Appalachian Mountains, the more speakers use verb phrases such as "I might could go," and replace "when" with "whenever," as in, "Whenever the carriage came, the lady got in."

The authors don't argue that all Midland speakers say these things, only that they show up in dialect surveys as characteristic of the region, crossing lines of sex and economic class.

Minority groups in the Midland provide linguists with some

---

of *The New Oxford American Dictionary* (*NOAD*) doesn't have it (though it does have "analyzable").

A Google search yields about 700 examples of the word. A quick scan of these results suggests the word usually uses a prefix to connote excess, as in "over-analyzations" and "hyper-analyzations."

carefuller: comparative form of "careful." A clang in the kitchen will elicit: "Be carefuller!" I thought this was an invented inflection, but *MWC* has it, though *AHD* and *NOAD* don't. The word gets more than 1,000 results on Google but only five results in a search of the LexisNexis news database for the last five years.

complexly: adverb meaning "in a complex way." This also sounded like an invented inflection to me, but it's in all three of

fascinating variations to study. In West Virginia, the fading Appalachian Heritage dialect still uses the "causative 'to,'" as in "He had me to get my license," and "the" with an illness, as in "She had the toothache." The so-called "Swiss Amish" of northeastern Indiana speak a dialect of German found in Switzerland; they refer to all outsiders, both Americans and German visitors, as "the English." Some of the 200,000 speakers of Deitsch, or Pennsylvania German, have formed new German-speaking pockets as far west as Montana.

Not only is the Midland a diverse region, but many individual states in the Midland are themselves a mix of influences. In a chapter called "Tracking the low back merger in Missouri," University of Missouri linguist Matthew Gordon finds an uneven adoption of one recent vowel change.

The "low back merger" leads speakers to pronounce "Don" to rhyme with "dawn," and "collar" with "caller." Gordon's survey found that the state seems split—about one-third (more concentrated on the west side of the state) rhymes these words this way, one-third rhymes them somewhat, and one-third (on the east side) doesn't.

You can't talk about the American Midland without talking

my dictionaries and gets more than 100,000 results in Google. A LexisNexis search finds eight examples from one publication alone: the prestigious *New Yorker*, which talked about "the most complexly intelligent and sophisticated, and yet the most keenly enthusiastic, study of the life and work taken together."

Go, us: "We did well," as in, "Good thing we got our grocery shopping done before Tuesday night. Go, us!" Possible first-person plural adaptation of the second-person singular exclamation, "You go, girl!" Virtually unsearchable on Google because the search engine does not distinguish between "us" as a word and "US" as an abbreviation for "United States."

ish: approximately. Isolation of the suffix "-ish," normally used as in, "We'll be there about seven-ish," to produce the following:

about Pittsburghese, with its "yinz" ("you'uns") and "dahn-tahn" ("downtown"). Linguist Thomas Donahue takes a novel approach, comparing Pittsburgh with another Heartland industrial city: Youngstown, Ohio, in an eight-page side-by-side comparison of sounds, words and grammatical features. Youngstown's dialect is more recent and more influenced by Cleveland, Donahue finds, but both dialects are "eclectic combinations of native and foreign speech forms found in industrial workplaces at the turn of the twentieth century," he writes.

It's too bad the publisher gave *Language Variation and Change in the American Midland* a price ($156) only a library could love. Although some of the material is technical, the topics are of enough interest and presented with enough visual help to give general readers plenty to enjoy.

anxious vs. eager

I recognize "anxious" to mean "to anticipate with nervousness," but I very often hear it used interchangeably with "eager" (which I would define as "to anticipate with enthusiasm"). I've gotten so picky about it that now my 10-year-old

"What time will you be there? Ish?"

monumentous: conflation of "monumental" and "momentous." Not in any of my dictionaries. "Monumentous" gets fewer than 7,000 hits on Google, compared with nearly 5 million for "monumental" and nearly 1.4 million for "momentous."

moment: significant conversation. Interrupting such a conversation to celebrate a development in the football game on TV will produce the protest, "Hey! We were having a moment." Possible adaptation of the term "Kodak moment," though that commercial catchphrase refers to a visual scene worth capturing on film. "Having a moment" conveys a conversation's importance more than its memorability.

Oh well, right?: Rhetorical question conveying, "It is not impor-

11

son corrects people by saying, "You mean you're *eager* to see us." Is "anxious" in such a context evolving to mean "looking forward to"?

—*Betty Schulz, Lisle, Illinois*

IT EVOLVED long ago, according to *The Oxford English Dictionary.* The *OED* quotes Scottish poet Robert Blair, who wrote in 1742 about "the gentle heart, anxious to please."

This usage is older than the complaint about it, says *The American Heritage Guide to Contemporary Usage and Style.* "People have been using 'anxious' as a synonym for 'eager' for over 250 years, and for over 100 years language critics have been objecting to it." The *Guide* argues that "people who like using 'anxious' to mean 'eager' can justify the usage on the grounds that it adds emotional urgency to an assertion."

All dictionaries I checked recognize the "eager" meaning of "anxious." It's interesting, though, that the word "anxiety" has not, in turn, evolved to serve as a synonym for "eagerness." There's only one way that English speakers interpret a sentence such as "We have anxiety about meeting you!"

tant." "Oh well" is an interjection—an exclamation that has no grammatical function but does communicate meaning (in this case, unimportance). "Oh well, right?" gets a handful of hits on Google and LexisNexis.

I was curious whether the word "right" here is what linguists call a "quotative marker," or a word that signals a quotation. So I brought this phrase to University of Pennsylvania linguist Mark Liberman for a diagnosis. He said quotative markers tend to be used only when the speaker is known, not for generic statements or clichés, as in, "No pain, no gain, right?" "Such fragments don't need to be full phrases normally interpreted," Liberman said, "but can instead be allusions to the projection of ideas or attitudes stereotypically associated with the referenced expression."

-o: suffix attached randomly to English words, not restricted to words derived from Latin, Italian or Spanish (in which "-o" end-

Arkansas, punctuation of possessive form of

It could go down in history as the Arkansas Apostrophe Act of 2007. Or maybe "Arkansas's Apostrophe Act of 2007."

In May of that year, the Arkansas State Legislature passed a non-binding resolution declaring that the proper way to punctuate the possessive form of the state's name ends with apostrophe-S: "Arkansas's," and not apostrophe-only, as many newspapers write it.

Although the resolution cannot be enforced, the state government has started to use the apostrophe-S form in all its documents. "No official stationery or signage will have to be changed," promised a news item at the state legislature's website. But the office of Gov. Mike Beebe, who supported the measure, had to scramble to change a graphic on its home page from "Ginger Beebe: Arkansas' First Lady" to "Arkansas's First Lady."

The man behind the resolution is historian Parker Westbrook, who says the extra S is needed because the S before the apostrophe is silent. In fact, he told the press he considers the apostrophe resolution to be an amendment of the state legislature's 1881

---

ings are common); as in, "Let's go in the house-o."

peanut: baby or toddler, as in, "That was back when I was a peanut." (Plural references tend to be "munchkins"). Since Googling this word brings up the website for The Peanut Institute, and since the most recent volume of the *Historical Dictionary of American Slang* only goes through the letter O, this usage is tough to track.

potatoest: containing the most potato, as in, "You take that french fry; it's the potatoest." Notable since "potato" is not usually an adjective, much less a comparative one. Not in *MWC*, *AHD* or *NOAD*.

See also **neologisms, presticogitation.**

resolution recognizing the pronunciation of the state's name as "AR-kin-saw," rather than "Ar-KAN-sas."

The Arkansas Times already uses apostrophe-S, calling itself "Arkansas's Newspaper of Politics and Culture." The *Arkansas Gazette*, which published from 1819 until 1991, was using apostrophe-S even before Arkansas became a state.

But Arkansans, or Arkansawyers, or whatever you call residents of Arkansas, are far from agreed. The *Arkansas Democrat-Gazette*, the state's largest newspaper, uses the apostrophe-only form. So does Katherine Shurlds, who teaches journalism at the University of Arkansas at Fayetteville and hosts "The Militant Grammarian" on her local public radio station.

"There are too many S's and it just looks silly," Shurlds said about the apostrophe-S form in a University of Arkansas news release.

Outside Arkansas, opinions are just as divided. The Associated Press opts for apostrophe-only Arkansas'. So does the *Chicago Tribune*. The *New York Times* uses apostrophe-only when a name ends in S-vowel-S—such as Pegasus and Jesus. But the *Times* switches to apostrophe-S when the word's final S is silent. So last month the *Times* wrote about "Arkansas's Gary Ervin" but "Kansas' Russell Robinson."

"I don't think any self-respecting editor will make a style change based on a non-binding resolution by a state legislature, but I do agree with Arkansas's over Arkansas'," Bill Walsh, chief copy editor of the national desk at *The Washington Post* and author of two books on usage, wrote me by e-mail. "With the apostrophe alone, there's no letter to represent the 's' that's pronounced in the possessive."

The Chicago Manual of Style leans toward apostrophe-S but allows apostrophe-only. "Although the collective heart of *CMOS* leapt for a moment at the idea that punctuation might be legislated, ultimately we must endorse a pro-choice position on the matter," Carol Saller, an editor at the University of Chicago Press, which publishes the *CMOS*, wrote to me by e-mail. "That is, *The Chicago Manual of Style* prefers to add apostrophe-S to form possessives of nouns that end in a silent 'S' (Arkansas's,

Illinois's), but also sanctions the alternative of omitting the final 'S' (Arkansas', Illinois')."

"Illinois," incidentally, has never caused the same level of controversy. The *Chicago Tribune*, the Illinois General Assembly, the *Springfield State-Register* and the website of the University of Illinois at Urbana-Champaign all use the apostrophe-only possessive for "Illinois," as in "Illinois' unemployment rate."

Saller continued: "A more radical solution, though it would cause an even greater legislative headache, would be for the states to eliminate the silent 'S' in favor of a more phonetic spelling. Of course, we would still be left with the knotty problem of Kansas."

Maybe the only clear way out of this mess is to go back to ending our possessives in "-es," as English used to do. In fact, the apostrophe was introduced as a replacement for the E in the "-es" ending, just as the apostrophe stands for O in contractions such as "wasn't" (from "was not").

Shakespeare, for instance, wrote in *A Midsummer Night's Dream*, "swifter than the moones sphere"—instead of "moon's sphere" (although linguists say the apostrophe had already emerged in Shakespeare's time, and the playwright kept the E in that line for rhythm's sake).

And as long as we're looking to history for guidance, we should also use an apostrophe in plurals, since the S ending of plurals is the remainder of an ending such as "-as." The word "fathers," for example, was spelled "faederas" in Old English.

But other than turning back time, what should we do with Arkansas? "I teach AP style [which calls for apostrophe-only in 'Arkansas'], so I won't be changing anything," Shurlds wrote me by e-mail, "except to crack jokes at the state's expense, and to warn those who may be going into state service that they'll have to get their esses in gear!"

as best

SOME ENGLISH words and phrases fall into the category of technically wrong but widely accepted, much to the chagrin of purists.

A few entries in that category seem to escape the notice of sticklers and puzzle the experts. Take the phrase "as best as I can," for instance.

I heard a version of it during Senator Barack Obama's 2006 appearance on *The Daily Show With Jon Stewart*. When Stewart asked him who was the worst senator, Obama, a Democrat and the junior senator from Illinois, said, "Most of the folks really are trying to represent their constituencies as best as they know how."

"As best as" is striking, because "best" is the superlative form of "well," and English doesn't use any other superlative in this phrase. We say "as much as" but not "as most as"; "as red as" but not "as reddest as." The phrase "as best as I can" may be a mix-up of "as well as I can" and "the best that I can."

Obama could have said either "as well as they know how" or "the best that they know how." In fact, in his next comment, he used a form of "the best that . . .": "If I try to work hard and do the best possible job that I can, then I think things will work out pretty well."

English speakers seem more comfortable using "the best that" when it follows the verb "do," as in the Mac Davis song "Hard to Be Humble": "Oh, Lord, it's hard to be humble, but I'm doing the best that I can."

So "as best as" is either a grammatical error or an exception to a firm rule of English syntax. Which is it? Experts disagree.

"As best I can recollect, I don't say or write this," Geoffrey Pullum, co-author of *The Cambridge Grammar of the English Language* (Cambridge University Press), writes by e-mail with deliberate irony. "But neither do I notice it or feel that it strikes me as wrong. It certainly slips by the grammar radar."

"The syntax is idiomatic," says Geoffrey Nunberg, chairman of *The American Heritage Dictionary* Usage Panel, but adds, "it's [a] normal way of saying this."

Others say the phrase is improperly formed. "I've always considered this an inoffensive though ungrammatical colloquialism," says David Mulroy, author of *The War Against Grammar* (Boynton/Cook).

"I hadn't thought about it before, but, yes, that has to be considered substandard," e-mails Bill Walsh, chief copy editor of the national desk at *The Washington Post*, and author of *The Elephants of Style: A Trunkload of Tips on the Big Issues and Gray Areas of Contemporary American English* (McGraw-Hill).

Standard or not, the grammatical oddity "as best I can" (and its alternate form, "as best as I can") has been in use for a while. A Google search for the phrase "as best I can" turns up nearly half as many results as a search for "the best I can," while "as best I can" gets about three times as many results as a search for "as well as I can."

The phrase may be rather informal, but it is sometimes used by reputable speakers in formal situations. A Brookings Institution senior fellow told Knight Ridder newspapers in November 2005 that the situation in Iraq was "closer to stalemate militarily than anything else, as best I can tell." A search on Google Scholar, a section of Google that searches published academic writings, finds over 1,000 cases of "as best I can" (about half as many as "the best I can").

Cary Grant once said, "My formula for living is quite simple. I get up in the morning and I go to bed at night. In between, I occupy myself as best I can."

"This [phrase] and related patterns are pretty old," says Mark Liberman, linguist at the University of Pennsylvania. "I think it's pretty well established."

Liberman found several examples from centuries past, such as a 19th century poem by John Greenleaf Whittier that says, "I will tarry, and serve ye as best I can." In Shakespeare's *The Taming of the Shrew*, Petruchio says, "Happily to wive and thrive, as best I may." The oldest example on record is from 1377, in *The Oxford English Dictionary*: "as best is for the soul."

So is it all right to say "as best as"? The most conscientious users of Standard English will probably try to avoid it, especially because the alternatives—"as well as" or "the best that"—are so simple. But as best as anyone can tell, "as best as" is an acceptable alternative.

at, ending in

> One word that really bothers me is the word "at," in "Where did you park your car at?" I was kidding my wife and said, "Never write a sentence that ends with at."
>
> —*Herman Fasnacht, Pontiac, Illinois*

THIS USE of "at" is informal and widely condemned, but I detect a subtle nuance and purpose in it. Ending a question with "at" indicates that the speaker expects the answer to be a particular location. I've never heard, "Where is the loyalty at?" But I do hear, "Where is he at?" The speaker may even expect the answer to begin with the same word: "At the mall."

I ran my theory past linguist Carmen Fought of Pitzer College in Claremont, California, who said, after generating some examples, "the pattern does seem to hold." No one, she observes, says, "Where's the logic at in that?" but they do say, "Where's your sister at?" So ending with "at" is hardly Standard English, but it's probably not just careless; that "at" may have a linguistic function.

AUSTRALIAN IDIOMS

If all you know about Australian English are the word "crikey!" and the greeting "Good day, mate!" then you need to learn some Australian idioms.

Australian linguist Pam Peters introduces us to some choice Aussie phrases in her chapter in the 2007 book *Phraseology and Culture in English*, a collection of linguistic studies edited by Paul Skandera (Mouton de Gruyter). It's a technical book for academics, but many of Peters' examples had me chuckling. Feel free to spice up your own conversation with some of these phrases, but be prepared to explain them!

alone like a country dunny: A "dunny" is an outhouse in Australian English. An outhouse in the country stands all alone.

at the end of the day

Why is it suddenly a requirement for anyone attempting to sound intelligent to use the phrase, "at the end of the day"? At the end of the day, I find it produces the opposite effect.

—*John Marcet, Naperville, Illinois*

I MUST be in the minority—I like "at the end of the day" much better than its banal predecessor, "when all is said and done." When, exactly, is all said and done? "At the end of the day" reflects the fact that we tend to make summary judgments when the day is done—on the way home from work or before falling asleep—and those judgments have a broader scope than when we're in the middle of our daily duties. But as with any phrase, overuse saps its impact.

attorney general, plural of

I was helping a candidate draft some marketing material and the flier remarked that he had worked for two "attorney generals." Seeing that the candidate had already printed about

---

busy as a one-armed bill-sticker in a gale: Busy as someone putting up fliers in a storm. I'm ashamed to say this was the first time I understood those signs that say "post no bills." All I could think of was dollar bills, and I couldn't figure out why anyone would nail those to a phone pole. But if "bills" means "fliers," then it makes sense. Australians also say "busy as a one-armed milker on a dairy farm," and "busy as a blowie at a barbie," meaning busy as a blowfly at a barbecue. Peters says these phrases are said with criticism, not admiration; if someone says them about you, they think you're working too hard.

bald as a bandicoot: A bandicoot, Peters says, is a small ratlike marsupial that lives in Australia. "Bandicoot" is such a fun word to say—and such an unsympathetic animal to make fun of—that it shows up in many Australian idioms, including "poor as a

19

5,000 of these I didn't ask if it should have been "attorneys general." Which form do you prefer?

—Joe Clark, Yonkers, New York

MY ANSWER will get me in trouble with my English teachers. I prefer "attorney generals."

Like you, I was taught that the plural here should be "attorneys general," because "general" is actually an adjective modifying "attorney" (which is why they should just call it a "general attorney," although that sounds less prestigious). And so you had good reason to flag this problematic plural.

But because we almost never put an adjective after the noun it modifies in English, "attorneys general" sounds very strange. "Attorney generals" sounds much more natural, and much less distracting to anyone except English teachers (though I realize you risk losing their votes over this one).

Besides, "general" is a good word for a leader. I like to think of an attorney general leading her troops into battle against injustice (some more faithfully than others), or a surgeon general guiding the war against disease. That's overstating the power they actually

bandicoot" and "miserable as an orphan bandicoot"; if a piece of land is worthless, you could say, "A bandicoot would starve on it." "No other Australian animal seems to be as deeply embedded in idiom as the bandicoot," Peters says.

cold as a polar bear's backside: Self-explanatory, though I wonder how this phrase gained currency in balmy Australia!

couldn't blow the froth off a glass of beer: Weak. Similar phrases include "couldn't knock the skin off a rice pudding."

doesn't know whether it's Tuesday or Bourke Street: Utterly confused. You would hear this in Melbourne, the home of Bourke Street, and would hear "Pitt Street" substituted in Sydney, Peters says.

have—both over injustice and over other attorneys—but it helps "attorney generals" sound right.

I still believe in "editors-in-chief" and even "heirs apparent," where the adjective or suffix is more obviously not a noun. I'll get back to you about the plural of "sergeant major."

In his handbook *The Elephants of Style*, Bill Walsh endorses "attorneys general" as the correct plural, but adds, "If 'attorney generals' is the worst error you ever commit, you're a genius. If you do it on purpose, you're a visionary." That's good enough for me!

Walsh also quotes the satirical newspaper *The Onion*, which once ran a headline about a well-known language guru: "William Safire Orders Two Whoppers Junior."

back in the day

NEWSCASTER SOLEDAD O'Brien once owned a lavender Citroen, she recalled on CNN.

"Wow! That was back in the day," her guest remarked.

"That was so back in the day it's not even funny," O'Brien replied. "I don't want to talk about it anymore."

---

dressed like a pox-doctor's clerk: Overdressed. A doctor's clerk doesn't need to dress up.

flat out like a lizard drinking: This phrase can mean either taking the physical posture of a lizard leaning forward to drink, or just working hard, Peters says.

gone to Gowings: This phrase has a remarkable history, Peters says. Back in the 1940s, ads for the Gowings department store in Australia used the slogan "gone to Gowings," showing scenes in which people had left quickly to go shopping. One memorable ad showed a bride left at the altar, reading a note left by the groom that said, "Gone to Gowings." "This would account for it becoming a general excuse for someone's absence, doing something else which cannot or should not be specified," Peters comments. But

Which "day" we are talking about is not always clear, but there has been a lot of going back to it lately.

For example, one week in September 2004 saw several references to it. *Auto Week* wrote that the new Pontiac GTO "has standard features galore and build quality unheard of back in the day." *Fortune*, in an article about airlines, observed, "Back in the day, bad service was the trade-off for low prices [before higher quality discount airlines emerged]." *Newsweek* said Slash, the former guitarist for Guns N' Roses now strumming with the band Velvet Revolver, "looks exactly as he did back in the day."

A Nexis search for "back in the day" returns more than 3,500 results for the first five months of 2004, compared with about 2,000 for the same period in the year 2000 (although Nexis does not distinguish between "back in the day" and "back in those days," which could skew the results). Google yields more than a quarter of a million results for "back in the day," five times as many as "back in those days" and 10 times as many as "back in my day."

The origins of "back in the day" are obscure, but the consensus among linguists and word watchers on The American Dialect Society's online forum seems to be that "back in the day" arose from hip-hop music circa the 1980s.

---

eventually, the phrase would get even more vague and versatile. Now "gone to Gowings" can mean going broke, losing a game, sleeping off a hangover, or most recently, suffering dementia. All from an advertising slogan.

if it rained soup, I'd be left with a fork: Unlucky; the equivalent of the British phrase "if it rained porridge, he would lack his dish."

kangaroos loose in the top paddock: Crazy; the equivalent of having "a few screws loose" or "bats in the belfry."

mad as a gumtree full of galahs: Peters explains, "The galah is a medium-sized Autralian parrot, which roosts above ground in noisy flocks."

"I teach at Hampton [Virginia] University, an historically black college," writes linguist Margaret Lee by e-mail. "I remember my students using 'back in the day' as early as 1984 to refer to the relatively recent past, but usually a time before they were born. Before that, I remember it being used occasionally by hip-hop artists in TV interviews in the early 1980's."

"I don't know that it originated in African-American English or hip-hop speech, but it has certainly gotten currency in those discourse communities," says Drew Danielson, an administrative assistant at Carnegie Mellon University in Pittsburgh, by e-mail.

Danielson cites hip-hop songs titled "Back In The Day" by Young MC and Ahmad in the early 1990s. More recent albums by artists Erykah Badu and Missy Elliot have tracks called "Back in the Day." *Newsday* wrote in 2004 that the new Beastie Boys album features "the same kind of East Coast beats that Run-DMC and The Sugarhill Gang would have busted out back in the day." A 2005 movie starring rapper Ja Rule is called *Back in the Day*.

As the phrase is currently used, "back in the day" seems to have two basic meanings: "long ago" and "was it really that long ago?"

For the first sense, consider O'Brien and her lavender Citroen.

sleeping in the Star Hotel: This sounds nice, but it means sleeping under the stars because you're out of a job.

things are crook at Musselbrook: That town is in bad condition. It can be any town; Musselbrook is used because it rhymes. Also: "things are weak at Werris Creek" and "there's no work at Bourke."

wet enough to bog a duck: It's so wet, a duck would get stuck in the mud.

She was really saying, "That was so long ago it's not even funny." Here, "the day" could mean "the days of my youth" or "the days when lavender was in style."

"The day" can also mean "heyday," which *The American Heritage Dictionary* defines as "the period of greatest popularity, success or power; prime."

Former Detroit Pistons player Rick Mahorn compared the crowds that cheered his championship team in the late 1980s to those who followed the 2004 champion Pistons. "I remember the crowd being just as loud, just as vocal, back in the day," he told the *Detroit News*.

One quirk of context: when someone uses "back in the day," it's generally a sign of pleasant nostalgia for days past. If you hear "back in my day," get ready for a pronouncement on modern moral decline: "Back in my day, kids respected their elders" carries an overtone very different from "kids respected their elders back in the day."

Sometimes "the day" isn't really so long ago: "Compared to what it was like to start your own Web page back in the day, starting a blog is a breeze," wrote the *Macon Telegraph* in 2004.

Younger generations may be latching onto the catchphrase as a rite of passage, says James Vanden Bosch, English professor at Calvin College in Grand Rapids, Michigan. "I hear it only from twentysomethings," he says. "It strikes me that this is early evidence of these youngsters' awareness that they, too, are growing old, and suddenly their quite recent past—7 or 8 years ago—constitutes a significant period of time and development. It's a way of claiming to be old enough to have an interesting past already."

beg the question

Are you as maddened by the ever increasing misuse of the phrase "begs the question"? My understanding has always been that "begging the question" means to avoid the real issue, not that something begs for a question to be asked.

—*Steve Rooney, Chicago, Illinois*

THE ORIGINAL meaning of "begging the question" was to base your argument on unspoken assumption. The phrase is a rough translation of the Latin phrase *petitio principii* (meaning "seeking the beginning [question]").

If you argue, "She is innocent, because she would never do something like that," then you're begging the question. You were supposed to demonstrate how to arrive at the conclusion that she is innocent, but instead you just assumed that the conclusion was true along.

"Beg the question" has gradually expanded to generally mean "raises the question," whether or not someone's logic is faulty.

For example, a *St. Louis Post-Dispatch* story of August 2006 reported that the Cardinals' losing streak "helped beg the question whether the Cardinals are merely slumping or being exposed [as a bad team]." Here, "beg" just meant "raised."

"All the evidence has shown that the usage and the meaning have forked and that there exist two or three meanings for the expression 'beg the question,'" says Grant Barrett, author of *The Official Dictionary of Unofficial English* (McGraw-Hill). "All of them have more than 100 years in the written record."

Most usage guides assume people who say "begs" to mean "raises" are misusing the phrase out of ignorance—and indeed, the "logical fallacy" meaning is not widely known. But Barrett says people have not come up with this new meaning out of thin air; they have connected it to the original meaning.

"I think it's no surprise that, probably through reanalysis (what others call misinterpretation) of a phrase they didn't understand, English speakers found a far more common way to put the phrase to use," Barrett wrote in an e-mail. "I mean, really, how many of us outside of a logic and rhetoric class our freshman year have a use for the logical fallacy sense of 'beg the question'?"

The New Oxford American Dictionary, in a note in its entry for "beg," says "begs the question" must have morphed from "assuming the conclusion" to "avoiding the real question" to, finally, "raising an obvious question."

You can easily replace "begs" with "raises" if you think "begs" is bad, but you might lose that sense of how urgent and essential

25

the unasked question is. The question isn't just related; it's begging to be asked.

between you and I

See **Recency Illusion.**

bird, as a verb

PETER CASHWELL leads a double life: he's an English teacher who likes to bird. But using the noun "bird" as a verb can get you in trouble in English teachers' lounges.

"Even as I draw my pay for teaching grammar . . . 'to bird' is a regular part of my vocabulary," Cashwell confesses in the opening pages of his book *The Verb 'To Bird': Sightings of an Avid Birder* (Paul Dry Books).

Cashwell, who lives in rural Virginia, apologizes for this apparent infelicity but explains that "bird-watching" won't do. "The term suggests that we . . . sit passively and stare at [birds]," he writes. "In reality, those who bird pursue birds, observing them, memorizing their names, learning their field marks and calls, chasing them over hill and dale . . . . I doubt that clock-watchers act this way around clocks."

The verb "to bird" is first recorded by *The Oxford English Dictionary* in 1576, but then it referred to hunting and trapping birds. Only within the past two decades, Cashwell says, has "birding" begun to replace "bird-watching."

Cashwell's love of birding often overlaps with his love of English, as when he looks at the history of the name "cardinal." Cashwell says he was skeptical of the standard story that the bird was named for the resemblance of its red feathers to the robes of Catholic cardinals.

"It seemed a stretch to me that in the Southeastern portion of the country [where cardinals are most prevalent], a heavily Protestant area, people would see a red bird and the first thing they think of is a high-ranking member of the Vatican," Cashwell says by phone. "I found out that it was the explorers, not the Protestants, who had done the naming, and they were from Catholic nations or were Catholic themselves."

Birding has inspired or appropriated a whole flock of words, as you can see at the online version of Peter Weaver's *Birdwatcher's Dictionary* (www.birdcare.com/bin/searchdict). Among Weaver's entries:

anvil: A hard surface a bird uses to smash the shells of snails or clams to obtain the soft insides. According to legend, as recorded by the first century Roman Historian Pliny the Elder, the Greek playwright Aeschylus was killed when an eagle dropped a tortoise on his head, mistaking its bald surface for a stone.

billing: This has nothing to do with accounting. Billing is the practice of touching bills in an affectionate way during courtship, and is often observed in pigeons. A British variant is "nebbing."

Cain and Abel situation: A colloquial term for siblicide, or the killing of one sibling by another (usually the younger sibling is the victim, as in the biblical story of Cain and Abel). "It probably showed up in a paper somewhere, and someone decided to get cute," says Jeff Brawn, associate professor of animal biology at the University of Illinois at Urbana-Champaign and treasurer of the American Ornithologists' Union.

guano: A Spanish word for a pile of droppings, such as what accumulates under a roost. Bat guano is sold as fertilizer.

LBJ: Not the nation's 36th president, but a little brown job—a bird that alights and then flies away too quickly to be described in any detail.

lek: An assembly of birds in which males strut and dance in hope of attracting a mate. The word, which can be used as a verb or noun, apparently comes from the Swedish word "leka," meaning to play. "It's a great Scrabble word," Peter Cashwell says. "I've been challenged about that one a couple of times."

life list: The list of all the bird species a birder has seen in her lifetime. An addition to the list is called a "lifer." Someone who earnestly seeks to add to her life list is called a "lister" (see "twitcher" below).

mobbing: The harassment or attack of a larger bird by a gang of smaller ones. "This is something I've observed fairly frequently," Cashwell says. "I've seen a handful of swallows chasing a hawk. It was like a small Apache attack helicopter attacking a bomber."

pen: A female swan. A male swan is a "cob." "There are literally scores of terms for the males and females of individual animals," Cashwell says. A male duck, for example, is called a "drake," the female a "hen."

pish: The approximate sound a birder produces through pursed lips in an attempt to draw a bird closer. "It sounds strange, but it really works," Cashwell says. "You can get a bird to fly out of the brush or down from the higher branches of a tree by saying 'pish' toward it."

twitcher: Someone who goes to great lengths to spot a certain species. Weaver suggests the name refers to the nervous anticipation of a birder on the lookout for a new addition to his life list. "Twitchers will drive great distances to see a rare bird in a particular area that may have blown in because of a storm or gotten lost," Cashwell says.

yaffle: The common name for the European green woodpecker, named for its laughing call.

blurb and bromide

THE 140TH birthday in 2006 of the humorist Gelett Burgess gave cause to celebrate the lexical legacy he left by adding the words "blurb" and "bromide" to the English language.

"Bromide" began in science to describe a compound made from the chemical bromine—including a kind of sedative. So Burgess used "bromide" to mean a boring person who sedated listeners with clichés. (His antonym to "bromide" was "sulphite," which didn't survive—maybe because there are more bromides than sulphites in the world.) Soon, "bromide" came to mean the clichés those boring people said.

"Blurb" came from "bromide"—actually, from Burgess' 1906 book *Are You a Bromide?* For the jacket of a special edition of his book, Burgess drew an illustration of a glamorous young woman and gave it a breathless caption. He named the woman "Miss Blinda Blurb," and eventually "blurb" became the word for lavish praise on book flaps.

Since "bromide" and "blurb" have had such useful lives, it's a shame the English language couldn't make room for Burgess' even more delightful creations, which he offered in his 1914 dictionary, *Burgess Unabridged.*

Proudly vowing to "give the diction of the year 1915," Burgess not only listed and defined his 100 words, he included a full page of commentary and an eight-line poem for each one. "We have no [French] Academy, thank heaven, to tell us what is real English and what isn't," Burgess wrote in his introduction. "We need so many new words, and we need 'em quick." Burgess urged readers to try his words out. "Little by little," he wrote, "as their sharp corners and edges are worn smooth by use, they will fit into your conversation and nestle into place, making your talk firmer, more expressive and wonderfully adequate to your daily needs."

agowilt: "sickening terror." The feeling you have the instant you have done something without considering the dire consequences. "The minute after you throw the burnt match into the waste-paper basket," Burgess wrote, "the agowilt comes."

alibosh: blatant lie or exaggeration. When your boss or your curfew-defying teen tells you a whopper today, you know what to call it.

bimped: to be jilted or cheated out of something. The would-be husband of the runaway bride or the customer who gets a nickel back instead of a quarter can say, "I got bimped."

bripkin: one who puts forth mediocre effort. "The bripkin invites a girl to the theatre, but he takes her in a street-car—on a rainy night, too!" Burgess explained.

29

cowcat: "a person whose main function is to occupy space." Of the many possibilities, Burgess suggested, "Your wife's relatives?"

diabob: garishly ugly decoration; kitsch. Burgess rhymed, "This object made of celluloid, This thing so wildly plushed, How grossly Art has been annoyed, How Common Sense has blushed!"

frime: a reliable, thoughtful person. "The frime knows when you are hungry, when you are thirsty and when you would be let alone," Burgess wrote.

gloogo: a person who displays notable loyalty and devotion to a task, thing, or another person. "You are a gloogo if you read *Burgess Unabridged* all the way through," Burgess wrote.

gubble: meaningless social chatter.

huzzlecoo: private conversation between friends, business people, or flirts.

igmoil: a bitter dispute over money.

jirriwig: a traveler who ignores, or is indifferent to, dazzling surrounding sights.

kipe: to scrutinize with jealousy or contempt. "Up and down, from hat to heel, women kipe each other insolently as they pass," Burgess wrote.

lallify: to delay; to painstakingly extend. "The preacher, barren of fresh thoughts, lallifies his meager sermon," Burgess wrote.

looblum: something enjoyable but harmful. "Human nature," Burgess wrote, "woos the looblum."

mooble: unremarkable attempts at greatness. "Moobly novels are written by—well of course you know already," Burgess said.

oofle: "a person whose name you cannot remember."

paloodle: person who provides unwanted advice or information.

quisty: useful but not beautiful.

quoob: person whose behavior is constantly out of place. "If you are a natural born quoob, you are the only one of all the audience to applaud, or cheer," Burgess wrote.

rizgidget: state of indecisiveness.

skyscrimble: to go off topic, obliviously or evasively.

tashivate: "to reply without attention." What readers of this article may currently be doing to their chattering spouses.

unk: a gift that is not wanted or appropriate.

vilp: one who wins or loses in bad form, either gloating or making excuses.

whinkle: disingenuous or manipulative politeness. Burgess wrote: "How whinkles the pallid clerk at his employer's jokes."

yowf: "one whose importance exceeds his merit."

Update: *Burgess Unabridged* has since been re-released by Walker & Company, with a foreword by Paul Dickson.

birthmate

A word I always thought was a legitimate word but apparently isn't is "birthmate." It is someone who shares your birthday and year of birth—that is, born on exactly the same day. Celebrity case in point: Doris Day and the late Marlon Brando. What do you think?

—*Phil Schwimmer, Skokie, Illinois*

I DIDN'T find "birthmate" in any dictionary I checked, but I did find this title of an out-of-print book published in 1988: *The Birthmate Book: A Collection of Heroes, Rogues, Villains, and Stars*

31

Who Share Your Special Day. Most of the top search results for "birthmate" on Google, however, are brand names for treatments and medications for pregnant women.

brand names

THERE IS a moment every marketer both dreams of and fears. It is the time when a brand name, by decree of the dictionary or whims of the zeitgeist, becomes a common noun or a verb. This can be a blessing—the ultimate validation of a name that is both catchy and meaningful. But it can also be a curse. The more widely a word is used, the harder it is to legally protect as a trademark. So we "xerox" a memo, "fedex" a package, or "google" a blind date, to the chagrin of squads of copyright attorneys in corporate headquarters.

In a brand name's infancy, however, the thought of gaining this kind of cultural currency is an inspiration to professional namers, says Alex Frankel in his 2004 book *Wordcraft: The Art of Turning Little Words Into Big Business* (Crown).

Namers long to launch their creations into the vernacular, until they show up around water coolers and in online chat rooms. The lawyers, they figure, can worry bout the rest.

Frankel's book, like a tour of a sausage factory or the U.S. Capitol building, shows readers places they've never seen to explain processes of which some would rather remain unaware. He describes how names are born—usually in magic marker on

Could you tell me the English term for when a brand name becomes synonymous with a product, such as Kleenex for tissue and Coke for cola?

—*Molly Rooney, Shorewood, Illinois*

Chicago-based lexicographer Erin McKean includes the word "antonomasia" in her eclectic collection *More Weird and Wonderful Words* (Oxford University Press). She defines it as "the practice, abhorred by lawyers, of using a trademark (like Kleenex or Xe-

whiteboards, alongside myriad other suggestions—and how a select few make it big, sometimes bigger than the name of the company itself.

The trick for corporations is to contrive a word that doesn't sound like a corporate contrivance. The more corporate it sounds, the greater the risk of a backlash against brand names among consumers.

Frankel, a journalist who started his own short-lived naming firm in Silicon Valley, chose five names to tell his story: Accenture, BlackBerry, Cayenne, e-business and Viagra.

Along the way, he introduces little-known but hugely influential naming firms such as Lexicon Branding in San Francisco—which coined Dasani, Febreze, Pentium, PowerBook, Zima, among hundreds of others—and Wood Worldwide in Manhattan, which has christened many best-selling drugs, including Paxil, Viagra and Zocor.

It was Lexicon that came up with the name BlackBerry for an electronic palm device. With the help of linguistics consultants, it analyzed possible names' semantics (meaning), phonetics (sound) and something namers call "sound symbolism."

For the Blackberry, Lexicon was seeking a name that would communicate the ideas "easy access" and "quick response." One namer thought the hand-held communicator looked sort of like a strawberry, its tiny keys resembling the seeds on a berry's surface. But he thought the word "blackberry" sounded better.

Lexicon brought in a linguistics professor to examine why.

---

rox) as a generic term," noting that the word's Greek roots mean "instead" and "to name."

This word is a delightful bit of etymological trivia, but most English speakers have never heard of it. You could call it making a proper noun (a capitalized name) into a common noun (a lowercase word for an object). You could also call it giving a legal headache to the squads of lawyers charged with guarding trademarks.

"Black," he noted, has hard and quick consonants that move the word along; "straw" begins with the sluggish hiss of the "S" and ends with a vowel, slowing the speaker down. Dubbing the device "BlackBerry" also benefited from alliteration and symmetry—two five-letter parts, each beginning with a capital "B" (thanks to "intercapping," or capitalizing a letter in the middle of a word).

Frankel credits the name for BlackBerry's success; it has sold millions, including 435 to the U.S. House of Representatives.

Viagra was even more of a verbal phenomenon, landing in *The Oxford English Dictionary* just three years after the product was launched in 1998.

The drug itself—sildenafil citrate—was patented by Pfizer in 1991 as a heart treatment. When researchers noticed the drug offered other benefits, Pfizer turned to Wood Worldwide for a name. Wood offered "Viagra," noting the aptness of the word's sounds for the nature of the drug's remedy—"Vi" for virility or vigor and "agra," suggesting the energy of "aggression" and the fertility of "agriculture."

Seeing the birth of brand names may lead readers to look at the ever-growing place of brands in their own lives and speech, Frankel says by phone. "Part of my hope is that the reader would come away from this book and look at the world in a slightly different way," he said. "They would see their own vocabulary filled with brand names and wonder if that's good or bad."

Of course, this kind of inspection could backfire, as Geoffrey Nunberg observed in *The New York Times* in 2004. "As advertisers have known for a long time," he wrote, "no audience is easier to beguile than one that is smugly confident of its own sophistication."

bring vs. take

Please discuss the differences between "bring" and "take." I hear people say, "I will bring the clothes to the dry cleaners." I would say, "I will take the clothes."

—*Jeanne Martineau, Chicago, Illinois*

THE OLD rule is that "bring" is an action that comes toward you and "take" is an action that goes away from you. But this is a two-dimensional model for a three-dimensional world.

If you throw a party, should you ask your friends to "bring" or "take" their own beer? The beer bottles will be moving in a direction toward you but away from them (as they read the invitation). In this case, the power of the abbreviation "BYOB" probably influences people to say "bring," but the direction of action—and the point of view of the person saying or hearing it—doesn't really matter.

Then there's the fact that "bring" can mean "escort," as in, "Let me bring you to your car." That usage might lead people to think of themselves as escorting their clothes to the cleaners, or their beer bottles to your party—"bringing" them.

So you can try to follow the "bring here, take away" rule. But if you need to pause to draw yourself a map of a proposed action before you choose which word to say, or if you can't decide if you're taking or escorting, then worrying about this distinction (and imposing it on others) is probably a waste of time.

by and large

I want to ask you about the term "by and large." In my naivete, having heard the phrase only spoken (not in print), I interpreted it as "by enlarge." What is the origin?

—*Sally Hering, Lincolnshire, Illinois*

TO THE high seas! "'By and large' is nautical in origin, originally referring to the sailing qualities of a vessel," writes Dave Wilton at his *Word Origins* website (www.wordorigins.org). "To sail 'by the wind' is to sail directly into the wind (or as close into the wind as is possible)," Wilton writes. "A 'large wind' is one that comes from [behind]. Therefore, a ship that sails well 'by and large' sails well in all directions."

cc, as an abbreviation

I vaguely recall some years ago a language authority explaining that that little abbreviation at the end of memos or other messages, "cc:" did not actually stand for "carbon copy" as is generally assumed, but in fact is an abbreviation for a Greek or Latin phrase that in effect states: "This message has also been communicated to others." Can you support or refute this?

—*Dennis Allen, Wilmette, Illinois*

I E-MAILED Michael Quinion, editor of the *World Wide Words* website (www.worldwidewords.org) and author of *Ballyhoo, Buckaroo, and Spuds* (Smithsonian). He replied, "*The Oxford English Dictionary* finds the first example of 'cc' only from 1936, in which it is specifically explained as meaning 'carbon copy.' This seems pretty definitive. I've looked in my standard resources but can't find anything earlier." So without more evidence, the standard explanation stands.

Canadian English

THE TERM "Canadian English" and the study of Canadian vocabulary and speech patterns are only about as old as the career of linguist Jack Chambers.

Chambers began teaching linguistics in 1970 at the University of Toronto, from which he formally retired in spring 2005. He created and taught the first course on Canadian English in 1975, the same year a book he edited, *Canadian English: Origins and Structures*, was published. It was the first full-fledged book in the field.

It surprises many Canadians to know the field is this young; after all, "we're so self-conscious about not being American," he says.

"Chambers was the first and thenceforth pre-eminent Canadian sociolinguist," says Michael Adams, editor of *American Speech*, the journal of the American Dialect Society. "He has always been more than a great sociolinguist—a widely interested, willing scholar of language in its many shapes and sounds."

In studying how Canadians speak English, Chambers has discovered and documented an array of Canadian expressions, slang and speech patterns. "You get a very clear notion of what does not cross the border," says Chambers, who served as editorial adviser to *The Canadian Oxford Dictionary* and co-editor of *The Handbook of Language Variation and Change* (Blackwell). "Things that Americans call 'sneakers' are increasingly being called 'runners' in Canadian English. 'Runners' does not cross the border."

Reflecting Canada's roots as a British colony and its continuing ties to Great Britain, the British influence on Canadian English remains apparent—for example, in the Canadian spelling of "colour," the pronunciation of "been" to rhyme with "seen" and the name "zed" for the letter Z. But other features of Canadian English are unique, such as the practice of ending sentences with "eh" as a way to convey, "right?" Several hockey terms, including "puck" and "poke check," originated in Canada. "Tuque" is a Canadian word for a knitted winter hat. By some estimates, 2,000 words are exclusive to Canadian English.

Despite the vast size and sparse population of Canada, the nation's brand of English is relatively consistent across the continent, Chambers says. The pronunciation differences between Vancouver and Toronto, for example, are far less noticeable than the differences between speakers in Los Angeles and New York City.

"Canadian English is virtually identical from coast to coast," Chambers says. "It has much less [regional] diversity than America. . . . It shows that a single speech community can in fact encompass thousands of miles, which didn't happen in the United States." Chambers says this may be because Canada had more stable settlement patterns than the United States did. Many settlers of the Canadian West came from Ontario, while the United States has had a variety of regional and ethnic influences on its language.

The establishment of Canadian English as a legitimate field in linguistics was evident in January 2005, when the University of Toronto hosted the first academic conference on the topic. The gathering drew attendees from the U.S. and Europe and featured papers on the speech of Canadian adolescents, regional variation and the decline of the "yod"—the insertion of a Y-like sound that makes "news" sound like "nyooz."

"It sort of crystallized what's been going on for 30 years in many aspects of the way Canadians speak English," Chambers says of the conference. "Canadian English is an equal partner with the other varieties of North American English, along with New England English and Upper Midwest English and Texan English," he says. "It represents an entire nation, not just a region. It has that kind of impact and importance."

It was Chambers who coined the term and pioneered the study of "Canadian raising," which refers to the distinctively Canadian pronunciation of the vowel in "out" by forming the sound higher in the mouth than Americans do. One of the trademarks of Canadian English, the sound may have its origins in the influence of Scottish settlers on Canadian English, Chambers says.

English remains the dominant language in Canada, but Chambers points out that French is still thriving there. Though some French speakers sense their language is losing ground, Chambers says it will continue to coexist with English.

"Canada is more bilingual now in French and English than it has ever been in its history," he says, noting that a recent census showed an increase in the number of bilingual Canadians. "The monolingual French community is being more restricted to internal parts of Quebec, [but] there's a tremendous boom of bilingual belts on the eastern and western frontiers of Quebec. . . . If you're bilingual and interested in the survival of French, it is not endangered."

canvass

My question is about the word "canvass," which means "a solicitation of votes or orders," or "an examination or discussion." The explanation I heard is that it comes from "to toss in a canvas sheet as punishment."

—*Nann Blaine Hilyard, Zion, Illinois*

THAT IS the origin, according to *The Oxford English Dictionary*, but it's not clear exactly how the word went from sheets to votes.

"Canvass" first meant "to toss in a canvas sheet . . . to blanket, as a sport or punishment," according to the *OED*. The violence of this action apparently led the word to more broadly mean "attack," as when historian Sir John Hayward wrote in 1599, "The north parts were many times canvased, and . . . almost consumed by the Scots."

But how do you get from that to canvassing votes—which can mean both verifying election results, and soliciting votes? The *OED* admits this development "has not been explained." I always assumed the idea was covering a voting district as though spreading a sheet over it, so that no one is left out. That could indeed be the metaphor at work, but it's not clear.

As if all that weren't bizarre enough, it turns out "canvass" comes from the same Latin root word as "cannabis," a word for hemp. The fiber of this herb is good for making a canvas—among other uses.

chat

"LET'S TALK. Let's chat," invited Senator Hillary Clinton, announcing her candidacy for president in a video message on her website in 2007.

"Chat" may seem like an unlikely word to use for a discussion of serious issues—more apt for coffee shops than presidential campaigns. It depends on how you hear it.

Historically, the word "chat" has not been taken seriously. It's a shortened form of "chatter," which *The Oxford English Dictionary* says originated as "an onomatopoeic word"—that is, a word that imitates the sound it signifies. The word "chatter" first referred to birds; it seemed to capture the noise they made, as when 14th century writer John de Trevisa wrote, "Small birds cry and chatter more than great [ones]."

"Human 'chattering' was originally transferred from the chattering of birds," the *OED* explains. It wasn't a flattering term: The definition for this meaning was "to talk rapidly, incessantly, and with more sound than sense." Even today, when we say "chitchat" or "idle chatter," we're talking about speech that doesn't amount to much.

Sometimes "chat" and "chatter" do carry heavier weight. The phrase "terrorist chatter" refers to messages that are intercepted by intelligence agencies. When someone tells you, "we need to have a chat," it's generally a euphemism for a serious talk about something uncomfortable. But it's a euphemism only because the word "chat" usually means something more pleasant and light-hearted.

In the last 10 or 15 years, we've added a new definition for the word "chat": "to take part in an online discussion in a chat room," as *Merriam-Webster* defines it. The book *High Definition: An A to Z Guide to Personal Technology*, by the editors of American Heritage Dictionaries, defines "chat" as "to communicate in real-time on a computer network using typed messages."

This new use of "chat" has now become so common that the old-fashioned sense of "chat" sometimes needs a clarification. In fact, it wasn't clear what, exactly, Hillary Clinton meant when she said, "Let's chat." Was she evoking a casual, comfortable conversation? Or was she previewing her forthcoming week of what she calls "Web chats"—a series of videotaped interviews in which she answered questions (mostly friendly and flattering) sent in by website visitors and read aloud by Clinton aides?

"The [older] meaning of chat is fully alive and functional," says Grant Barrett, author of *The Official Dictionary of Unofficial English* (McGraw-Hill). "She simply means an informal, unstructured conversation. It doesn't have to be online."

It was this meaning that led columnist Jan Tuckwood to quip in the *Palm Beach Post*, "Hillary Clinton wants to chat with me. She'd like me to pull up a dainty chair next to her pastel couch . . . and swap girl talk about our kids and their future." Tuckwood was being sarcastic, but President Franklin D. Roosevelt used the word "chat" the same way when he called his radio addresses during the Great Depression "fireside chats."

Today, though, the meaning of exchanging online messages has given "chat" some different overtones. "'Chat' is used both ways, and I think she deftly used the word," Steve Kleinedler, senior editor of American Heritage Dictionaries, said of Clinton's announcement. "To people for whom it meant face-to-face, it had resonance, and to people for whom it meant online communication, it also had resonance."

Either way, the word "chat" serves an illusion of intimacy in modern politics. We want our politician to be someone we'd like to sit and share small talk with, even though most of us never will. We want to feel close to that person, even though lights, cameras, and handlers keep them at a distance. Even when their communication is controlled and calculated, we want it to feel casual.

Chicago, pronunciation of first syllable

Why do Americans pronounce Chicago with a "sh" sound at the beginning (as in "she"), instead of a "ch" (as in "chick")? You might have noticed that Spanish speakers, even bilingual speakers (such as myself) make a very clear distinction between the CH sound and the SH sound. My lips refuse to conform to anything but a "Chick-ah-go" pronunciation.

—*Stephanie Pringhipakis Guijarro, Chicago*

ALTHOUGH "CH" usually stands for the sound in "chick," English also uses it sometimes for a "K" sound, as in "character," the German guttural sound in "Bach," and, yes, the "sh" sound in "champagne" and "chandelier." These soft "ch" words tend to come from French. One of those words is "Chicago."

"Most sources agree that the present-day pronunciation of 'Chicago' derives from the variation of a Native American term by early French-speaking settlers, but there's also evidence to suggest the distinctive 'shh' goes back to its Indian origins," says Tim Samuelson, cultural historian for the city of Chicago. He points to an early 19th century source that describes the Native American pronunciation as "Shig-gau-go" and defines the name as "the skunk."

Some historians make a stink about this theory of the name's origin, Samuelson warns, but to make a long story short, the "Shicago" pronunciation is probably older than the city itself.

41

Chicago, pronunciation of second syllable

As an expatriate Chicagoan, I particularly enjoyed your discussion about the pronunciation of the city's name (*see* **Chicago, pronunciation of first syllable**). I have a follow-up question. Why do some people pronounce the second syllable of "Chicago" as "cah" while others (including me) say "caw"?

—*Kevin McCarthy, New Haven, Connecticut*

LAURA DICKEY, linguist at Northwestern University, says this "aw" to "ah" change is part of the Northern Cities Shift, a series of changes in vowel pronunciation in many Midwestern cities. The "aw" sound is starting to sound different because many of us are pronouncing it from a slightly different position in our mouths. "This isn't confined to the word 'Chicago'; it's part of the whole vowel system," Dickey says. "How you say this word is related to how you say things like 'pot' and 'block' too."

A professor of mine once had a student complain about the Midwestern pronunciation of "God" as "Gahd," saying that "Gawd" is the more reverent pronunciation (except, presumably, when the word is used to curse).

ciao

In Italian, how or when did *ciao* (hello) evolve to regular usage for *arrivederci* (goodbye)?

—*Daniel J. Smith, Chicago, Illinois*

I ASKED Max Braglia, an Italian native and Floridian who produces a podcast on learning to speak Italian at www.learnitalianpod.com.

"I wouldn't say that 'ciao' has evolved to regular usage for *arrivederci*," Braglia writes by e-mail. "*Ciao* and *arrivederci* are two different types of greeting—both still widely used in Italian. While *ciao* is informal, and used at all times among relatives and friends or with children, both when meeting and leaving, *arrivederci* can be . . . both formal and informal, and it's always used upon leaving."

Braglia adds, "In those instances where *ciao* and *arrivederci* have the same meaning (when leaving and saying goodbye in an informal way), then you could say *ciao* is actually more popular—I guess for no particular reason, other than the fact that *ciao* is easier to pronounce than *arrivederci*. Still, the word *arrivederci* is very widely used in Italian."

clichés

MARCH IS the season of the NCAA men's basketball tournament, and, as they inevitably say, you can throw the records out the window. And the mathematics. In pregame pep talks and post-game press conferences, players and coaches repeatedly make the math-defying pledge to give 110 percent and offer up boundless other basketball banalities.

"If anybody watches 10 seconds of sports on TV or reads anything between quotation marks in the paper, it's almost all clichés," says Steve Rushin, columnist for *Sports Illustrated*. "We all know those ready-made phrases so well you can almost predict them before they come out of someone's mouth: 'It was a team effort; we gave 110 percent.'"

In 2000, Rushin wrote a column composed entirely of clichés (deliberately, he hastens to note).

"Men, if we play our game, bring our 'A' game, take it one game at a time, stick to the game plan, stay within ourselves, dictate the tempo . . . step up our intensity, execute, focus, convert and leave it all on the floor, it's anybody's ball game," Rushin wrote. "But there's no tomorrow, our backs are against the wall, it's crunch time, gut-check time, do or die. . . . We'll need good chemistry, and you can't teach that."

In 2003, Rushin wrote a column comparing television coverage of the NCAA tournament with coinciding coverage of the invasion of Iraq, noting how overwrought the militaristic jargon of basketball seemed. "The cataclysmic and the inconsequential sounded almost identical," Rushin wrote. "Said [one player], after his team's not-quite-epic victory, 'It was a war out there.'"

But if reporters tire of the blather of athletes, they should watch their own jargon, Rushin says.

"Many athletes, sportswriters and fans really do think that way, because they're conditioned to think that way," he says by phone. "When a player is asked repeatedly about the chemistry of the team, nobody would naturally think of a team as having chemistry unless they had heard that so many times."

"Coaches have been living inside of this rhetoric their entire lives, since the time they started playing basketball in junior high," said David Shields, who spent a season covering the NBA's Seattle SuperSonics for his book *Black Planet: Facing Race in an NBA Season* (Three Rivers Press). "After a while their language becomes reality, and they have no way to see outside of that. It's never acknowledged that it's just a game, the result of which carries no larger meaning."

The Oxford English Dictionary defines "cliché" as "a stereotyped expression, a commonplace phrase." The word is derived from a French term for a printer's template.

As pretentious as they may sound, clichés sometimes serve as a defense mechanism for players in the glare of the media, Shields said. "It's a way to let no feeling come into the mix," said Shields, author of *Body Politic: The Great American Sports Machine*. "By presenting bland language to you, it makes sure you can never penetrate my inner being. . . . There's actually very little communication going on."

As a result, hollow statements preserve the mythic quality of athletic feats, Shields said. "The words tell you nothing, so the deeds stay magical," he said. "If the words started to become beautiful, interesting and dense, we would say, wait a minute, that's a complete human being who really does get nervous at the plate."

Though emptied of significance by their overuse and hyperbole, clichés can be succinct and rhythmic, especially in basketball. "Take it to the hole," "crash the boards," and "nothing but net" all hit the ear in a way that "make a basket" does not.

"When you put them all together they take on [the quality] of a mad poetry," Shields said. "The reason they have become part of the vernacular is that they're weirdly evocative."

"Most clichés became clichés because they were colorful phrases in the first place, and people wanted to use them." Rushin said. "The first person who said, 'We were backed into a corner but came out swinging,' was being very colorful."

"Sometimes athletes can go on in Shakespearean soliloquies entirely in clichés," Rushin said. "By writing a column in clichés, I was trying to elevate clichés to a perverse art form."

Clueless, linguistic legacy of

THE YEAR 2005 marked a milestone—a tragic one, some would say—in the history of American English. Ten years earlier, in July 1995, the movie *Clueless*, starring Alicia Silverstone, was released. And our language was, like, forever changed.

"The interesting thing about *Clueless* is that the language was basically another character in that movie," says Carmen Fought, linguist at Pitzer College in Claremont, California. "A lot of research was put into it to really capture how Californians talked at the time, and I think that was the first time that people in different parts of the country got a clear exposure to all the features of the California dialect."

Clueless spread its share of slang words, including a fleet of synonyms for "good" and "bad." Writer and director Amy Heckerling keeps a list of them in her personal *Clueless* thesaurus.

Heckerling, who loosely based her story on Jane Austen's classic novel *Emma*, was out of the country as her movie's 10th anniversary approached, but in the 2005 PBS documentary *Do You Speak American?* she read some of the words for "good" from her thesaurus: "kicking, juice, keen, funky, monster, proper, rad, noble." As for "bad": "random, heinous, cheesy, blows, bites, bogus, bunk, brick, bum, bug . . . clueless."

Clueless of course, also popularized the interjection "Whatever!"—with emphasis on the second syllable, and thumbs joined with forefingers extended to make a "W."

Clueless didn't invent these words; many were already well-established in Californian speech. In the 1980s, some (such as "like" and "totally") already had appeared in Heckerling's 1982 movie *Fast Times at Ridgemont High* and Moon Unit Zappa's song "Valley Girl" the same year. But Fought says *Clueless* may have helped circulate this language like never before.

"Now we're starting to see some sporadic Californian features in other areas of the country, . . . and even as far away as Canada and Scotland," Fought says. "So it seems very clear that that's something that's been exported from California, and I think movies like *Clueless* did have a role in that."

Slang words from television shows and movies tend to have a short life span. But *Clueless* may have helped introduce more subtle and durable linguistic features to American English, including the function of the words "all" and "like," as in this line from *Clueless*: "This weekend he called me up and he's all, 'Where were you today?' and I'm like, 'I'm at my Grandmother's house.'"

"All" and "like" are used here as what linguists call quotative markers, introducing a quotation. These words aren't just casual alternatives to "said"; they often have their own function. "Said" precedes an exact quotation, "all" and "like" can also set up an approximate quotation in the tone of the original speaker.

Fought says linguists now need to take a new look at whether movies such as *Clueless* can even influence certain sound changes, such as "oo-fronting." The Californian pronunciation of "oo" is initiated toward the front of the mouth, so that the word "dude" sounds more like "dewd" than "dood." Fought says some Americans outside California have started to adopt "oo-fronting."

Linguists have long rejected the possibility that TV and movies change the way we speak. Regional dialects remain the biggest influence on people's pronunciation and vocabulary; people tend to sound like the people around them.

But many teenagers outside of California apparently have picked up on the kind of dialect Silverstone uses in *Clueless*.

"Now there's more dissemination of casual speech [in the media]," Fought says. "I think *Clueless* was really one of the first to get those new trends started and raise the question for linguists."

Fought has done studies that show people associate the California dialect with the state's pleasant climate, outdoor sports and its stereotypical relaxed, laid-back spirit. But what some consider relaxed, others call lazy. Few words have raised the ire of language purists the way the quotative "like" has in the years since *Clueless*. Any tirade about the state of the language is sure to say something about "like" as a plague on the language.

Fought says older speakers of any language tend to have the most negative response to language change. She says older speakers associate the constant use of "like" with being less intelligent, less ambitious and less serious about life.

"People in their 30s, 40s, and 50s are focused on getting ahead, having a career," Fought says. "To older people, hearing kids talk that way is like, 'Oh, they have no ambition.' Of course, linguists know that there's absolutely no connection between using the word 'like' and being stupid or having no ambition."

Fought says reading social doom into linguistic change is nothing new. "Older people have always criticized new words and [ways of speaking]," Fought says. "Go back to the 1950s to 'scram' and 'be cool,' and people were saying, 'The youth are ruining the language.' I'm sure if you go back to Shakespeare's time, people were saying, 'sooth sounds so bad, you really should say forsooth.'"

See also **I'm all** and **like totally.**

Coca-Cola, translation of slogan into Chinese

IN HER 2007 book *Biting the Wax Tadpole: Confessions of a Language Fanatic* (Melville House)—a compendium of language oddities—Elizabeth Little looks into the urban legend that Coca-Cola's slogan translates in Chinese as "bite the wax tadpole."

You might have heard a marketing consultant warn you about how your company's name or slogan translates into another language, and give you the cautionary tale of Coca-Cola. As the story goes, when Coca-Cola tried to sell its product in China in 1928, it used Chinese characters whose pronunciation sounded like "ke-kou ke-la," not realizing that in Mandarin this meant "bite the wax tadpole."

This marketing urban legend has a grain of truth Little says. Yes, some Shanghai shopkeepers advertised that they were selling "kekou kela." But there's no evidence this unappetizing translation deterred anyone from buying the soft drink. And the Coca-Cola company, Little says, anticipated the problem and found a solution: a combination of Chinese characters that sounded like "ke-kou ke-le" and roughly meant "delicious happiness."

co-family

MORE THAN 10 years ago, sisters Kathy McGrath and Jeannie McDonald encountered a dilemma when introducing the members of their new stepfamily.

"We found ourselves dealing with awkward situations when introducing someone: 'This is my dad's wife,'" McGrath said. "There was always a hesitation in our voice. Saying 'stepmother' and 'stepson' never seemed to convey the true family sentiment, the sense of belonging. We wanted to find different language."

It doesn't help that the words "stepmother" and "stepsister" come with connotations of wickedness, thanks to the timeless story of Cinderella. It also doesn't help that the "step-" prefix originated in the Old English word "astieped," which meant "bereaved," and led to such Old English words as "steopbearn," meaning "orphan."

Recent portrayals of stepmothers are more benign but still negative. In the 1998 movie *Stepmom*, Susan Sarandon plays a caring and capable mother who watches the immature and incompetent Julia Roberts character hook up with her ex-husband and try to take care of her kids.

So what can you say besides "step-"? McGrath and McDonald started combing books about stepfamilies. "In our research, we came across a lot of 'comfort,' 'confidant' and 'in care of,'" McGrath said. "All of us were really in care of each other. So we made it 'co-,' such as 'co-mom,' 'co-dad.'"

They had their new prefix. Now it was just a matter of introducing it to the English language. The best way to do that, they decided, was to start their own greeting card business: Co-Family Expressions Inc.

"Greeting cards are a means by which people express themselves on holidays or even every day," McDonald said. "We thought that maybe this would be an avenue to introduce the co-family concept, to bring about an awareness of co-families, and to help to give them some relational clarity."

The cards read, "For My Co-Sister," "Happy Birthday, Co-Son!" and so on. McGrath is in charge of design, and McDonald writes the text. They've heard from hundreds of customers, and from organizations such as the Stepfamily Association of America, who like the new word.

But Co-Family Expressions has yet to take the greeting card industry by storm. McGrath and McDonald, both full-time mothers, continue to operate their business out of their homes and through their website (www.co-family.com). They hope to place their cards in stores next year.

Wayne Glowka, chairman of the New Words Committee of the American Dialect Society, who happens to live in a "co-family" situation, says the word may be an improvement, but it can only begin to ease the tensions among relatives by remarriage.

"'Co-family' is probably a wonderful euphemism for some people, but at my house we try our best to call our arrangement a family," Glowka says. "People create euphemisms and 'politically correct' language to disguise ugly things, but new words do not disguise the ugly things any better than the old words did."

"The co-family concept isn't for everyone," McDonald said. "Our cards don't all convey a warm, fuzzy feeling. Not everyone is uncomfortable using 'step-.' 'Co-family' is for people who are looking for an alternative."

collective singulars

> WITH A noun subject that denotes a group, do you use the singular or plural? "The staff is (are) all going to the meeting. The group of girls is (are) having an overnight campout."
>
> —*Dorothy Schmidt, Chicago, Illinois*

YOU MIGHT be sorry you asked. This is one of the grayest areas of English. Some people call these cases "collective singulars"—a term that's right up there with "virtual reality" and other oxymorons.

The usage guides I consulted say it depends on what you subtly mean by "group." If the group is being considered as a whole, a singular verb applies. If group members are being considered as individuals, a plural verb is used.

Bill Walsh, who spills a lot of ink on this in his book *The Elephants of Style* (McGraw-Hill), gives these examples: "A group of surgeons is calling for new warnings on cigarette packaging," but "A group of surgeons are going to the club for open-mike night." His explanation is that in the first sentence, you're "talking about the group," while in the second, you're "talking about the surgeons." My guess is he would take your example and say, "A group of girls has decided to have a campout," but "A group of girls are going camping."

The problem is that it's not always clear whether a collective action is unanimous or composite. How can we follow or enforce this distinction when we can't always understand it? Walsh says he doesn't know what to do with the sentence, "A series of specials on PBS document(s) the civil-rights movement."

You can often insert "members" to make it easier on yourself: "All staff members are going to the meeting." Or you can move to Britain, where they say, "The family are coming."

"In an effort to make the world a better place, I cleave to Conan the Grammarian's Three Rules of Correcting Others," writes best-selling language maven Richard Lederer, a.k.a. "Conan the Grammarian," in a cover article in the Chicago-based language magazine *Verbatim*.

His first: "Are you right?" Second: "Will it make a difference?" If the answer to both questions is "yes," Lederer concludes, then you may proceed to the third rule: "Do the correcting in private."

Lederer's three rules are fairly simple and straightforward, but to me, they illustrate the flaws of the entire enterprise of giving grammatical advice. "Says who?" is always an appropriate response to Lederer's first question, because what he means by "Are you right?" amounts to this: Do manuals on English usage and style recommend the correction you're about to make?

But usage manuals are seldom written by linguists, who actually study how language works. The manuals tend to make subjective, selective and shaky suggestions. The authors pass off their own personal preferences or folk customs as gospel truth. Arnold Zwicky, a linguist at Stanford University, writes at his website that linguists' "foundational assumptions diverge strikingly from those of the advice literature at almost every turn." He cautions, "The advice literature on language is [merely] advice, comparable to advice on diet, exercise, gardening, child rearing, relationships, and the like."

For example, usage manuals keep perpetuating the myth that it's an error to use the adverb "hopefully" in a sentence such as "Hopefully, my in-laws will leave tomorrow," arguing that your in-laws will not literally be "full of hope" as they depart. But usage manuals don't usually condemn the similar use of adverbs such as "clearly," "fortunately" and "admittedly." So the "hopefully" rule isn't really a rule, it's just a custom for English usage.

Lederer himself shows how arbitrary the grammar advice business can be. He writes in *Verbatim* that he was annoyed by a nurse who asked him to "lay down on the table," instead of "lie down." Lederer writes, "Enough . . . of us standard English speakers and writers adhere to that distinction that I feel that I'm right about enforcing it in reasonably formal situations."

But many educated speakers of English use "lie" and "lay" interchangeably in everyday conversation, and not all usage manuals ban this. "For many expressions," says *The American Heritage Guide to Contemporary Usage and Style* (Houghton Mifflin), "nonstandard 'lay' is actually more common than standard 'lie,' and in many contexts 'lay' sounds more natural." Besides, since when is a doctor's office a "reasonably formal situation"? If the patient is in his underwear, how formal can it be?

Lederer's second condition for bestowing grammatical advice—"Will it make a difference?" —raises even more doubts, because the answer almost always is, "No."

Lederer figures that "in the case of the nurse, who's probably misusing 'lay' many times each day and could lose the doctor business, I feel that my interposition will make a difference."

I've never met anyone who switched doctors because of a nurse's English usage, and I hope I never do.

However they justify it, some people consider it their calling in life to enforce customs of English usage as though they were actually moral principles. But trying to preserve picky usage "rules" is like trying to make a fashion trend permanent. Fashion merely reflects subjective and often conflicting judgments about good taste—and fashion is always changing.

People have been complaining about the state of the English language for centuries, and they almost always overstate the doom English faces. John Dryden whined in the year 1660 that "our language is in a manner barbarous." Jonathan Swift wrote an essay in 1712 called "Proposal for Correcting, Improving and Ascertaining the English Tongue."

But you can't freeze language in time. If English were supposed to stay put, we'd all talk like they did in *Beowulf*, that first-millennium Old English poem that begins, "Hwaet! We Gardena in geardagum . . . " Lederer acknowledges that because of his degree in linguistics, "I'm supposed to see language change as neither good nor bad but natural evolution," but he says this grudgingly.

When I answer questions about usage and style, I try to be honest about how subjective my reply is and stress that deciding whether or not to conform to usage customs always depends on the situation. Lecture halls and board rooms are different from city streets, living rooms, and, yes, doctor's offices. Many gurus of grammar suggest everybody should follow their advice in every situation. But they're just writing hopefully.

Update: In a letter to the *Chicago Tribune*, Richard Lederer complained that "Bierma contends that no one is in a position to offer anyone else any tips about any matter linguistic." No, I was merely distinguishing between informed, useful advice and arbitrary, irrelevant advice. Everyone is potentially in a position to offer the former, though too few actually do.

Lederer also wrote that most usage writers "are trained scholars who understand that effectiveness and power in language result in part from the ability to code-switch depending on the relative formality of a situation." In my experience, a usage writer with these linguistic sensibilities (such as Lederer himself, to a refreshing extent) is the exception, not the rule.

He also insisted, "I continue to believe that nurses' instructions to 'lie down' will work for all patients, that nurses generally appreciate the privately proffered advice to use 'lie down,' and that some nurses will actually make the change."

I agree that "lie down" will indeed "work for all patients," but "lay down" will work for all patients too—even the needlessly picky ones, who will suffer no ounce of misunderstanding of the nurse's meaning, despite looking down their noses at her (or his) style of expressing it. I can't imagine a nurse who would sincerely appreciate a correction in this situation, much less change his usage in future similar situations. No doubt a few exist, but they, too, are unusual—as they should be.

See also **grammar, descriptive; National Grammar Day; pedantry; prepositions, ending sentences with;** and **usage.**

could care less vs. couldn't care less

Besides the common "I could care less," my second-ranking pet peeve is the use of "and" rather than "to" in the phrase "try and do something" as though these were two separate actions, like "eat and drink."

—*Peter G. Haag, Elmhurst, Illinois*

"COULD CARE less" and "try and do" can be considered idioms— phrases whose meaning is understood separately from the meanings of the individual words. "Could care less" is a variation of the phrase "couldn't care less"; strangely, these two phrases would seem to be opposite but actually have identical meanings.

The American Heritage Guide to Contemporary Usage and Style says that "try and" is "commonly used as a substitute for 'try to,'" but it cautions that "the usage is associated with informal style and strikes an inappropriately conversational note in formal writing."

dasn't

> I found myself recently about to write in an e-mail, "But you dasn't say that." Just how archaic is "dasn't"? Am I the only one on the planet who remembers using it?
>
> —*Rhita Lippitz, Evanston, Illinois*

THIS ONE was new to me, although maybe I should have remembered reading it in Mark Twain's *Huckleberry Finn:* "We dasn't stop again at any town, for days and days." Editor Enid Pearsons wrote at the website of Random House in 2001, "'Dasn't' is a contraction of 'dare not,' found chiefly in dialects spoken in northern parts of the United States." She says the "S" probably comes from either the archaic inflected forms "durst" and "darst," or the third-person singular form, "dares not." I dasn't challenge what Pearsons says.

decimate

> When did the word "decimated" come to mean wiped out or annihilated? I've been hearing it used this way for some time now, and it's driving me crazy.
>
> —*Robert Janke, Des Plaines, Illinois*

THIS ONE probably falls into the category of obscure etymological trivia—too obscure to make a rule out of it.

The trivia is that "decimate," derived from the Latin "decem" for "ten," originally meant "to reduce by one-tenth" or, more specifically, "to kill every tenth person," a punishment reportedly practiced by the ancient Roman military. But so few people know this gruesome history that you'll probably confuse people if you try to use the word to mean "destroy a tenth of." Besides, why base language rules on ancient Roman military practices?

"Decimate" was used in the sense of "to destroy or wipe out a large part of" at least as early as the 19th century, when author Laurence Oliphant wrote, "Cholera was then decimating the country."

deceptively

We have had a long-standing disagreement about how to interpret the phrase "deceptively simple." Once at a dinner party we surveyed our very smart guests, and the group was evenly divided. What is your opinion? Does "deceptively simple" mean that something is truly simple but appears difficult, or does it mean that something is truly difficult but looks as if it were simple?

—Terry Sukenik, Chicago, Illinois;
Terry Imber, Los Angeles, California

THIS BET will be hard to settle. The answer is not simple, and I'm not deceiving.

"When 'deceptively' is used to modify an adjective, the meaning is often unclear," says *The American Heritage Guide to Contemporary Usage and Style.* The *American Heritage* editors surveyed their Usage Panel back in 1982, and got similar results to your dinner-party poll. In the sentence—"The pool is deceptively shallow"—half of the panel thought the pool is shallower than it appears, while 32 percent said it was deep, and 18 percent said it was impossible to determine.

I agree with the 50 percent. Because "deceptively" modifies "shallow," I would think the pool is shallow but deceives you into thinking that it isn't shallow. But there's so much ambiguity in the phrase that the *American Heritage Guide* suggests that you reword it, saying that the pool "is shallower than it looks" or "is shallow, despite its appearance."

dentist

What is happening to the English spoken language? Have you noticed the disappearance of the "T" when it is preceded by an "N"? For example: "She is going to the denist" (dentist) or "It was very inneresting" (interesting), or "He attended an innernational (international) meeting."

—Elise Glassenberg, Chicago, Illinois

I DON'T know if I've ever pronounced the "T" in words such as "center," "wanted," "twenty," or "international." To me, the clear articulation of the "T" in these words sounds snobby, British, or both.

Linguists say it's natural for the "T" to blend in with the "N" sound, because these sounds are produced so similarly. "The 'T' and the 'N' are made with the mouth in the absolutely identical position (tongue tip touching at the ridge behind the top teeth)," Laura Dickey, linguist at Northwestern University, explained to me by e-mail. "The only difference between them is [that] the 'N' lets air flow through the nose and the 'T' doesn't."

Without special effort to supply extra breath to the "T," it naturally gives way to the "N." "What happens is that the part with no nasal airflow (the 'T') just gets shorter and shorter until it disappears," Dickey says. "So, the 'T' is gone and only the 'N' remains."

Two of your examples, though, actually strike me as exceptions. I tend to pronounce "interesting" as "intra-sting," skipping the second "E" rather than the first "T." And I do hit the "T" more firmly in "dentist" than in other words, at least when "dentist" ends the sentence.

Maybe the word "dentist" reminds me to use my teeth!

diagramming sentences

SENTENCE DIAGRAMMING is the long division of English. It involves a bewildering array of lines and diagonal branches. It is loathed as an elementary school chore. And it is presumed to be obsolete.

"Today, diagramming is not exactly dead, but for many years it has been on a steep slide into marginality," writes author Kitty Burns Florey at the online *Vocabula Review*, in an essay reprinted in the December 2004 issue of *Harper's*. But with students' writing skills widely presumed to be in dire straits, sentence diagramming may be ready to make a comeback.

To diagram a sentence—if you have blocked this memory from your school days—you place the noun phrase and verb phrase (subject and predicate, if you prefer) on a straight line, separated by a vertical line. Modifying words and prepositional phrases go on corresponding diagonal lines underneath. (For an introduction and examples, see www.tinyurl.com/y6kq8b.) The result, Florey says, is "a picture of language."

The practice was introduced in an 1877 textbook called *Higher Lessons in English*, but it fell out of favor beginning in the 1960s. Around that time, progressive theories emerged that said students should be encouraged to express themselves in writing without being subjected to grammatical nitpicking. Today, *The New York Times* says, sentence diagramming has become "a symbol of everything old and stodgy."

Even Florey concedes that the skill of diagramming is of limited use. "Diagramming may have taught us to write more correctly—maybe even to think more logically—but I don't think anyone would claim that it taught us to write well," she writes. "And besides, any writer knows that the best way to learn to write good sentences has always been not to diagram them but to read them."

Florey recalls diagramming as her favorite part of the school day and says she liked "the way the words settled primly along their horizontals like houses on a road." Her fondness for the exercise is shared by some linguists who see it as a way to improve students' knowledge of grammar.

"It's a very direct way to visualize the function of the different parts of speech," David Mulroy, professor of classics at the University of Wisconsin-Milwaukee and author of *The War Against Grammar* (Boynton/Cook), says by phone. In his book, Mulroy laments the fact that many of his college students don't even know what a clause is (it's a string of words containing both a noun and verb, as opposed to a phrase, which has just one or the other). Diagramming, he says, is a place to start. "A diagram is a natural way to teach structure," he said. "Human memory works with structure. If information is structured, it's retained."

Diagrams aren't perfect, says Bill Poser, a linguist at the University of Pennsylvania. "The downside of diagramming is that it's a limited representation," he says. "It shows constituency, but it doesn't provide any labeling of grammatical categories, parts of speech and phrases. It also doesn't represent the word order."

Linguists, Poser says, prefer to write sentences in their original word order and use sets of brackets or branches to indicate parts of speech and relationships between phrases. But if diagramming sentences can help students grasp grammar, Poser says, he's all for it. He adds that diagramming doesn't have to be dull. "[The problem is] diagramming has not been presented as an exploratory activity," Poser says. "It should not be a matter of memorizing diagrams the teacher gives you. It should be exploring how sentences are put together."

Maybe Gertrude Stein was right. She once wrote, "I do not know that anything has ever been more exciting than diagramming sentences." Mulroy might not go that far, but he does say diagramming should not be considered tedious. "Sentence diagramming, if it's taught well, can be very stimulating," he says.

Mulroy has observed that students respond well to diagramming when they are encouraged to be creative—for example, by filling in a blank or partial diagram with words of their choice, as long as they fit. This way, he says, students "find it empowering to master when it's done correctly."

With students' writing abilities widely lamented by teachers and parents alike, the time may be ripe to reintroduce diagramming. In 2004, the state of Virginia passed a requirement that all sixth-grade students study sentence diagramming as a way to improve their writing.

If grammar does make its way back into the curriculum, it should be taught more effectively than it was in the last century, Mulroy urges. "There's a tendency in discussing grammar to focus on superficial usage," he says, "when really the need is for students to understand the foundational concepts of grammar."

Update: In 2006 Kitty Burns Florey published the book *Sister Bernadette's Barking Dog: The Quirky History and Lost Art of Diagramming Sentences* (Melville House).

dictionaries, coexistence with handheld technology

ERIN MCKEAN'S job is not just to change the dictionary—daunting as that is—but also to change the idea of a dictionary, from a heavy book to a handy tool.

"I want to make a dictionary as easy to use as a pencil," says McKean, editor in chief of U.S. dictionaries for Oxford University Press. "Now I can look up something walking down the street. You can have full access to it whenever you want, without having to drag a heavy book down from the shelf. You can look up a word with two fingers."

That's because the second edition of *The New Oxford American Dictionary* (Oxford University Press), released in 2005 and produced under McKean's supervision, can be downloaded onto a PDA or smartphone. It's the largest dictionary ever to be released for hand-held technology. "I checked five things during dinner last night," McKean says. "If a question comes up, I have the answer in my pocket." The new edition of the *NOAD* has also been published the old-fashioned way, as a 2,088-page bound book, with the trademark blue cover of Oxford University Press.

Of the new dictionary's more than a quarter million entries, about 2,000 were added since the first edition came out in 2001. Words that gained currency in American English over the last four years, and gained entry in the *NOAD*, include "bridezilla" ("an overzealous bride-to-be who acts irrationally or causes offense") and "speed dating" ("a social activity in which equal complements of potential partners spend a few minutes in short interviews with all other participants in order to determine whether there is interest").

McKean says that while the *NOAD* doesn't add every new word that comes along, it does reflect changes in the language. "The dictionary is not supposed to validate words, it's supposed to record them," she says. "It's like a phone book or a map—it tells you if something is there. . . . What it all comes down to is what's useful, what's helpful."

The second edition of the *NOAD* was released the same month as the 250th anniversary of Samuel Johnson's landmark *Dictionary of the English Language*, one of the first major English dictionaries.

Johnson defined "lexicographer" as "a writer of dictionaries, a harmless drudge." But McKean is anything but a drudge. For one thing, "I don't have to produce the whole thing by myself by candlelight," she says. Instead, she does her work digitally, e-mailing collaborators, revising entries and checking computer databases for examples of word usage.

Dubbed "America's lexicographical sweetheart" by National Public Radio, the 33-year-old word whiz and self-proclaimed "dictionary evangelist" gets excited as she talks about what went into the new *NOAD*. "It's the difference between getting a new house and renovating an old house," she explains. "If you can just fix the squeaky door, you wouldn't want to build a new house. We're always trying to say, can we find a better example sentence, write a new definition, add a couple of derivative forms. There's no such thing as a perfect dictionary, but we always strive for that."

See also **lexicography, in an online era.**

did you not

How do you answer the question: "Did you not kill your wife?" if you did?

—*Dick Hartop, Wheaton, Illinois*

DOG-RELATED VOCABULARY

The annual Westminster Kennel Club Dog Show in New York City gives us a sampling of dog-show terminology and reminds us of the many dog-related words and phrases that have trotted their way into the English language.

bark is worse than his bite: The phrase has been traced to the early 1800s, but the thought goes back to the 1600s, according to *The Oxford English Dictionary*, which quotes an anonymous writer as saying, "It is intended that [this] letter shall be a great bark if not a bite."

brace: In dog shows, a competition in which one handler shows two dogs of the same breed who look and act alike. "The two dogs are supposed to be as much alike as possible. They're judged on

I **WON'T** ask why you need to know; I'll just stick to the grammar.

In theory, you should be able to answer "yes" to mean "yes, I did not kill my wife," and "no" if you're guilty. But in reality, a one-word answer to this question, whether you're guilty or not, will confuse people.

The problem is that we tend to use the phrases "did you not" and "didn't you" for rhetorical questions—when we want confirmation rather than information. The person who asks you, "Didn't you go to Northwestern?" is checking her facts, not your class attendance record. Or she might be teasing you for doing something dumb: "Didn't you go to Northwestern, smart guy?"

If a "didn't you" question has a flawed assumption in it, you have to say "no" to clear things up. If the Cubs lost yesterday, the correct answer to "Didn't the Cubs win yesterday?" would not be "Yes, they did not win"—even though that checks out grammatically. The only answer that makes any sense is, "No, they lost."

Lately, of course, people are less likely to assume the Cubs have won.

---

how close they are," says David Frei, longtime television co-host of the Westminster Kennel Club Dog Show. (The word "brace" got its meaning of "pair" from its French root, which means "two arms.")

Canary Islands: These islands in the Atlantic off the African coast were named for the dogs found there, believe it or not. The little singing birds also found there were named for the islands, not the other way around.

The ancient explorer Juba landed on one of these islands and reported seeing a number of large, wild dogs, according to Martha Barnette in her book *Dog Days and Dandelions: A Lively Guide to the Animal Meanings Behind Everyday Words* (St. Martin's Press). Juba named it "Dog Island," and historian Pliny the Elder, writing in Latin, wrote this down as "Canaria Insula" ("Island

dilemma

See eon and dilemma.

disgruntled

The other day I saw a billboard that read, "Arrive Gruntled" (to your destination). Now I know that "disgruntled" has become a rather common word, but is there really such a word as "gruntled" to describe people who are content?

—*Nina Gaspich, Chicago, Illinois*

ONLY WHEN it's used playfully, as this billboard was doing, and as P.G. Wodehouse did back in 1938 when he wrote, "I could see that, if not actually disgruntled, he was far from being gruntled."

Etymologist Michael Quinion credits Wodehouse with starting this play on words and calls "disgruntled" an "unpaired opposite." He looks at a few other examples at his *World Wide Words* website (www.worldwidewords.org), including "disconsolate," "ineffable," "innocuous," "unruly" and "unscathed."

of Dogs"). (The Latin word for dog was "canis," the root of our word "canine.")

dog days: I always thought this phrase meant days when people are lazy, or "dogging it," because of the heat. But Barnette tells a different story in *Dog Days and Dandelions.* The mythical hunter Orion, whom we know as a constellation of stars, had a dog, and the Romans named a star for the creature: "Canicula," meaning "little dog." We call this star "Sirius." In the summer, Sirius rises and sets with the sun, and the Romans called this period "dies caniculares," or "days of the little dog."

dogging it: It's interesting that "dogging it" means being lazy while "dogged pursuit" means just the opposite. *The Oxford English Dictionary* added "dogging it" to its online edition in 1993, defining

The "dis-" in "disgruntled," Quinion explains, is actually an intensifier, making the word more true, rather than untrue. This use of "dis-" used to be more common in English. "For example, the unusual word 'disannul' was used in the sense 'to make null and void, bring to nothing, abolish' and 'dissever' means 'to divide, separate, disjoin,'" Quinion writes.

In the same way, "disgruntled" means "very gruntled," with "gruntled" originally meaning displeased — or, literally, in a state of sustained grunting (Quinion calls the "-le" ending a "frequentative" marker, suggesting sustained activity, as in "curd" and "curdle," and "game" and "gamble"—and "grunt" and "gruntle"). But I don't think "sustained grunting" is what the billboard you saw had in mind.

double negative

To HEAR linguist Richard Ingham tell it, the double negative wasn't nothing unusual in the history of the English language.

In a revealing study in a 2002 issue of *Language Variation and Change*, a quarterly language journal, Ingham shows how double negatives—such as "wouldn't never" and "not give him

---

the verb "dog" in this sense as "to act lazily or half-heartedly; to shirk or avoid responsibility, risk, etc."

Back in the 1500s, the verb "dog" meant what today we would call "giving dogged pursuit to," or "hounding" someone—pursuing them like a dog chasing its prey. Shakespeare, for instance, wrote in "Richard II," "Destruction straight shall dogge them at the heeles."

doggone: Most sources say this has always been a euphemism for "gosh darn"—or the harsher form of "gosh darn." As *The Oxford English Dictionary* puts it, "dog gone" may be "a deformation of the profane [phrase]." But the *OED* adds: "Some think the original form was 'dog on it,' to be compared with 'pox on it!'"

Flexi: A thin leash that retracts into a hand-held spool. Popular

nothing"—were common in Old English (English before the year 1000).

Many linguists assume the double negative was used randomly in Old English—a speaker had a choice whether to say either "wouldn't never" or "would never." But Ingham, of Birmingham, England, argues that the use of the double negative depended on what dialect of Old English you spoke.

Dialects are hard to study in Old English, because so little Old English survived in writing. But Ingham says there's enough evidence to show that the double negative was far more common in an Old English dialect called "West Saxon," spoken in the west and south of Britain. Outside those regions, the double negative was used sparingly.

People who used the double negative in Old English probably did it for grammatical reasons, Ingham says. They figured that when you used a word like "naefre" (the original spelling of "never"), or "naenig" (meaning "not any"), you needed another negative word in the sentence to match it. So they put the word

---

among everyday dog walkers, Flexis (presumably adapted from the word "flexible") are usually banned at dog shows, Frei says, because "the handler has less control over the dog."

going to the dogs: "[It is] most likely that a person or thing that was said to be going to the dogs was compared to the scraps thrown to the dogs—so worthless that people did not want to eat them," writes Berlin linguist Elke Gehweiler in the *International Journal of Lexicography*. Gehweiler's article notes that German has the identical idiom—"geht vor die Hunde"—and studies the relationship between the two phrases.

pooper-scooper: "That has a pretty universal meaning, I think," Frei says.

raining cats and dogs: No one knows for sure how this expression got started, though there are plenty of theories, according to Michael Quinion of *World Wide Words* (www.worldwidewords. org). One says cats and dogs used to hide in thatched roofs dur-

"ne," meaning "not," before the verb. They thought that "ne" made the verb "agree" with the word "never."

Ingham found hundreds of examples of double negatives by Old English writers who spoke the West Saxon dialect. One wrote, "thaet heo nanne aefter hyre ne forlete," meaning, "that she should not leave none behind her." Another said, "he nowiht to gymeleste ne forlet," meaning, "he allowed nothing to not be neglected." Ingham says he studied prose rather than poetry, because poetic language might take liberties with usage for artistic reasons.

The dialect differences in the use of the double negative, Ingham argues, lasted through the Middle English period, but gradually the double negative disappeared. It was almost gone by Shakespeare's time, although it does show up occasionally in Shakespeare's plays. In *As You Like It*, for example, Celia complains, "I cannot go no further." But beginning in the 1700s, language purists said the double negative was illogical and improper in English.

Ironically, back in Old English, the West Saxon dialect—the

---

ing storms, and heavy rain would cause them to fall out. Another explanation is that in Northern European ancient mythology, cats had power over (or at least symbolized) the rain, and dogs ruled the wind, so when you had both rain and wind together, cats and dogs were to blame. Still another theory says that "cats and dogs" is a malapropism of the French word "catadoupe," meaning "waterfall." Pick your favorite story.

see a man about a dog: Quinion and others say that over time, "I need to see a man about a dog" has been used to express an urgent need for a bathroom, an alcoholic drink (especially during Prohibition) or a sexual partner.

underdog: The word presumably comes from dogfights, either figuratively or literally, because the dog who loses the fight often ends up under the other one. At some point the word became attached to competitors who were expected to lose.

dialect that used the double negative—was considered the "proper" dialect of English, according to Ingham. He writes by e-mail from England, "I came across some beautiful examples of people actually 'correcting' single negation to double negation at that time!"

Ingham notes that neither double nor single negation can be called the "normal" linguistic way to negate a verb. The double negative, he writes by e-mail, "is common in many languages of the world, but single negation is common too."

Incidentally, can a double positive ever equal a negative? According to an old grammar joke, a professor lecturing at Columbia University claimed that no language used two positives to make a negative. Another professor shot back, "Yeah, yeah." . . .

Update: A few readers heard the closing story, as I first did, with the retort "Yeah, right"—which is even better, since it uses two different words. I went with "Yeah, yeah," since that's what was given in the 2004 obituaries in *The New York Times* and *New York Sun*—and subsequently quoted at *Language Log*—for philosopher Sidney Morgenbesser, who was credited with saying the remark.

druthers

I couldn't find this in my dictionary: "If Michael had his druthers . . ."

—*Rhita Lippitz, Evanston, Illinois*

THE WORD is a slang version of "would rather." The verb phrase is collapsed into one word, "d'ruther," and made into a noun. The American Dialect Society has traced this word back to 1833.

dwarf planet

ASTRONOMERS TRIED to settle the 2006 debate over Pluto's status by changing the definition of "planet" and renaming Pluto a "dwarf planet." But critics say that only led to linguistic confusion.

"We now have dwarf planets, which are in fact not planets. I consider this a linguistic catastrophe," Owen Gingerich, chairman of the official planet definition committee of the International Astronomical Union, told the British press. "I think the union is going to get a lot of flak for this, in doing it in such a muddy way."

The confusing terminology could even benefit Pluto fans, one astronomer told the IAU gathering. "It could be argued that we are creating an umbrella called 'planet' under which the dwarf planets exist," said Jocelyn Bell Burnell, who oversaw the IAU proceedings. According to reports, she tried to lighten the mood by holding up a stuffed toy of the Disney character Pluto under an umbrella.

That argument is true linguistically, wrote Benjamin Zimmer at *Language Log* (www.languagelog.org). It's hard to exclude Pluto as a planet by using a term with the word "planet" still in it. "In a compound noun of the form A-B, we generally assume that the compound is composed as a hyponym, [with A as] a particular type of a more general category B," wrote Zimmer, who is senior lexicographer for American Dictionaries at Oxford University Press. "So alley cats are types of cats, rocking chairs are types of chairs, bay windows are types of windows, and so forth."

Zimmer concluded: "The fact that the IAU would like us to think of dwarf planets as distinct from 'real' planets lumps the lexical item 'dwarf planet' in with such oddities as 'Welsh rabbit' (not really a rabbit) and 'Rocky Mountain oysters' (not really oysters)."

This isn't the first time astronomers have used the word "planet" for something they don't think is a planet. For years, astronomers have used the term "minor planet" for asteroids and other smaller objects that aren't really planets. The IAU ruled that a "minor planet" will now be known by the clunky name "small solar system body."

Dictionary editors were following the news from the IAU's General Assembly in Prague almost as closely as astronomers were—waiting to see if they would have to change their dictionaries. "It's much easier to downgrade Pluto and asterisk the planet chart than it is to try to cram in a bunch of new planets," said Steve Kleinedler, senior editor of *The American Heritage Dictionary*.

But Kleinedler added that "dwarf planet" isn't necessarily a done deal. It has to have staying power. "As a lexicographer, as of this moment I would have to make an entry for 'dwarf planet,'" he wrote by e-mail. "If the IAU reverses course, we would revisit the term."

Before it settled on "dwarf planet," the IAU was mulling using the word "pluton" for Pluto and similar objects. "Pluton" has been tossed around by astronomers at least since 1991, when it appeared in *Science News* as a term for Pluto-like objects. But geologists complained that the word "pluton" was already in place as a term for a kind of igneous rock (adapted from "plutonian") and feared that a new sense would be confusing.

The word "planet" originated in ancient Greek, derived from "planasthai," meaning "to wander." To ancient astronomers, the stars in the sky seemed to stay put, while the planets constantly changed their position, as though they were wandering around. "Pluto" was the Greek name for the god of the underworld.

Geza Gyuk, director of astronomy at the Adler Planetarium in Chicago, said revisiting the meaning of the word "planet" has been long overdue, because of discoveries in recent years of multiple Pluto-like objects in the solar system.

"People have been trying to figure out whether the term 'planet' has any meaning as such, or is just a useful [generic] term," Gyuk says by phone. "It's important to have terms mean something that we can all agree on, but it's also not absolutely essential that we nail down everything, with no gray area. It's generally true about language: It's never precise."

Changing the classification of Pluto is the easy part, Gyuk said; it's harder to change the definition of the word "planet" and get it to stick. "The IAU has absolute authority to classify objects, but I'm not sure they have the authority to define 'planet' as such," Gyuk said. (The IAU added the criterion that a "planet" must "clear the neighborhood around its orbit"; Pluto swings into Neptune's orbit, and so it's disqualified.)

Gyuk said the Pluto episode is a reminder that astronomy involves language, as well as science. "Children frequently ask what it takes to become an astronomer," Gyuk said. "I always say math and science are important, but don't neglect English and history. You need to get your ideas across. You need good language to describe your discoveries."

effect vs. affect

Is there a short method to differentiate in the usage of "effect" and "affect"?

—Eugene O'Connell, Des Plaines, Illinois

THE RULE of thumb is that in most cases, "effect" is a noun and "affect" is a verb. So you affect something, and it has an effect. The rare exceptions are when "effect" is a verb that means "bring about," as in, "to effect change," and when "affect" is a noun that means "emotion." But these usages are nearly nonexistent in informal speech.

Elements of Style

THE 2005 release of *The Elements of Style Illustrated* (Penguin), with illustrations by Maira Kalman, will breathe new life into what many English teachers consider a classic composition manual: *The Elements of Style* by William Strunk and E.B. White. But some linguists wish the book—and its collection of what they call ill-advised rules—would be forgotten.

E.B. White, the author of the children's books *Charlotte's Web* and *Stuart Little*, published *Elements of Style* in 1959 as an edited and expanded version of the handbook written by his English professor, William Strunk. With its classic commandments such as "Omit needless words" and "Keep related words together," *Elements* (now in its fourth edition) has been praised by *The New York Times* as "as timeless as a book can be in our age of volubility."

In the new edition, Kalman's colorful art illustrates the example sentences of *Elements:* for instance, the phrase "somebody else's umbrella"—given as an example of the proper punctuation of possession—now appears with Kalman's painting of a woman in a yellow dress gazing at a red umbrella hanging in a closet.

The pictures soften the brusque manner of the book; even

White, in an introduction published in 1979, described his writing mentor as "Sergeant Strunk," acknowledging that the book's prescriptions come off as "sharp commands."

Of course, those who believe the English language is "deteriorating" continue to appreciate this pious propriety. But some linguists say *Elements of Style* is filled with misinformation about the English language.

Geoffrey Pullum, linguist and co-author of *The Cambridge Grammar of the English Language* (Cambridge University Press) and *A Student's Introduction to English Grammar* (Cambridge University Press), is an outspoken critic of *Elements*, and airs his rants at the linguistics blog *Language Log* (www.languagelog. org). Pullum has called Elements "a horrid little compendium of unmotivated prejudices, arbitrary stipulations, and fatuous advice." So Pullum was none too happy to hear about *Elements of Style Illustrated*.

"There is an ILLUSTRATED edition of *The Elements of Style* coming out?" he replied by e-mail. "Oh, how pathetic, how horrible. . . . You have depressed me."

The problem, Pullum says, is that some of what Strunk and White prescribe actually contradicts historical precedent and the intuition of any native speaker of English. "Strunk and White are so willfully ignorant of the history of the language," Pullum says, "that they say things that are not true now, were not true when they were writing it, and have never been true at any time in the history of the language."

Take the insistence in *Elements* that the pronoun "they" should never correspond to the indefinite pronouns "anyone" or "everyone"; the book calls for sentences such as, "Every one of us knows he is fallible."

"Anybody in the last 500 years of English has used the words 'they' and 'them' with singular antecedents," Pullum says. "It's in Shakespeare, Chaucer, Milton, Jane Austen. It's in everybody's writing and everybody's speech. I have no doubt that it would have been in Strunk's writing and White's writing if they hadn't consciously scanned for it. But if you do scan for it and eliminate it, you're not writing like Jane Austen; you're just tampering with your own prose for no point." (*See also* **they, singular**.)

Pullum says other rules in *Elements*, such as the book's bans on beginning a sentence with "however" and using "hopefully" to mean "we hope that . . . " also go against the grain of English. To see how unnatural the rules of *Elements* can be, Pullum says, look at White's own fiction (which Pullum praises for its elegance).

White goes only two paragraphs of *Stuart Little* before breaking his rule that only the word "that," not "which," can introduce a clause not enclosed by commas (as in the phrase "the sight that I saw"). White writes, "Every morning, before Stuart dressed, Mrs. Little went into his room and weighed him on a small scale which was really meant for weighing letters." (To avoid breaking his own rule, White should have made the phrase "that was really meant for weighing letters.") As White himself shows, Pullum says, "that" and "which" have been used interchangeably in English for centuries.

"Rather than accuse [White] of being a lying hound who tells people not to do things and then does them himself, like a minister who visits prostitutes, I think he's just ignorant of what the evidence shows," Pullum says. The rule for "which" and "that," he says, "doesn't in any way match educated usage."

For a more reliable guide to how the English language really works, Pullum recommends *Merriam-Webster's Dictionary of English Usage* (Merriam-Webster). Pullum's *Student's Introduction to English Grammar* includes sidebars on the "myths" of grammar guides and how the evidence shows they're wrong.

Pullum wrote at *Language Log*, "If I have one ambition for my professional life, it is to do something to drive back the dark forces of grammatical fascism of this kind, to help get English-language teaching back into a state where the things that are taught about the grammar of the language are . . . the things that are true, rather than ridiculous invented nonsense."

English 101

I TAUGHT English 101 for the first time in spring 2005. Here are six things I learned on the other side of the desk at my alma mater, Calvin College, a liberal arts school in Grand Rapids, Michigan:

1. It only takes a few weeks to be able to identify each student's individual writing voice. Word choice, sentence length, comma use, vocabulary range and choice of topic all bear the fingerprint of the author. It helped that I had only 22 students, but I thought it would take all semester to recognize their distinct styles. When I could, I told them so, both to discourage plagiarism and to make the point that a discernible, seemingly audible voice can emerge when you put words on paper.

2. There's no good way to talk about grammar to a generation that hasn't been taught it. Anytime I diagrammed a sentence or talked about relative clauses, I felt I was speaking a foreign language. Luckily, grammar was just one of four things I graded in assignments, along with content, structure, and style.

   I could never go as far as former University of Illinois at Chicago dean Stanley Fish, who wrote in *The New York Times* in 2005 that his freshman writing course focused entirely on sentence structure. He assigned students to invent a language of their own and explain its grammar in terms of tense, singulars and plurals, subjects and objects, and so on. But that's not a writing class; that's a linguistics class. On the other hand, I'm not convinced, as are some English teachers I talked to, that the relationship between knowing grammatical terms and writing well is distant.

3. Practicing what you teach confronts you with your own hypocrisy. No sooner did I scoff at my students' whining about their deadlines than I would start whining about my own deadlines. No sooner did I warn of excessive passive voice in a student's paper than my editor would tell me I was doing the same thing. I kept thinking to myself, "Writing would be so easy to teach if only I didn't have to do it myself."

4. The comma is the most dastardly punctuation mark there is. In my students' work, commas were overused, underused, inserted superfluously, and omitted conspicuously. Sometimes explaining comma placement was straightfor-

ward, but other times I almost had to apologize for the density of the rules I was trying to teach: Put a comma after a conjunctive adverb ("However, it is reasonable . . .") but not, as some students did, after a coordinating conjunction ("But, it is reasonable . . .") You try to explain that one. And after a while, I gave up pointing out that book titles are not considered appositive phrases enclosed by commas. I constantly came across constructions such as, "as it says in the book, *Cross-Cultural Perspectives.*" I knew the comma didn't belong there, but I wasn't positive why it wasn't an appositive.

5. It's hard to be a descriptivist and an English 101 teacher at the same time. Descriptivist linguists say—and I'm convinced—that commanding people to write and speak in a certain way is an ill-intentioned and ineffective way to stabilize or change a language, and it usually is condescending. So while I was determined to enforce the writing rules of English 101, I explained this enforcement in the context of dialects.

    Standard English, I said, was a dialect, appropriate in some settings (a college classroom) and inappropriate in others (a dorm room). And it's standard not because it's morally superior or more logical (it isn't always), but simply because it has been standardized, or agreed upon.

    At times I wondered if this disclaimer dulled the students' response to my insistence on particulars—subject-verb agreement, dangling modifiers and so on. But I remain convinced that presenting Standard English as a dialect among other dialects is the best way to show the purpose of teaching it. We follow the rules of Standard English not to please the picky and pedantic, but to be intelligible and taken seriously in the settings where people speak it and write it.

6. Reading student papers can be rewarding as well as tedious. Some students' writing displayed good insight and fresh wording, and many seemed to engage and enjoy the

73

readings I assigned them. That made the whole experience worth it.

Every time I teach English 101 I do with my course what I kept telling my students to do with their papers: revise, revise, revise.

Update: My professor Jim Vanden Bosch faithfully wrote me to say that in the ending example in #4 above, "the book title is an appositive, but it should be seen as a restrictive appositive because it provides essential identifying information. That's why the comma doesn't belong there."

eon and dilemma

My native language is Greek, and I notice when a word is used in English with a different meaning than the original Greek one. This makes me wonder if those words really have a different meaning or they are simply misused. For example, "eon" in Greek means 100 years, but in English it means a very long but unspecified time. "Dilemma" is used in English to mean "problem." In Greek it means a difficult choice between two (and only two) options.

— *Theo Vlahopoulos, Chicago, Illlinois*

"'**Aion**' **is** pretty flexible in Greek," says Helma Dik, a classics professor at the University of Chicago who specializes in Greek linguistics. "The specific 'century' meaning is relatively recent. For the ancient Greeks, standard time reckoning as we know it didn't exist."

The word "eon" doesn't appear in English until about the 1600s, usually with the meaning of "eternity," especially in religious and poetic use, according to *The Oxford English Dictionary*. Since then, scientists have assigned "eon" as the standard term for one billion years, because British English used to use "milliard" for the American "billion" and "billion" for the American "trillion."

"Dilemma" literally means "two assumptions," because the Greek "lemma" means "thing taken" or "assumption," according to *Merriam-Webster's Collegiate Dictionary*. A usage note in the *Merriam-Webster* entry says we shouldn't worry about the literal meaning. People who say "dilemma" are not trying to talk about how many choices they have, *Merriam-Webster* argues, but rather "the unsatisfactoriness of the options."

Eskimo snow vocabulary, compared with English

ONE OF the most influential linguistic urban legends of all time is the idea that Eskimos have an unusually high number of words for "snow." In truth, Inuit and Yupik language families (there is no one "Eskimo language") don't have many more terms for snow than other languages do.

In January 2007, after nearly 20 years of dogged debunking, linguist Geoffrey Pullum posted "The Snow Words Myth: Progress At Last," on *Language Log* (www.languagelog.org) a blog where he and a group of academic linguists sound off on the news of the day.

A friend had sent Pullum, an article called "Snow Words" from the *Holland Herald*, the in-flight magazine of KLM airlines, which tried to set the record straight: "The idea that Inuit people have many more words for snow than English speakers is a myth," the article said. Some of the article's grammatical explanations weren't quite right, Pullum said, but "it was a lot closer to being accurate than the familiar nonsense that has been repeated so many times," he wrote on *Language Log*.

The truth is out there, and it has been since at least 1986, when linguistic anthropologist Laura Martin wrote an article in the *American Anthropologist* called "Eskimo Words for Snow." She argued that anthropologists were throwing around all kinds of figures for the number of words Eskimos supposedly had for snow without any facts to back them up.

Martin traced the Eskimo-vocabulary myth back to 1911, when Franz Boas wrote in his *Handbook of American Indians* that Eskimo languages had four unrelated terms for snow: "aput," meaning "snow on the ground"; "qana," for "falling snow"; "piq-sirpoq," for "drifting snow"; and "qimuqsuq," for "snow drift." Boas' point was simply that languages can have words with similar meanings but different etymologies—the same way the English words "liquid," "river," and "dew" appear unrelated in origin but all mean something like "water."

So far, no big deal. But then came legendary linguist Benjamin Whorf in the mid-20th century.

Whorf's source isn't clear, but he probably had Boas' book in mind when he wrote in 1940, "We have the same word for [different kinds of] snow. . . . To an Eskimo, this all-inclusive word would be unthinkable." Inexplicably, Whorf claimed there were at least seven Eskimo words for snow.

The Eskimo example was incidental to Whorf, but linguists and anthropologists seized on it as a primary example of Whorf's influential theory that the way we think and look at the world around us is influenced in part by the words our native language gives us. They taught that Eskimos see the world differently than the rest of the non-arctic world does, and that you can tell this by all those terms for snow in their language.

Martin wrote in her 1986 article that the Eskimo example "has transcended its source and become part of academic oral tradition." Martin found a 1978 play that said the Eskimos had 50 words for snow and a *New York Times* editorial that said there were 100. I've found media references as high as "a zillion." "It sort of pumped its way up into being a remarkable factoid through a series of popularizations uncritically embellishing each other," Geoffrey Pullum writes by e-mail.

Pullum was already furious about Eskimo misinformation in 1989, when he explained Martin's research in his column in the journal *Natural Language and Linguistic Theory*. In 1991, the University of Chicago Press included the article in a collection of Pullum's essays published as *The Great Eskimo Vocabulary Hoax and Other Irreverent Essays on the Study of Language*.

"The truth," Pullum wrote in *Great Eskimo Vocabulary Hoax*, "is that the Eskimos do not have lots of different words for snow, and no one who knows anything about Eskimo (or more accurately, about the Inuit and Yupik families of related languages spoken by Eskimos from Siberia to Greenland) has ever said they do."

The number of root words for "snow" in Inuit and Yupik languages is about four or five, Pullum says—no more than English (which has "snow," "sleet," "slush," "powder," and "blizzard," to name a few).

What's more, trying to count the exact number of words for any term in those languages is pointless, because Inuit and Yupik languages are "polysynthetic," meaning they can take a small number of roots and, with several endings, build countless words on any subject.

"Eskimoan languages are really extraordinary in their productive word-building capability, for any root you might pick," wrote Pullum at *Language Log*. "But that very fact makes them exactly the wrong sort of language to ask vocabulary-size questions about, because those questions are virtually meaningless—unless you ask them about basic non-derived roots, in which case the answers aren't particularly newsworthy."

Things are looking brighter to Pullum after seeing the *Holland Herald* article earlier this month. But he's still cautious about the long-term prospects of debunking the Eskimo vocabulary myth.

"To a modest extent, things have improved a bit," Pullum wrote me by e-mail. But he added, "I think there is a very rational reason for pessimism, and it is this: Once a myth or legend establishes a useful role for itself, it starts to spread faster than scientists can write and publish corrections or criticisms."

Pullum concluded: "I imagine it will spread forever—the number of people who know it is false (though that number is growing) will never outstrip the number of people who believe it is true."

Esperanto, among English speakers

"Saluton!" The greeting rings throughout the Sulzer Regional Library auditorium in Chicago as members of the Esperanto Society of Chicago gather for their monthly meeting. They have come to study and celebrate the language of Esperanto, invented in the late 19th century to be an international language.

The meeting is conducted almost entirely in Esperanto, but

the non-Esperantist visitor can pick out words here and there: "ne" for "no," "dankon" for "thank you," "estas" for "is," and "unu" for "one."

The headings on the membership roster sheet speak for themselves: "telefonnumero" for "telephone number," "urbo" for "city," and "Cxikago" for "Chicago."

The 12 people at this meeting are preserving the dream of Polish physician Ludovic Lazarus Zamenhof, who in 1887 published a brochure titled "Lingvo Internacia" ("International Language") under the pseudonym Dr. Esperanto ("one who hopes"), outlining the basics of his invented language. If everyone could learn Esperanto as a second language, Zamenhof believed, different cultures could maintain their own identities and still communicate with each other.

Zamenhof designed Esperanto to be simple to learn, consistent in structure, and clear in meaning. He used root words derived from Latin, English, and French, among other languages.

According to Esperanto educational materials, students can expect to take about a year to become fluent in Esperanto—a fraction of the time it takes to master other languages. There are only 16 rules of grammar (compared with the book-length grammar guides for English) and no silent letters or irregular spellings. All singular nouns end in "o," plural nouns in "j," verbs in "i," adjectives in "a," and adverbs in "e." The vowel endings give Esperanto an elegant sound, evoking Italian or Spanish.

As a would-be world language, Esperanto's advantage is also its disadvantage. Because it has no nation of native speakers, Esperanto is culturally neutral and non-threatening. But its nomad status also means there has never been much political push for anyone to adopt it.

Still, Esperanto has a core following of hundreds of thousands of people around the world, "possibly millions," who have some degree of proficiency in the language, according to the Netherlands-based Universal Esperanto Association (UEA), which lists members in more than 100 countries.

Six Nobel Prize winners spoke the language, and everyone from Leo Tolstoy to Eleanor Roosevelt to Robert F. Kennedy has endorsed using Esperanto as a global second language.

So have six popes; the Vatican makes its radio broadcasts available in Esperanto. Hundreds of people worldwide register for free Esperanto lessons at www.lernu.net.

Most members of the Esperanto Society of Chicago (www.esperanto-chicago.org), including natives of Austria, Germany, Hungary, the Netherlands and the Ukraine, are advanced or fluent in Esperanto.

President Bill Mania opened one meeting by reading a report he wrote in Esperanto about attending a conference of Esperantists in "Sankta-Luiso," or St. Louis, with his daughter Sarah, 9, whom he is teaching Esperanto.

Mania then suggests a group exercise: translate a short story by Guyanese author Pauline Melville into Esperanto, one page per person. Les Kordylewski, who learned Esperanto in his native Poland, gets a laugh when he says he would prefer to be assigned the "lasta pagxo"—the last page, which has only three lines.

Gertrude Novak, an Austrian native and a delegate to the UEA, closes the meeting with the report of a phone call she received earlier that day from a man in Congo who conducted the conversation in Esperanto—a reminder of how useful a universal language can be.

Like the majority of Esperantists, members of the Chicago society are idealistic but not delusional: They like the spirit of international goodwill that enlivens Esperanto but are not under the impression it is about to become a major world language. "Esperantists tend to be well-read, environmentally aware, politically involved," says Mania. "There's a geekiness to it," adds Robert Stalzer.

Marc Shafroth drove down from Madison, Wisconsin, for the opportunity to converse in the language with other enthusiasts. "There are four parts to a language: speaking, hearing, reading and writing," he says. "With Esperanto, you can do all of them on your own except speaking. There's no place to speak it except here. That's the benefit of this."

The Chicago club is mourning the loss of one especially tireless proponent of Esperanto, Kent Jones, a longtime member who died in February 2004. A civil engineer, Jones promoted Esperanto as a way to reduce airline accidents involving pilots and control tower operators for whom English was a second language.

He also believed teaching Esperanto in schools would provide students with an effective building block. "The formal study of English requires preparation . . . in the form of a model language—one without the snaggle-toothed problems of English," he wrote in a 1996 letter to the *Chicago Tribune*. "Esperanto should precede the formal study of English, because Esperanto can prepare the mind for it."

esquivalience

A TERM dictionary editors invented as a lexicographical "gotcha" has given word lovers a chuckle. *The New Yorker* reported in 2005 that the editors of *The New Oxford American Dictionary* (Oxford University Press) had inserted a false entry in their dictionary as a trap.

Mapmakers and creators of dictionaries, encyclopedias, and other reference works sometimes include fake information to expose people who lift the material for their own publications. (It's considered unethical to lift information directly from a source without researching and verifying it yourself, which people duped by fake information obviously haven't done.) Though traps can result in a copyright infringement charge, usually the most severe punishment is egg on the guilty party's face.

Since the practice is discreet, it is difficult to document, though Erin McKean, the *New Oxford American*'s Chicago-based editor in chief, calls it "not uncommon."

The *New Oxford American*'s trap appeared in the dictionary's first edition published in 2001, before McKean was appointed editor in chief, But it wasn't until after the second edition came out in 2005 that talk began to spread about a trick entry.

"I was pressed, and I said, 'It's in "E,"' that's all I'm saying,'" McKean says. *The New Yorker* presented a short list of the possible fakes to a group of word experts. The majority of them fingered the word "esquivalience" as a suspect.

The *New Oxford American*'s entry for "esquivalience" defines it as "the willful avoidance of one's official responsibilities; the shirking of duties," as in, "After three subordinates attested to his esquivalience, Lieutenant Claiborne was dismissed." The word's etymology is traced to the late 19th century, "perhaps from French esquiver, 'dodge, slink away.'"

But while "esquiver" is a real French word, "esquivalience" is an invention. McKean confirmed this for *The New Yorker*, saying the team of editors behind the *New Oxford American* set out to make up a word for "working hard," which they were. But one editor, Christine Lindberg, came up with a word that meant just the opposite.

"I wanted the word to suggest character weaknesses," Lindberg writes by e-mail, "and words like 'quivering' and 'vacillating' went through my mind and became the glob of brain putty that eventually got fashioned into 'esquivalience.'"

The copyright trap worked. "Esquivalience" showed up at *Dictionary.com*, attributed to the electronic dictionary *Webster's New Millennium Dictionary of English*. (The word has since been removed from *Dictionary.com*.)

McKean says although the definition of "esquivalience" had been altered at *Dictionary.com*, there was no question that the entry came from *The New Oxford American Dictionary*.

Both *Dictionary.com* and *Webster's New Millennium Dictionary* are online reference works offered by Lexico Publishing Group, a privately owned company. Barbara Ann Kipfer, editor of *Webster's New Millennium Dictionary*, deferred comment to a Lexico spokesman, who did not respond to repeated inquiries.

McKean says she doesn't lose any sleep over dictionary pirates and that Oxford University Press, publisher of the *New Oxford American*, is not contemplating legal action. As crime waves go, dictionary piracy isn't even a trickle. "Piracy is low on our list of concerns," McKean said. "We don't have hordes of lawyers watching for it or anything." Still, doesn't her team find it satisfying to say "Gotcha!"?

"I shouldn't say," McKean says. "That should be a 'no comment.'"

A more serious question is whether publishing a copyright trap damages a source's credibility. McKean says there's no harm in listing an entry nobody actually uses. "We wanted it to have as little a footprint as possible. We didn't want to find a [fake] synonym for 'yellow,'" she says.

Of course, in the world of lexicography, a made-up word can become real simply by having people discuss it—and then use it. Lindberg, the inventor of "esquivalience," says the word is real to her. "It is only this recent bit of attention to my infamous little neologism that has reminded me of its fauxness," she says.

"I find myself using the word regularly, and I've grown quite fond of it. I especially like the critical, judgmental tone I can get out of it: 'Those esquivalient little wretches.' Sounds literate and nasty all in one breath. I like that."

Word histories are like self-help programs: they're always unfinished, and you can seldom trust anyone offering easy answers.

A massive 2008 book on English word origins shows how true this is. *An Analytic Dictionary of English Etymology: An Introduction* by Anatoly Liberman (University of Minnesota Press), gives an in-depth look at words whose origins are unclear or controversial.

Look up a word in any major dictionary, and you'll see a line or two about the word's etymology, or origin. Occasionally a dictionary will shrug its shoulders and simply say "origin unknown"—as *Merriam-Webster's Collegiate Dictionary* does for the words "drab" and "traipse," for example.

Liberman says that when it comes to etymology, sometimes dictionaries are too sure of themselves, and other times they give up too easily. In most major dictionaries, Liberman writes in his introduction, "etymology is only one of their concerns, and they have little space for discussion. But discussion should be the prime goal of an [analytic] etymological dictionary."

And so Liberman, a Russian native and longtime professor of German philology at the University of Minnesota, offers his own book as an extended commentary on tricky etymologies, tackling 55 words that puzzle etymologists.

Liberman puts brief summaries of his conclusions at the front of the book: he traces both "drab" and "traipse," for instance, to—spoiler alert!—the German word "traben" and related words meaning "tramp, wander." But after this sneak peak, Liberman plunges into extended explorations of each word, all of them fascinating tours of linguistic history for word lovers.

etymology

"EVERY WORD was coined by a resourceful individual or borrowed as a result of language contact in a certain place at a certain time," writes Anatoly Liberman in his book, *Word Origins and How We Know Them: Etymology for Everyone* (Oxford University Press).

It may sound simple, but etymology—the study of word origins—is in fact murky and tedious, if unfailingly fascinating. Liberman's book is an examination of the process of determining how a word originated, and it shows how complex his craft can be.

For the word "bird," Liberman analyzes all the possible root words, and says the two most plausible are the Old English "bredan"—meaning "brood, keep warm"—or a Germanic root "beran"—meaning "bear, give birth." He says there isn't enough evidence for either one, but says "beran" is "possible" and that many etymologists have been too quick to settle on "bredan."

Or take "skedaddle," which some etymologists have traced to the Greek word "skedannumi" (meaning "to disperse"), the Irish "sgabaim" ("scatter"), or the Danish "sgone" ("hurry")—all of which Liberman analyzes and rejects. He settles on the regional British word "scaddle," meaning "frighten."

"Tracing word origins is a game of probabilities," writes Liberman, who has also written *Word Origins and How We Know Them* (Oxford University Press) and keeps *The Oxford Etymologist* blog at blogs.oup.com. (For more fun with English etymology, see Sol Steinmetz's new book *Semantic Antics: How and Why Words Change Meaning* [Random House Reference]). "The language historian often reaches a stage when all the facts have been presented and it becomes necessary to weight several hypotheses and choose the most probable or . . . the least improbable one."

Liberman's attention to detail makes his *Analytic Dictionary* a monumental achievement—and he hopes it's only a start. "I think I will have to write about five or six hundred English words without known cognates [relatives], which means seven or eight volumes like the one I have now brought out," he writes by e-mail.

"The art of etymology consists in seeing through a word's disguise," writes Liberman, a professor of medieval literature and linguistics at the University of Minnesota.

Take the word "speed." Liberman says the root of "speed" can only be determined by what linguists call "internal reconstruction," which basically amounts to an educated guess. Liberman writes that by analyzing a family of related words, including the Old English word "spowan," the Old Slavic word "speti," and the Latin "spes," etymologists can speculate that the root of all of these words must have been "spodi." But they put an asterisk by the word to show the existence of "spodi" is hypothetical.

"Speed" disguised its origins by changing not only its spelling but its meaning, too. The word originally meant "prosperity," as in the phrase, "God send you good speed," but over time, "speed" came to mean the manner in which prosperity is presumably achieved.

The number of unexpected turns words can take is nearly infinite. Liberman explains the phenomenon of "misdivision," or an unintended combination of words. The word "nickname" is a misdivision of the phrase "an ekename"—in which "ekename" is Old English for "other name." The "N" of "an" was accidentally added to the second word, and it stuck as "nickname."

"Tawdry," Liberman says, is a misdivision of "Saint Audrey." Medieval historians wrote that Saint Audrey, queen of Northumbria in the 7th century, died of a throat tumor. They claimed this tumor was divine retribution for the fancy necklaces she liked to wear. Eventually, "tawdry" came to mean "gaudy" or "showy."

"Every decipherment presupposes that the code can be broken; in this respect, the etymologist is like a decoder," Liberman writes.

Word Origins also shows word lovers that English etymology means more than just knowing Latin and Greek. The number of languages that influenced English, and the complexity of the ways they did, go well beyond what Latin and Greek can teach us.

In his closing chapter, Liberman asserts that most popular books about words merely recycle examples listed by *The Oxford English Dictionary*—a 20-volume set of definitions and notable citations of words throughout history.

Liberman says by e-mail that while the *OED* is a masterpiece, it "gives the user the results rather than tracing the paths of research. It never tries to explain how thousands of cognates have been netted and why other candidates have been rejected."

Meanwhile, many people continue to confuse the word "etymology" with "entomology," the study of insects. If nothing else, Liberman's book should at least help clear that up. But in spite of misunderstandings and outright myths (no, the word "sirloin" did not originate when a king knighted his meat "sir loin"), Liberman's book shows that while it takes specialists to make confident claims about word origins, the rest of us can enjoy the fruits of their labor.

"Etymology, like geometry and physics, is for experts," Liberman says by e-mail. But he adds: "My title [*Etymology for Everyone*] means that every person interested in language and knowing the most elementary things about it can be told how engrossing the science of etymology is, and how professionals arrive at their results."

except, as preposition or conjunction

How can I determine which is correct? "Everyone has read the book except me." "Everyone has read the book except I."

—*Sanford Franzblau, Arlington Heights, Illinois*

GRAMMAR BOOKS say that when "except" is a preposition, as it is in your example, it takes an object: "me." When "except" is a conjunction—as in, "except I didn't want to"—it's usually followed by the subject of a new clause.

farther vs. further

Is it "farther" or "further?" I was taught that the word "farther" denotes physical advancement in distance while "further" denotes advancement to greater degree, as in time. Yet I hear many people, most notably Chicago meteorologists and traffic reporters, when denoting distance, use the word "further"

85

instead of "farther." Is "further" another one of those words, because of repeated incorrect usage, whose definition has been broadened to denote distance as well?

—*Mark Zurblis, Geneva, Illinois*

IT'S ACTUALLY one of those words whose definition has always been flexible in the history of English, but which language elites—the same folks who enforced the bizarre ban on prepositions at the end of sentences—decided to insist could only mean

---

Try to guess the language each of these words came from and their original meanings, which have mostly faded away over time but are preserved in *The Oxford English Dictionary*.

acute: from the Latin "acus," meaning "needle."

altruism: from the French "altruisme," from the Latin "alteri huic," meaning "to this other."

apart: from the French "a part," meaning "to the side."

bedlam: a shortened version of "Bethlehem." Founded in the 1200s, the Hospital of Saint Mary of Bethlehem in London was a well-known insane asylum.

but: from Old English "be-utan," literally "by the outside."

butter: from the Greek "boutyron," supposedly formed from "bous" ("cow") and "tyros" ("cheese").

chauvinism: named for Nicolas Chauvin, a man "noted for his excessive patriotism and devotion to Napoleon," according to *Merriam-Webster's Collegiate Dictionary*. The sense of "excessive devotion to a cause" was eventually transferred to sexism.

depot: French for "deposited," from the Latin "depositum."

diabolical: from the same Greek root as the word "devil." The Greek "diabolos," like the Hebrew word "satan," literally means "accuser" or "slanderer." In religious use, both "diabolos" and "satan" became proper names for an evil being that opposes God.

"degree" and not "distance."

So it's advisable to try to follow the distance-or-degree distinction between "farther" (if you can go "far," you can go "farther") and "further" (a synonym for "more"—"let's discuss this further") in formal settings but disregard it in informal ones.

But note that the line between distance and degree can be blurry; the *American Heritage Guide to Contemporary Usage* points out that most educated users say "far from the truth" but also "Nothing could be further from the truth."

eavesdrop: originally the English word for the ground on which water drips from the eaves (the edges of the roof) on a building—the ideal location to overhear something going on inside.

eccentric: from the Greek *ekkentros*, meaning "outside the center."

emergency: from the Latin *emergere*—the same root as "emerge"—meaning "to come forth." So "emergency" etymologically just means something that has come up.

geyser: from the Icelandic *geysa*, meaning "to gush."

heritage: from the Old French *heriter*, meaning "to inherit," from the Latin "heres," meaning "heir."

infant: Latin for "unable to speak."

mausoleum: from the Greek *Mausoleion*, the name of a Greek king in the 4th century B.C., and subsequently the name of his tomb, which was one of the seven wonders of the ancient world.

maverick: named for Samuel Maverick, a Texas rancher who left his cattle unbranded. Eventually, any unbranded cattle were called "mavericks," and today "maverick" means simply "nonconformist." Maverick's grandson, incidentally, is credited with coining the word "gobbledygook," making the Maverick family quite lexically productive.

nice: from a French version of the Latin word *nescio*, meaning "to be ignorant of." Over time, the sense of meaning went from "ignorant" to "unthreatening" to "kind."

nightmare: compound of the Old English words "night" and "mara"—the latter meant "evil non-human being"—which were combined in the belief that an evil spirit or monster would perch on a sleeping person and give him or her bad dreams.

pacifier: from the Latin *pacificare*, meaning "to make peace." (The Latin translation of the biblical saying "Blessed are the peacemakers" is *beati pacifici*.)

robot: from the Czech *robota*, meaning "forced labor." The word was popularized by Karel Capek's 1921 play *Rossum's Universal Robots*, in which artificial workers are produced in a factory and eventually revolt against humans.

serendipity: presumed to have been coined by writer Horace Walpole in the 18th century. Walpole claimed he named the word for the characters of the fairy tale "The Three Princes of Serendip"—who, he said, "were always making discoveries, by accidents and sagacity, of things they were not in quest of." *Sarandip* was the Persian name for Sri Lanka.

February and jewelry

My two pronunciation pet peeves are dropping the first "r" in February (although this is so common, I feel I must be the only one who still pronounces it), and mispronouncing jewelry as "joo-la-ree." I have even heard this mispronunciation in TV and radio ads for jewelry stores!

—*Bob Jagla, Chicago, Illinois*

The New Oxford American Dictionary says this alternate pronunciation of "jewelry" is "regarded as uneducated," though it notes that the British spelling of the word is "jewellery." That, and the fact that "L" and "R" are hard to pronounce consecutively with-

stigma: Greek for "mark made with a sharp object." The English word "stick" has the same Greek root. The English word "stigmatize," formed with the Greek suffix "-ize," originated as a word for branding with a hot iron as punishment, often with a letter of the alphabet that indicated the crime.

stoic: from the Greek *stoikos*, from *stoa*, meaning "porch," named for the "Stoa Poikile," the "Painted Porch" in Athens, where Zeno taught and founded Stoicism, a philosophy of self-control and detachment from emotion as a route to happiness.

swab: from the English noun "swabber," meaning a sailor who mopped the decks, presumably from the Dutch *zwabben* for "to mop."

tedious: from the Latin *taedere*, meaning "to grow weary."

teeter: from the Old Norse *titra*, meaning "shake" or "shiver."

town: from the Old English *tun*, meaning "enclosure" (such as a village enclosed by castle walls).

window: from the Old Norse *vindauga*, a compound of "wind" and "eye."

out a vowel between them, probably accounts for the alternate pronunciation.

"February" is a similar case. *Merriam-Webster's Collegiate Dictionary* says the "Feb-yoo-ary" pronunciation is "in frequent use and widely accepted," and sees it as another case of what linguists call "dissimilation"—changing a sound to avoid saying consecutive similar sounds.

"Dissimilation may occur when a word contains two identical or closely related sounds, resulting in the change or loss of one of them," *Merriam-Webster* says. "This happens regularly in 'February.'"

In the case of "February," we might also be trying to match the last three syllables of "January."

feel bad vs. feel badly

Is it correct to say, "I feel bad that you lost your job," or is it correct to say, "I feel badly that you lost your job?" Most people would say "badly," whereas I think the proper word is "bad." I think that feeling badly indicates the way that your fingers touch things.

—*Baiba Kahn, Vernon Hills, Illinois*

I'M WITH you, and most English teachers and dictionaries are too. When it refers to your emotions or your health, "feel" is a linking verb, linking the subject to a name or description. Linking verbs take adjectives, not adverbs. You say, "I feel glad," not "I feel gladly."

I've always thought that "feel badly" is a case of what linguists call "hypercorrection"—what you do when you're so worried about making a usage error that you try to correct what isn't even an error. That's what's going on when people say, "He talked to Jim and I," which is ungrammatical but may sound more proper to the speaker than "Jim and me."

With "feel badly," people probably fear the idiomatic use of "bad" as an adverb—"That hurt us bad" or "we needed it bad"—which is common in informal English but off-limits in Standard English. So the person about to say, "I feel bad," might have a mental red flag go up that says "feel bad" sounds like "hurt bad," and therefore it must be unacceptable. So they say "feel badly" instead.

The American Heritage Guide to Contemporary Usage and Style tells a more complicated story, explaining that some speakers have come up with distinctions in meaning for "feel bad" and "feel badly."

For "many speakers of English," according to the *Guide*, "bad" means "unwell" or "sad," while "badly" is a more benign emotional state, such as regret. To me, that distinction seems too subtle to be of much use.

The *Guide* offers a second possible distinction. "Some speakers would restrict 'feel badly' to refer to emotional distress and let 'feel bad' cover physical ailments, but not everyone maintains this distinction."

To make things even more confusing, the *Guide* notes that some dialects of English use "badly" or "poorly" to mean "sick," though it adds, "this usage has never been considered standard." *The Oxford English Dictionary* quotes the novel *The Rainbow* by D.H. Lawrence, in which Mr. Brangwen says of his wife, "Ay, but she's badly." This lends to the confusion.

One thing just about everyone can agree on is that "want it badly" or "badly needed" are finally acceptable in Standard English, even though this means allowing "badly" to take on a new meaning of "very much." This usage "is now considered standard," the *Guide* says.

By the way, it's not necessarily true that adjectives can't end in "-ly," as word watcher Richard Lederer points out in the current issue of the language journal *Verbatim*. Lederer lists "costly," "elderly," "friendly," "kindly," "sickly," and refers to "more than a hundred other adjectives that wag '-ly' tails." Lederer argues that "badly" should also be allowed to be an adjective, but concludes, "to avoid the disapproval of others, I recommend that you feel bad, not badly."

fifth

When did it become common practice to drop the second "F" in "fifth"? Everyone is doing it, including news announcers and people in commercials. It is driving me crazy!

—*Robin Bangs, Chicago, Illinois*

I CHECKED four dictionaries; two recognized this alternative pronunciation and two didn't. But *Fowler's Modern English Usage Dictionary* backs up your condemnation, saying that in "fifth," "both the '-f' and '-th' should be clearly sounded." I assume that the "F" is often dropped for the same reason the "T" was dropped from "often" (*see* **often**): It's easier to say that way. The "-fth" combination really gives your mouth a workout.

forte

> Should I continue to mangle the pronunciation of "forte" with one syllable in the phrase "juggling is my forte"? Or follow the crowd that continues to say "forte" with two syllables?
>
> —*Dan Steidl, Bolingbrook, Illinois*

It's true that many people don't realize that the word in your example actually comes from the one-syllable French word "fort" ("strong"), and not the two-syllable Italian word "forte" ("loud") used in music. But the word has been so Anglicized—we changed it from an adjective to a noun and pronounce the silent "T"—that I am underwhelmed by those who argue that using one syllable will preserve the word's French heritage.

Friends, language of

See **so, as intensifier.**

Frisian, as a cousin of English

With a vague sense of ethnic pride, a vaguer sense that I owed it to my great-grandfather and a complete ignorance of the Frisian language, I attended the 50th and final annual Frisian worship service in Grand Rapids, Michigan, in May 2006.

For me, the service hammered home a key distinction about my own ethnicity. I usually say that my ancestors were Dutch. But my great-grandfather, who immigrated to the U.S. in 1890, might have objected to that claim. Technically, he was Frisian, and for Frisians, that is more than just a technicality.

Friesland is a province of the Netherlands along that country's northern coast, but dating back to the ancient days when it was a vast kingdom and maritime power, it has always been its own country, in a way. The Frisians are one of the oldest ethnic groups in Europe and one of the most doggedly independent. A famous Frisian slogan is "Frysk en Frij," meaning "Frisian and Free."

The Frisian language also represents a piece of linguistic trivia: Old Frisian was the closest relative of Old English, its sibling in the West Germanic language family. Linguists tend to say that in its earliest days, English used to sound a lot like German. But it's closer to the truth to say that English used to sound a lot like Frisian.

So as a Frisian descendant and an aspiring linguist, I had two good reasons to attend the final Frisian-language worship service in Grand Rapids, where an annual Frisian service has been held since 1957 in a local church. In recent years, attendance has dwindled to fewer than 100 people, but last month, more than 250 people came, some from around the U.S., Canada and yes, Friesland. The language intimidated me at first, especially when the room erupted in laughter at a Frisian quip while I sat silent and oblivious. Sitting next to me, my father knew German and Dutch well enough to pick out some key words and give me the gist of what I missed.

Soon I caught on to a couple of basics as I studied the bulletin: the "tsj" sound in Frisian is basically the English "ch," so the word "tsjerke" sounds something like its English translation, "church." The first hymn was "Hillich, hillich, hillich," which I identified as "Holy, Holy, Holy," and in the first line, the word "almachtich" gave itself away as "almighty." Fortunately, the ushers handed out an English text of the sermon.

The service happened to be held the same week that the U.S. Senate approved two language proposals, including one that would single out English as our national language. Even if neither measure becomes law, the Senate sent the message that linguistic diversity is unwelcome and even threatening. But on that Sunday in Grand Rapids, in a congregation that was all white and mostly gray-haired, the church was surging with immigrant pride.

"I knew it would be emotional," said Louis Tamminga, who preached the sermon. Fifty years ago, Tamminga was the young seminary student and Frisian immigrant who preached the sermon in the first Frisian service in Grand Rapids, in his native language.

Notably absent from the Frisian service was its founder, Bernard Fridsma, who died in December 2005. Fridsma immigrated from Friesland at age three, and taught a course on Frisian at Calvin College in Grand Rapids, where I work (and where, today, one of the most common surnames is still "De Vries," meaning "the Frisian"). Fridsma wrote an "Introduction to Frisian" workbook for the course, with the dream of eventually publishing it as a textbook.

That dream has now been inherited by Frisian native and retired English professor Henry Baron, who was raised speaking Frisian, educated in Dutch, and learned English after immigrating to the U.S. after World War II. Baron taught courses on Dutch and Frisian at Calvin College, and still has lunch every other week with 10 to 20 other Frisian natives living in West Michigan.

"No other Dutch province has anything like that," Baron says about these gatherings of expatriates. "It's an extension of this Frisian solidarity. . . . You come across a Frisian anywhere in the world, and you identify each other as Frisian, and you immediately have a bond there. It's as if you're long-lost buddies."

This Frisian pride has helped keep the Frisian language alive, despite the constant threat of extinction. So has the Dutch government; in 1955, the Netherlands officially recognized Frisian as its second language and dropped a 19th century ban on teaching Frisian in Frisian schools. Today, out of Friesland's population of about 600,000, about 400,000 speak Frisian, Baron says, while most of the rest can understand it.

After the Frisian service in Grand Rapids, I met Koen Zondag, who traveled from Friesland for the service and gave a public greeting from the homeland. I asked him whether he considered himself Frisian or Dutch. He sighed and looked away, searching for a way to explain it, then looked me straight in the eye.

"Are you American or from Michigan?" he asked.

"I live, speak, and dream in Frisian," he said. "But the question of identity is complex."

gawk

WE ARE despicable people. We are the people who slow down when passing through the scene of an accident, trying to get a good look at the wreck. I do it. You do it. We all do it.

Traffic reporters have a word for us. We're "gawkers."

A gawker is an uninvited spectator. And that's putting it nicely.

Merriam-Webster defines the verb "gawk" as "to gape or stare stupidly." A Google search for the term "traffic accident gawker" turns up a personal ad on a website in Louisville that includes "traffic accident gawkers" in the category of "things that turn me off," between "religious freaks" and "smelly people."

But though "gawker" may seem like a loaded term, it isn't just slang or a put-down; it's used as a neutral and even technical description of passing motorists in news and government reports. "Gawkers were the cause of an accident on I-70 two months ago that injured two people," the *Columbia Missourian* reported in spring 2006. "Crashes produce long, but infrequent, delays to all motorists, made all the longer by gawkers who slow down even more than the altered traffic conditions require," wrote automotive analyst Leonard Evans in his relatively technical 445-page book *Traffic Safety*.

And so we gawkers are not just an annoyance, we snarl traffic with our gawking. We're such a problem that some state governments have decided one of the best ways to speed up traffic around an accident is simply to hide the accident: "The Massachusetts Highway Department, tired of traffic jams caused by accident-gawkers, has begun using large, portable screens to shield car wrecks from passersby," the *Boston Herald* reported in 2005.

You don't have to look for a traffic accident to find "gawkers," though. The word's basic meaning of "someone who watches danger rather than fleeing it" shows up in a news report in April 2006 about flooding along the San Joaquin River in Northern California. *The Sacramento Bee* paraphrased the warning of a county spokeswoman: "She warned residents to stay away from the levees, saying that gawkers would be at risk of being swept away, should a breach occur."

But the more general meaning of "unwanted spectator" led to the naming of the gossip website *Gawker.com*. Celebrities have complained about the "Gawker Stalker" feature at *Gawker.com*—a map of recent celebrity sightings in Manhattan. (The *London Observer* reported that George Clooney tried to sabotage Gawker Stalker by urging publicists to post fake celebrity sightings.)

While the meaning of "gawker" is usually clear, word experts say the history of the word remains a mystery. The first recorded use of the verb "gawk," according to *The Oxford English Dictionary*, was in American clergyman and scientist Manasseh Cutler's memoirs, written in the late 1700s but not published until 1888. Cutler wrote, "We . . . do little else than sit in the chimney-corner, repeating over the same dull stories, or gawking at one another with sorry grimace."

But how the word originated isn't clear. "There is no fully convincing etymology of 'gawk,'" says Anatoly Liberman, author of *Word Origins and How We Know Them* (Oxford University Press), who blogs as *The Oxford Etymologist* at blogs.oup.com.

The *OED* speculates that "gawk" could be a newer version of "gaw," an obsolete English word that meant "to gape or stare," which was first recorded back in the 1200s. "Gaw," the *OED* says, may have come from the Old Norse word "ga," which meant "to heed." Those are a lot of dots to connect, without much solid evidence, according to Liberman. He says the *OED*'s suggestion rests on an argument that other English words such as "lurk" and "walk" used to be three letters long and added the "K" later, as a suffix.

But Liberman isn't convinced. "The addition of 'K' to 'gaw' strikes me as a very remote possibility," he writes by e-mail. "In my opinion, the best etymology connects gawk with the Middle English word 'gowke,' derived from Scandinavian, meaning 'cuckoo,'" Liberman writes. "The cuckoo bird has always had a bad reputation (think of 'cuckold,' for example), and bird names designating simpletons are common ('You silly goose' and the like)."

After hatching this theory, Liberman says he was pleased to see it supported in *The Century Dictionary*, a 19th century dictionary edited by linguist William Dwight Whitney. It listed the definition of "gawk" as either "A cuckoo" or "A stupid, awkward fellow." It also lists the phrase "gawk's errand" as a synonym for "fool's errand." The connection between "gowke" and "gawk" requires less imagination than the possible connection between "gaw" and "gawk," Liberman says, though he emphasizes that there is no way to know for certain.

"All of it is guesswork, and hedging should be recommended in dealing with this word," Liberman says. "Yet the etymology in *The Century Dictionary* may be the most persuasive one."

gay

See **merry.**

gerund, with possessive

HERE'S A sentence from a good writer: "It's silly to tell a lie when there's a chance of your being caught." What's the difference between "YOU being caught" and "YOUR being caught"? The author of the sentence, Eric Ambler, used "your." I would use "you." What are your thoughts?

—*Matt Meisterheim, Arlington Heights, Illinois*

GRAMMARIANS HAVE historically frowned on "you being caught," saying it sounds awkward and emphasizes the person rather than the action. There's a chance that in the sentence, "I'm worried about Jim operating that chainsaw," the word "operating" serves merely to identify Jim among other Jims, rather than to serve as the cause of worry.

And when a (grammar warning!) gerund, or the "-ing" form of a verb that acts as a noun, begins the sentence, the possessive sounds much more natural: "His coming was eagerly anticipated." (Not "him coming.") But this debate has been raging for nearly a century.

gone missing

In the last three or four years, I've noticed news media using the phrase "went missing" to describe a disappearance, as in, "A child went missing today" rather than "A child is missing today." I have always assumed "went missing" to be informal slang or a colloquial expression, not a part of the more formal grammar generally used by the media. Have I missed a shift in "correct" grammar?

—*Elaine Truver, Chicago, Illinois*

FOR SOME reason, questions about "gone missing" and "went missing" are the most common queries I get by e-mail. A search of the LexisNexis news database suggests the use of "went missing" and "gone missing" has increased slightly but steadily over the last 10 years. But the phrase is well over a century old. In a 2004 column on "gone missing" *The New York Times'* William Safire quoted the *BBC News Styleguide* as saying, "'Go missing' is inelegant and unpopular with many people, but its use is widespread. There are no easy synonyms." At least not in news reporting, where the phrase is used specifically to describe a sudden and suspicious disappearance. "Is missing" doesn't do the job.

Incidentally, what about the *BBC Styleguide*'s seemingly redundant phrase "unpopular with many people"? So much for language fussiness!

graduate, as a transitive verb

When I was a high school student, an English teacher insisted that we should never say that we "graduated from" anywhere. It should be "we were graduated." Is there any validity to her idea?

—Elaine Werth, Lincolnshire, Illinois

HISTORICALLY, "WE were graduated" was more common. In the mid-1600s, for instance, according to *The Oxford English Dictionary*, author James Howell wrote in a letter, "transplanting me thence to Oxford, to be graduated."

The newer use of "graduate" as an intransitive verb—as in, "we graduated"—entered English at least as early as 1807, when Robert Southey wrote in *Letters From England*, "Four years are then to be passed at college before the student can graduate."

"In general usage, the older transitive sense has largely yielded to the more recent intransitive sense," says *The American Heritage Guide to Contemporary Usage and Style*. Its 1988 survey of its Usage Panel of writers and public figures found that 89 percent of the panel approved of the sentence "They graduated from

Yale," while 78 percent approved of "They were graduated from Yale." Meanwhile, 77 percent disapproved of the sentence, "She graduated Yale."

grammar, descriptive

IT MAY be a first: a grammar textbook that complains about grammar textbooks.

"There is a long tradition of prescriptive [books] that are deeply flawed: They simply don't represent things correctly or coherently, and some of their advice is bad advice," write Rodney Huddleston and Geoffrey Pullum in their 2005 book *A Student's Introduction to English Grammar* (Cambridge University Press).

Many grammar books, they say, tell readers that when it comes to writing or speaking English, only standard usage and formal style is "correct," and anything else is unacceptable. But many of the rules of self-appointed guardians of "good grammar," argue Huddleston and Pullum, turn out to be arbitrary, counterintuitive and without historical precedent.

Take the example of the common decree about "which" and "that" in relative clauses. Many grammar guides insist that only "that" can be used to start a clause not enclosed by commas ("The house that I saw was old"), and only "which" can be used in clauses between commas ("The house, which was built during the Civil War, was old").

But nobody minded when Franklin Delano Roosevelt declared the day of the Pearl Harbor attack to be "a date which will live in infamy," the authors point out. Besides, this rule was invented less than 100 years ago, after centuries of comma-less cases of "which" in English. The 17th century King James Bible read, "Render therefore unto Caesar the things which are Caesar's . . . ").

The strictest grammarians also insist that saying "It's me" is incorrect, since "is" cannot take an object; it should be "It is I." But all but a fraction of English speakers are oblivious to this rule, and would violate their linguistic intuition by following it. "Grammar rules must ultimately be based on facts about how people speak and write," Huddleston and Pullum write. "The rules are supposed to reflect the language the way it is, and the people who know it and use it are the final authority on that."

And so they fill *A Student's Introduction to English Grammar* with "prescriptive grammar notes"—blue boxes in each chapter that tell students what strict grammarians expect, and why they're wrong.

In between these disclaimers, Huddleston and Pullum provide a tidy summary of their magnum opus, the 1,859-page *Cambridge Grammar of the English Language* (Cambridge University Press), which was published in 2002. The authors trimmed their work to 290 pages for *Student's Introduction*, and tailored it to classroom use. "Everywhere I went, people were saying [about *CGEL*], 'It's lovely but it's very big. When is it going to be a textbook so we can teach this stuff?'" Pullum says by phone.

People whose native language is English may not realize how intricate their language is until they see it mapped by Huddleston and Pullum. The word "whose," for example, can be used to refer to inanimate objects, as in, "The book whose pages were falling out was historic." But when it comes to questions, "whose" only applies to people. No one looks at a stack of books and says, "Whose pages are falling out?" You don't need an English teacher to tell you that—it's just the way English works.

Other words have peculiarities we may not notice until we see them pointed out. The words "some" and "any" behave in opposite ways despite their similar meanings. It's ungrammatical—based on what native speakers naturally say—to use "any" instead of "some" in the sentence "I have some." But it's ungrammatical to say "some" instead of "any" in the sentence "I don't have any." (The authors call these words "polarity-sensitive," since "some" has a "positive orientation" and "any" has a "negative orientation.")

So Huddleston and Pullum's critique of dubious grammar rules doesn't make them wishy-washy about the particulars of sentence structure. Anyone who writes about "non-verbal clausal negation," "the partitive subtype" and "fused determiner-heads" cannot be dismissed as language lightweights.

"We're concerned with describing what the syntactic regularities of Standard English actually are, not trying to change them,"

Pullum says. "There are grammarians who see the point of their work not to change people's habits, but to interpret them. . . . It's not a recommendation, it's a characterization. A house appraisal is not a recommendation for how a house should be improved, it's a description of what the house is. The appraiser doesn't wander off into recommending that a skylight be installed in the family room."

Although their analysis is technical, Huddleston and Pullum write that they don't find it the least bit dull. "Some think the study of English is as dry as dust, probably because they think it is virtually completed, in the sense that nothing important in the field remains to be discovered," they write. "But it doesn't seem that way to us. . . . At the level of small but fascinating details, there are thousands of new discoveries to be made about modern English."

See also **National Grammar Day**; **pedantry**; **prepositions, ending sentences with**; and **usage**.

gravitas

"Gravitas" is losing weight. The discussion of Katie Couric's move from NBC's *Today* show to the *CBS Evening News* showed that the word is undergoing a definition shift.

The term traditionally refers to someone's dignity or serious behavior. It derives from the Latin word for "weight"—*gravis*—and entered English early in the 20th century with the meaning of "serious or solemn conduct or demeanor befitting a ceremony, an office, etc.," according to *The Oxford English Dictionary*.

In Couric's case, "gravitas" applied to her air of authority: Some wondered if a TV morning show personality with so many cooking, fashion and "happy talk" segments on her resume could credibly fill the news anchor chair once occupied by the legendary Walter Cronkite.

"Gravitas lurks at the heart of the concentric speculation about Katie Couric's television future," wrote Rebecca Dana in *The New York Observer* in spring 2006, when Couric was still mulling her move to CBS.

Sure enough, after Couric's CBS debut, her critics seized on the term to level their charges that the newscast didn't have enough serious news. A sentence in the *Baltimore Sun* read: "Gravitas be darned, Couric seemed to be saying." "Defying Gravitas," read the headline at the blog of *Broadcasting and Cable* magazine.

So what exactly is this enviable TV news attribute, "gravitas"? Dana tried to get to the bottom of it in her article.

"Industry types are vague about what constitutes gravitas, but an informal poll suggests it involves some combination of gray hair and a baritone voice," Dana wrote. Because of that, "Gravitas is essentially a chauvinistic word," former CBS co-anchor Connie Chung told Dana.

"I suppose people mean weight, seriousness, sobriety, author-ity," columnist Geneva Overholser offered Dana as a definition of "gravitas." But there's a danger, Overholser added, in "confus-ing it with . . . pomposity. This is the thing we make fun of in anchors."

It's the thing Stephen Colbert makes fun of, at least. The star of the satirical *Colbert Report* on Comedy Central is notorious for his imitations of self-important newscasters and pundits. In 2006 Colbert invited NBC anchor Stone Phillips to appear on his show for a "gravitas-off" in which the two men faced off to see who could read pretend news copy with the most earnestness. The exchange, Colbert said on the show, demonstrated that "if you possess sufficient gravitas, what you're saying doesn't have to mean anything at all."

These may be early indications "gravitas" is picking up an overtone of phoniness. In a 2006 *New York* magazine article entitled "Humor Is the New Gravitas," Kurt Andersen claimed Couric would succeed because "she's the first network anchor to have a quick, smart, mischievous sense of humor as a major part of her public persona."

"She has all the serious-news experience the job requires," Andersen writes, "but it's her lack of old-fashioned TV-news 'gravitas'—that perpetual default to careful . . . solemnity that any moron can fake—which makes her special."

If "gravitas" gets a new definition of "phony seriousness"—no major dictionary has added this meaning yet—then it will be a new turn in its roundabout journey over the last two thousand years.

In Latin, *gravitas* could mean "importance" or even "virtue." Cicero wrote about one politician: "the gravity of the man, his knowledge of the law, and his authority delight me." His original Latin in the phrase "the gravity of the man" was *hominis gravitas*.

The word was adopted into French as *gravite*, and then into English as "gravity," and both languages kept the metaphorical meaning of "seriousness" or "authority."

But then scientists grabbed the word "gravity" for the physical force of attraction that causes weight, and eventually writers had to find a new word for the old meaning, according to etymologist Michael Quinion at *World Wide Words* (www.worldwidewords. org).

"After Isaac Newton, 'gravity' became so closely attached to the concept that it slowly lost some of its associations with the older senses," Quinion writes. "Writers from the 1920s onwards began to use 'gravitas' instead, as a direct reference to the classical Latin authors like Cicero who employed it in much the same way."

But now, it seems, we're starting to take "gravitas" lightly.

Greece

The word for "Greece" in the native Greek is *Hellas*, so how did it become "Greece" in English? Even the word "Hellenic" is an English word meaning "having to do with Greek culture." And how did we get "Germany" from "Deutschland"?

—*Cathy Selin, Grand Rapids, Michigan*

I WONDERED this, too, while watching the 2004 Olympics in Athens on television and hearing the crowd chant "Hell-as! Hell-as!"

It turns out that both "Greece" and "Hellas" have Greek roots, but "Greece" was adopted by the Romans (as the Latin word *Graecus*), and later brought into English, according to *The*

Oxford English Dictionary. The *OED* says Aristotle uses *Graiko* as the name for the first inhabitants of the region.

"Germany" also comes from Latin. The Romans called a large European region *Germania*, which they apparently borrowed from the Gauls (the ancestors of the French), according to the *OED*. (The name may come from the Old Irish word *gair*, meaning "neighbor," or *gairm*, meaning "battle cry.") (The Romans also used the name *Teutoni*.)

English actually started out using "Dutch" (from an Old German word for "people" or "nation") as the adjective for both Germany and the Netherlands. But beginning in the 1500s, English speakers started to restrict "Dutch" to the Netherlands and picked up "German" for, well, Germany, even while the Germans held onto "Deutschland."

Update: My dad pointed out that "Deutsch" could simply be a Germanic derivation of the Latin name "Teutoni," and I figured it must be. But the truth seems complicated. A 1971 paper by Max Freund for the South Central Modern Language Association says that "Deutsch" does presumably go back to a hypothetical Aryan root "teut," meaning "people" but also says, "the words *Teutonic* and *deutsch* have the same origin although a totally different development."

groovy and grok

See **Hippie English.**

guts

I'm a volunteer tutor for a Polish girl and she asked what "guts" means in the phrase "I hate your guts." The idiom sources I've researched do not explain "I hate your guts."

—*Kathy J. Moran, Forest Park, Illinois*

THE HELPFUL *Dictionary of American Idioms* (Barron's), co-edited by Adam Makkai, defines "hate one's guts" as "to feel a very strong dislike for someone." The metaphor suggests that the speaker hates the person's innermost being, as far as hatred can extend, to the person's vital inner systems. "Gut" has the connotation of "deep down," as it does in "gut feeling."

gypsy

YEARS AFTER the rise of political correctness, offensive definitions can still linger in dictionaries. In July, a human rights agency called The Advocacy Project filed a complaint to the managers of *Dictionary.com* on behalf of "the Roma community" ("Roma" being the preferred term for "gypsies"). It found that one the definitions for "gypsy" given at *Dictionary.com* was "one of a vagabond race . . . living by theft, fortune telling, horsejockeying, tinkering, etc." The entry had been automatically uploaded from the 1913 edition of *Webster's Revised Unabridged Dictionary*, which itself was taken from an 1867 dictionary known as the *Webster-Mahn Dictionary*.

Lexico Publishing Group, which manages *Dictionary.com*, removed the entry in August. "We agreed with TAP that it was inappropriate," Lexico COO Daniel Fierro wrote by e-mail.

"It's interesting that such an obviously old definition was still up and that no one had complained before now," said Chicago lexicographer Erin McKean.

Harry Potter, language of

AMONG THOSE mourning the end of the Harry Potter series are those on whom J.K. Rowling cast her spells of wordplay.

Whether having fun with alliteration (Dudley Dursley and Poppy Pomfrey), word origins (the name Draco Malfoy comes from the Latin *draco* for "dragon" and the French *mal foi*, for "bad faith"), archaic words ("Dumbledore" is an Old English word for "bumblebee") or puns (Knockturn Alley is a play on "nocturnally"; "Erised" is "desire" spelled backward), Rowling stocked her books with linguistic tidbits.

"The Harry Potter books . . . are not just good literature but a treasury of wordplay and invention," wrote author and librarian Jessy Randall in the journal *Verbatim*, after the fourth Potter book came out. "In naming her characters, beasts, spells, places, and objects, author J.K. Rowling makes use of Latin, French, and German words, poetic devices, and language jokes."

Look no further than "muggle," Rowling's mundane-sounding word for non-magic people and things. "Muggle" was an Old English word for "tail," and later an American slang word for "marijuana." But Randall says the word works in the Potter series because of the way it sounds.

"'Mugwort' and 'mugweed' are names for the common plant also known as wormwood," Randall wrote. "'Muggle' sounds like a combination of 'mud,' 'muddle,' 'mug,' 'bug,' 'Mugsy,' and 'Mudville' . . . It's difficult, in fact, to find an echo of anything airy or light in the word, so it's a good one to describe regular, boring, non-magic aspects of life."

"Voldemort" is a linguistic double play: "vole" means "rodent" and *mort* is the Latin word for "death"; Randall also noticed that the phrase *vol de mort* is French for "flight from death," which Voldemort pulls off in the Potter series.

Some of Rowling's names have ordinary explanations: "Potter" was the last name of a neighborhood family from her childhood, and the cat Mrs. Norris was named for the character in Jane Austen's *Mansfield Park*, Rowling has said in interviews.

But other names betray Rowling's linguistic background; she studied French and classical languages at the University of Exeter. Her character Remus Lupin is a werewolf, and his name is a clear allusion to the ancient legend of Remus and Romulus, the founders of Rome, who were raised by wolves (*lupus* is Latin for "wolf"). As Randall points out, Rowling's words for casting spells all have telltale Latin roots—for example, "Sonorus!" (from the Latin *sonor*, for "sound") turns a wand into a microphone, and "Imperio!" (from the Latin *imperium*, for "command") grants total power.

You don't need to know Latin or French to enjoy the Harry Potter books, of course, but these linguistic touches add another layer of intrigue.

That raises the question: How intentionally did Rowling add

these linguistic overtones? Were they just a natural byproduct of her linguistically trained mind, or deliberate derivations? Potter experts say both.

"I would guess that Rowling knows exactly what she's doing with most of her word inventions—I'd say it's almost all deliberate," Randall wrote to me by e-mail. "It's when people start doing anagrams on 'Hermione Granger' and coming up with farfetched nuances of meaning that I get nervous. And some of my own guesses are perhaps farfetched, too, like my suggestion that Crookshanks comes from [19th century Dickens illustrator] George Cruikshank. That may be pushing it."

"I am convinced that she is very deliberate in the words and names she chooses—sometimes," says Steve Vander Ark, creator and editor in chief of *The Harry Potter Lexicon* (www.hp-lexicon. org). "Other times, she chooses a name because it 'feels right' or because she just likes the word."

"I tend to know what sound I'm after," Rowling told CBS' *60 Minutes* in 2002. "Then, I waste so much paper, I'm just experimenting and experimenting," she said, opening a notebook filled with trial versions of character names.

Language wizardry isn't unusual for writers of fantasy. The works of J.R.R. Tolkien, author of the *Lord of the Rings* trilogy, and C.S. Lewis, author of the *Chronicles of Narnia* series, reflect those authors' studies in philology—the study of words in ancient literature.

"Rowling is far from unique—in fact, her grab bag of literary allusions and Latin words is probably more pedestrian than that of many fantasy writers—after all, a non-expert like me can figure a lot of them out," Randall writes by e-mail. "Tolkien was a mastermind, even a showboater, in this respect."

"She draws from a wide range of sources, far more than either Tolkien or Lewis," Vander Ark says of Rowling. "But she is making no effort to create a systematic structure to the words and phrases used nor to create separate languages at all. . . . She gives every impression of just enjoying unusual words and wordplay."

healthy vs. healthful

> Is the distinction between "healthy" and "healthful" obsolete? Is the latter even a word in the English language anymore? All the foods on grocery store shelves are "healthy," and I'm glad for them that they are not sick. I feel like a pedant when I use "healthful."
>
> —*Rhita Lippitz, Evanston, Illinois*

IF THERE ever was a distinction, it was already ignored in Richard Huloet's Latin-to-English glossary in 1552, which listed "healthye or healthfull" as equivalent, according to *The Oxford English Dictionary. The American Heritage Guide to Contemporary Usage and Style* says, "Certainly, both 'healthy' and 'healthful' must be considered standard in describing that which promotes health."

height vs. heighth

See **often.**

Hippie English

PAGING THROUGH *The Hippie Dictionary* is a trip. Not necessarily, as the book defines it, "a mind-expanding experience brought on by the introduction of some sort of chemicals to the human body." But the 2004 edition of *The Hippie Dictionary: A Cultural Encyclopedia of the 1960s and 1970s* (Ten Speed Press) is at least a trip back in time, back to the days of antiwar protests and civil rights marches, free love and flower children, when America heard the words "peace," "love" and, yes, "dope" in a whole new way.

The thousands of entries were collected and defined by John Bassett McCleary, a California-grown hippie and former tour photographer for Tina Turner, The Doors and The Rolling Stones. They include terms sent in by readers after the dictionary's first edition was published in 2002.

"If you fell asleep in 1959 and woke up in 1980, you would not have been able to recognize the world you were in," McCleary says by phone. "I can't think of any other period of time that had so many changes."

McCleary recalls the '60s and '70s as an era when "we were expanding our minds and expanding our language." The lexical role of hippies was not to coin new words so much as to give existing words new meaning, new life or new combinations.

"The vocabulary of the hippie generation comes, in large part, from the beat generation, jazz and blues music, African-American culture, Eastern religions and the British musical invasion of the early 1960s," he writes in the introduction.

This blend of influences was remarkable, said John Ayto, editor of *The Oxford Dictionary of Slang* and *Twentieth Century Words*.

"Most [slang] arises out of self-contained communities within a single culture, but hippiedom quickly spread its tentacles around the world, and so it would have been open to a wider range of influences than most," Ayto said.

Hippie language was not only creative, it was mobile, says McCleary, who hitchhiked across the country more than once during the hippie era. "Language traveled very rapidly at that period of time," he said. "I'd be in New Jersey, and someone would use a new word I'd never seen before, like 'karma,' a Buddhist term, and the next day I'd use it in Iowa."

Blues and jazz may have inspired the most hippie words and phrases. Take "groovy," which was born in American jazz in the 1930s as a shortened form of "in the groove."

"It was a jazz term meaning the music that you're playing is good enough to be in the groove of a record," McCleary said. He added that he thought Simon and Garfunkel's "The 59th Street Bridge Song (Feelin' Groovy)" in 1966 ruined the word.

Ayto contends that "in the groove" referred not to a record but the state in which "the performer is freed from inhibitions and can improvise or create at will—rather like some present-day athletes and others speak of being 'in the zone.'"

The word "hippie" itself has its roots in jazz, where "hip" meant "aware" or "fashionable" as early as the turn of the 20th century. "Hippie" may have started as a synonym of "hipster," or someone who was hip.

"Hippies" came to describe the youth of the counterculture in the 1960s (after "beats" or "beatniks" started the movement in the 1950s), though not by hippies themselves, McCleary notes. Instead, hippies claimed the words "freaks" and "heads" in order to emphasize their differences with mainstream society. "We'd be hitchhiking and someone would yell, 'Freaks, get out of the country.' We just took what they called us and absorbed it," he said.

Just up the page from the entry for "groovy" is a rare case of a hippie word that originated in the hippie era—the verb "grok," meaning "to understand something deeply, to the point of feeling it," as McCleary defines it. The word was invented by Robert Heinlein as a Martian term in his wildly popular 1961 novel *Stranger in a Strange Land*.

You can spend a wistful (or for those of us who were born after hippiedom waned, educational) afternoon scanning some of the other entries—"acid rock," "afro," "bell bottoms," "cool," "dig it," "far out," "flower power," "keen," "psychedelic," and a good number of synonyms for marijuana and sex. The dictionary is a reminder that, as Ayto writes in *Twentieth Century Words*, "Words are a mirror of their times."

Hispanic vs. Latino

WHAT IS the proper term for an American of Spanish-speaking background? Is it "Hispanic" or "Latino"?

"That can be answered only regionally," says Sandra Benedet, professor of Spanish and Portuguese at Northwestern University. "The answer is very different from California to Miami."

In Miami, "Latino" has not gained currency, Benedet says, and the most common term is "Cuban" or "Mexican" followed by "Hispanic." In California, "Latino" is most prevalent, "Hispanic" is frowned upon, and "Chicano" is preferred by some Southern Californians of Mexican descent. In Chicago, Benedet says, "Hispanic" is well-established, but "Latino" and "Latina" seem to be gaining ground.

"I'm new to the Midwest, but what I've heard is that 'Latino' and 'Latina' [are] increasingly gaining popularity, but 'Hispanic' is still used quite a bit," she says.

Although the use of "Hispanic" and "Latino" vary from region to region, the entire United States is wrestling with the complicated question of what to call its largest minority. "Hispanic," many critics say, has problematic associations.

"For one thing, it's related to Spain," says Arlene Sanchez Walsh, who teaches religion and Latin American and Latino Studies at DePaul University. She observes that many Spanish speakers have no direct ties to Spain and are reminded of Spanish colonization when they hear "Hispanic." "Secondly," Walsh adds, "it's a term created for the purpose of taking the census. It's not a word that comes from the community. It's what the government chose to call us."

"Hispanic" gained currency in the United States when it was added to the census form in 1970. Since then, it's been dropped as a racial category. In the 2000 Census, the majority of the 29 percent of Americans who identified themselves as of "some other race" called themselves either "Hispanic" or "Latino."

That's another problem with the word "Hispanic," say critics. It's not an ethnic term. "Hispanic is not a race, and the term inadequately reflects the cultures of the different regions that make up Latin America," says Vera Teixeira, senior lecturer in Spanish and Portuguese at Northwestern. "The term 'Hispanic' attempts to blur all national and cultural identity."

That's because the Spanish language is the only common link among the diverse groups who speak it, say defenders of "Hispanic." "For better or worse, Latino-Americanos [Spanish for "Latin Americans"], and that includes those of us living in the United States, have a common root: Spain," says Duard Bradshaw, president of the Hispanic National Bar Foundation. "Even the indigenous people of Mexico, Guatemala, Ecuador, Peru, and Bolivia—countries that have the largest indigenous populations—cannot ignore the Conquista, for it not only affected their original culture but gave them a common thread in religion and language."

Bradshaw says he hears "Hispanic" and "Latino" used interchangeably or side by side in the United States. "Ironically," he adds, "I have found in my travels to Latin America that the term 'Hispanic' is used much more frequently than it had been even three or four years ago."

There's no ideal solution for Americans, Benedet says. "There's no one term that can adequately define all the peoples and the cultures. It's really quite a problem," she says. "'Chicano' is too exclusive to Mexicans. 'Hispanic' has too close a tie with colonial roots." Using "Mexican-American" or "Cuban-American," Benedet adds, implies "you're not a culture in your own right."

Even "Latino"—which rose to prominence in part as an anti-imperialist alternative to "Hispanic"—does not have a spotless history, Benedet says. She notes that the French used it in their attempted conquest of Mexico in the 19th century. And "Latino"—the Spanish equivalent of "Latin"—has strong associations with the Roman Empire and medieval Europe, where the Latin language thrived. "Latino" also is gender exclusive, although it is often used as shorthand for both males and females (who are "Latinas").

This dilemma makes "Hispanic" usable but limited, says Virginia Cueto, editor of *Hispanic Trends* magazine, based in Coral Gables, Florida. "Personally, as a Cuban immigrant and U.S. citizen raised in this country from the age of nine, I am not offended by either term, nor do I have a preference for either, although if I absolutely had to choose, I would choose 'Hispanic,'" Cueto says.

"When people ask me about my ancestry, I tell them I am Cubana. After all, that is what they want to know," Cueto says. "That does not mean that I do not feel one hundred percent American also. These are not mutually exclusive, and it is important that non-Hispanics realize this."

historical, with "a" or "an"

You quoted a source's e-mail as saying: "I teach at . . . an historically black college." I believe that this school is "a historically" black college. My understanding of the "rule" is that if the "h" is aspirated, it is preceded by an "a," and if the "h" is silent, it is preceded by an "an."

—*Stephen Reiches, Evanston, Illinois*

I THOUGHT so too (though I don't edit sources' grammar in their quotes), but then I checked *Fowler's Modern English Usage* (third edition), which gives "an historical" some support. It begins by saying, "Opinion is divided over the form to use before h-words in which the first syllable is unstressed: The thoroughly modern thing to do is to use 'a' (never 'an') together with an aspirated h." But *Fowler's* continues to say that there is currently "abundant evidence" of "an historical," and concludes, "the choice of form remains open."

holiday

"**Best wishes** for a holiday season of hope and happiness," reads the official White House seasonal greeting card. So technically, it's not a "Christmas card," although the White House, among others, has taken some heat this year for not using the term.

"It's a Christmas card," William Donohue, president of The Catholic League, told CBS News. "What's wrong with the president of the United States, who's a practicing Christian, saying 'Merry Christmas' in his Christmas card?"

The irony is that while the White House, along with other government officials and retailers this year, opts to use the word "holiday" as its generic, non-religious alternative to "Christmas," linguists point out that the word "holiday" itself has religious etymological roots. In fact, religious references are buried in the histories of many words we now use without thinking about their history.

While the religious roots of "Christmas" are transparent—the word began as a compound of "Christ's mass"—it's less obvious that the word "holiday" has the word "holy" in it, as in "holy-day." It began in Old English as two words, "halig daeg" ("holy day") that were combined into one as early as 1,000 years ago, according to *The Oxford English Dictionary*. A 13th century rule-book for nuns, for example, instructs nuns to pray more often on "helidawes" (holy days) than on "werkedawes" (workdays).

"Holiday" gradually came to mean any special day set aside for leisure or celebration. A 16th century poet, for instance, describes "holiday" as "a day to dance in and make merry at the Ale house." Soon, the *OED* says, the generic meaning of "holiday" became the most common definition, and sacred references again had to be written as two words, "holy day." Today, even non-religious days such as Presidents' Day and Labor Day are "holidays," and the British word for "vacation" is "holiday"—as in, "He's on holiday this week."

"Yuletide," by the way, is an old-fashioned but seemingly innocuous word—until you find out that "yule" actually began as the name of a pagan winter festival.

"A civilization with a long history, and formalized yet evolving religious practices going back for millennia, will have all sorts of bits and pieces of its religious and cultural history buried in the words and phrases of its languages," linguist Geoffrey Pullum writes by e-mail. Pullum points out that even though "Saturday," for example, was named for the Roman god Saturn, this history is so distant that the etymology is all but irrelevant. The same is true for the rest of the days of the week.

"The names of the days of the week commemorate the sun (Sunday) and the moon (Monday), and then five pagan gods: Tiw [Tuesday], Odin [or Woden, "Wednesday"], Thor [Thursday], Freya [Friday], and Saturn [Saturday]," Pullum writes. "If we were to start obsessively analyzing all of these names for religious links to object to, we would have our work cut out forever."

"Christmas," too, may soon (or already) function as a generic

HORSE RACING CLICHÉS

The Kentucky Derby puts horse racing at the center of American sports for one May weekend each year, and it reminds us that horse racing once had a huge influence on American culture and the English language.

"The words we've added to the American vocabulary reflect our undertakings and devotions," says lexicographer Grant Barrett. "Think of the gambling terms ('ace up his sleeve'), the gold-mining words ('pan out'). . . . Horse racing's introduction of new American words has been reinforced by its overlap with gambling and our greater past reliance upon the horse, which is still in our collective memory. But more importantly, who doesn't love a horse?"

In preparation for Derby Day, listen for the galloping hooves behind these familiar words and phrases.

name—not to mention a commercial name for this season of spending—more than as a religious name, Pullum suggests. "There is no hope of ever disguising the fact that the United States celebrates Christmas as a period of time off from work, exchanging of gifts, and rituals involving holly, ivy, mistletoe . . . tinsel, gifts, and a jolly white-bearded fat man wearing red," Pullum writes, adding, "And yes, for some people, a commemoration of the birth of a religious leader in Bethlehem."

See also **merry.**

I'm all

THE PHRASE "I'm all"—a staple Californian dialect over the last two decades—may be on its way out. And some Californians are all, "That's too bad."

A 2007 study in the journal *American Speech*, by a team of linguists from Stanford University led by John Rickford, looks at what linguists call the "quotative" use of "all"—when the word "all" introduces a quotation, as in, "I'm all, 'No way.'"

This usage showed up in American English in the early 1990s, say the Stanford linguists, but it's now giving way to an equally in-

across the board: covering all categories. If you place a bet that a horse will win, and then place additional bets that the horse will place (finish second or higher) and show (third or higher), you're betting across the board. No matter where the horse shows up on the board that displays the top finishers, you'll win. The phrase eventually expanded to mean any kind of comprehensive covering of categories.

also-ran: weak or forgettable competitor. A horse that "also ran" in a race but did not place or show is inconsequential. *The Oxford English Dictionary* quotes George Ade's 1896 novel *Artie*, which portrayed the life and speech of a Chicago Loop office worker, "They ain't even in the 'also rans.'" Presidential candidates who drop out early in the primary season are often called "also-rans."

formal quote signal: the word "like," as in, "He was like, 'No.'"

The Stanford team points to a 1994 study of the conversations of high school students in California. That study showed that students used "all" more than 45 percent of the times they introduced quotes, compared with "like" 18 percent of the time and "said" or "says" 11 percent.

Today, teens and twentysomethings still occasionally use "all" for quotes, as with one male speaker in the Stanford survey who said, "I was all, 'Keep at it'"—with "I was all" replacing "I said."

What the *American Speech* study doesn't say is that "all" and "like" usually go with approximate quotations, rather than exact ones. "He said" is an act of reporting. "He was all" or "He was like" just gives the gist of what someone said, often with an emphasis on that person's emotion or attitude. If you say, "My mom was all, 'Why are you late?'" your main intention is to say that your mom was mad, rather than to re-enact that conversation.

But now, "I'm all" is starting to disappear, the *American Speech* study says. In a survey of California high school and college students done in 2005, the Stanford team at Stanford University found that the quotative use of "all" had plummeted since the

dark horse: a competitor of whom little is known or expected. The *OED* quotes a line from Benjamin Disraeli's 1831 novel: "A dark horse, which had never been thought of . . . rushed past the grand stand in sweeping triumph." The darkness may be figurative—fans were "in the dark" about the horse's abilities—or it may be somehow literal. *The Phrase Finder* website (www.phrases.org. uk) speculates, "Horses that regularly won races were darkened to conceal their identity and increase the betting odds," but there is no proof for this theory.

front-runner: defined by *Webster's Third* in 1961 as "a contestant who runs best when in the lead; also, one who can set his own fast pace; [or] the leading contestant in a competition."

get one's goat: to deeply irritate someone. The most common theory is that the phrase comes from the practice of putting goats

early 1990s. In their study, speakers used "all" less than 5 percent of the time they introduced quotations, down from 45 percent in 1994. "All" had even fallen behind the word "said," which was used 12 percent of the time.

"Like" was the king of quotative words in the Stanford study, showing up nearly 70 percent of the time speakers began quotations. The researchers found a similar trend in archived online message boards.

In fact, "all" has lost so much ground to "like" that it now appears as a modifier of "like," as in, "She's all like, 'Well you have to.'"

"'All like' has become the primary sequence in which 'all' is used as a quotative, and the only one used by the younger speakers," say the Stanford linguists, adding that "all" may be "shifting from its new quotative [function] to its older intensifier function, reinforcing 'like.'"

Carmen Fought, linguist at Pitzer College in Claremont, California, conducted the 1994 survey discussed in the *American Speech* study. She says the Stanford researchers are probably right about "I'm all."

"Sadly, I believe it may be true that quotative 'all' is declin-

in the stables of racehorses as a calming influence. A trainer of a competitor's horse might try to steal the goat from the stable in order to disrupt the horse before a big race.

But etymologist Douglas Wilson doesn't buy it. He wrote last year at the e-discussion list of the American Dialect Society that goats were often used as sports mascots in the early 20th century, and if horse trainers used them, it was probably for their own benefit rather than their horse's.

Either way, Wilson says, he finds no evidence of goat theft at stables, so the metaphor was probably figurative to begin with. "I speculate that the race-horse's goat was a mascot kept out of superstition (whether or not the horse became attached to it)," Wilson wrote, "and I doubt that the specifically horse-related goat was the etymological ancestor of this metaphor."

ing," Fought writes by e-mail. "I think this is a great loss to the English language. Quotative 'all' has been a part of my life, as a Californian at heart, and I'm sorry to see it go."

I'm good

IF YOU want to download Google Earth, a computer program that uses satellite images to give driving directions, you'll get a message from Google that not all computers can run the application. To move past Google's list of the kinds of computers that won't work, you have to click on a button that says, "I'm good."

Google isn't asking visitors to flatter themselves. ("I sure am a good person!") Google is just picking up on one of the latest meanings of a very versatile adjective, "good." This sense of "I'm good" means "I'm all set," or "I'm adequately equipped to proceed."

The word "good" has more than two dozen entries in most dictionaries. Consider the nuances in meaning among "I'm good friends with her," "I'm good for him," "I'm good at that,"

---

hands down: The *OED* defines this phrase as "with ease, with little or no effort," and explains that it originated "in the racing phrase 'to win hands down,' referring to the jockey dropping his hands, and so relaxing his hold on the reins, when victory appears certain." The *OED* cites an 1867 book called *Lyrics and Lays* that includes this line: "There were good horses in those days, as he can well recall, But Barker upon Elepoo, hands down, shot by them all."

hedge your bet: "To secure oneself against loss on (a bet or other speculation) by making transactions on the other side so as to compensate more or less for possible loss on the first," the *OED* says. The phrase is first found in 1672 and apparently originated outside of horse racing, though it would become common at the racetrack. (One way to hedge your bets is to bet across the board.)

The sense of "hedge" meaning "protect" (in this case, the extra bets form a figurative hedge around the first bet) has an even longer history in English. The *OED* gives one definition of

"I'm good for nothing," "I'm good with kids," "I'm good for the money," and "I'm good to go," to name a few.

Google's use of "I'm good" to mean "I'm all set" is fairly informal. It's the kind of colloquial usage you will see in blogs or hear in conversations: "Want fries with that?" "No thanks, I'm good." Middle-school students submitted "No thanks, I'm good" to the Prevention Video Corp. (www.preventionvideo.org) as one of 190 ways to refuse cigarettes.

"The message is, 'I'm OK, I'm fine' with things as they are," says Arnold Zwicky, linguist at Stanford University. "So it conveys [the decline of] an offer, by giving a reason for declining."

"In online [language] usage forums, it's been suggested that the expression derives from draw poker—a player who stands pat, or doesn't need to draw any cards, will tell the dealer, 'I'm good,'" says lexicographer Benjamin Zimmer. "Of course, it has also long been a formulaic expression in bars, where 'I'm good' is a standard negative response to a bartender who asks if the patron wants another drink."

"hedge" as "to surround as with a hedge or fence," and cites this line from Shakespeare: "England hedg'd in with the maine, That Water-walled Bulwark."

run roughshod: run or carry oneself in an aggressive manner. According to the *OED*, Randle Holme defined "roughshod" in *The Academy of Armory* in 1688, "Rough-shod—when the nails are not yet worn that holds on the shoes." Protruding nails give the horse better traction but also damage the ground.

shoo-in: a heavy favorite. The term apparently originated as a reference to a fixed race, in which other jockeys would hold back and "shoo," or urge ahead, the predetermined winner. The *OED*'s first definition of "shoo in" is "to allow a racehorse to win easily," and quotes a 1908 book *Racing Maxims and Methods of "Pittsburgh Phil"*: "There were many times presumably that 'Tod' would win through such manipulations, being 'shooed in,' as it were." Eventually "shoo-in" came to mean a competitor expected to legitimately win easily.

In these cases, "no thanks" is implicit in the "I'm good," as one blogger noticed with dissatisfaction. "When did 'I'm good' replace 'no thank you'?" he wondered. "The other day I asked someone who works for me if they wanted sugar in their tea and the answer was 'I'm good.' I thought he was going to ask me for a raise."

But "I'm good" sometimes has a shade of meaning all its own. In some instances, "I'm good" appears to be an understatement, communicating "I really don't want that." One blogger writes about trying to hand out raffle tickets at a work outing, when one man responded by saying, "No thanks, I'm good."

Another blogger writes, "My friend just asked me if I ever thought about dating women. Um, no thanks. I'm good. I like men."

"No thanks, I'm good" is also used to reject lewd propositions on online message boards. In these cases "I'm good" amounts to an almost sarcastic statement—"yeah, right." The speaker isn't trying to provide a reason for declining as much as to say that a reason shouldn't be needed.

Maybe this even applies to Google Earth. When you click on "I'm good," you could be thinking, as I was, "I really don't want to read this fine print. Let's move on."

in harm's way

Four times during a 2004 presidential debate, and twice in the same answer, President Bush used the phrase "in harm's way" to refer to troops in Iraq.

"The hardest part of the job is to know that I committed the troops in harm's way and then do the best I can to provide comfort for the loved ones who lost a son or a daughter or husband and wife," he said. Bush added that he met with a young widow "knowing full well that the decision I made caused . . . her loved one to be in harm's way."

The phrase seems to be getting more common as the presidential campaign heats up; it registers nearly as many results on the Lexis-Nexis database for the last month as it does for July and August combined.

Although Bush uses the phrase more, Kerry also employed "in harm's way," as he did in his acceptance speech at the 2004 Democratic National Convention. "Before you go to battle," he said, "you have to be able to look a parent in the eye and truthfully say: 'I tried everything possible to avoid sending your son or daughter into harm's way.'"

The phrase's associations with battle go back several centuries, as *New York Times* columnist William Safire noted. American naval hero John Paul Jones—the commodore who uttered the famous line, "I have not yet begun to fight"— wrote in a letter in 1788, "I wish to have no connection with any ship that does not sail fast, for I intend to go in harm's way." According to a biographer, when Jones wrote that sentence, he underlined the words "fast" and "in harm's way." John Wayne played a naval officer in the 1965 movie *In Harm's Way*, based on a novel of the same name, who says, "A fast ship going in harm's way—a lousy situation, Commander Eddington."

Today, "in harm's way" is a euphemism, a tidy tagline for the brutality of battle, and now for the messy situation in Iraq. But unlike the military euphemisms "collateral damage" for "civilian deaths" or "delivering an ordnance" for "dropping a bomb," "in harm's way" is not coldly bureaucratic.

"In harm's way" pleases politicians who love to sound eloquent without much effort, because the phrase is "actually a bit on the literary side," says Arnold Zwicky, linguist at Stanford University. It helps that "in harm's way" is old-fashioned; Zwicky notes that the phrase's parent, "out of harm's way," dates to the mid-1600s.

Putting oneself "in harm's way" connotes sacrifice, the risk of one's life to keep another safe. But the distinction between a way that's safe and a way that's harmful may be getting outdated in this post-9/11 world. Who among the workers at the World Trade Center could fathom that they were in way of such horrific harm? Meanwhile, the most mundane acts, such as driving on the highway or eating fatty foods, are fraught with peril. To an extent, we all live in harm's way.

inch vs. inches

> We copy editors are going nuts! Is it 0.9 inch or inches?
>
> —*Jayne Bohner, Wheaton, Illinois*

I ASKED Bill Walsh, chief copy editor of the national desk at The *Washington Post* and author of *Lapsing Into a Comma* and *Elephants of Style*.

"I'd say inches," Walsh replied by e-mail. "In *Lapsing Into a Comma* I advanced the idea that it's incorrect to think of plural as more than one and singular as one or less. Rather, the singular is uniquely suited to the number one. If something is free and someone asks you how many dollars it costs, you might say 'zero dollars'; you'd never say 'zero dollar.'"

Update: Several readers have objected to this verdict, arguing that when saying this measurement aloud you would say "nine tenths of an inch." But printed versions of measurements don't always follow how they're read aloud; for example, "$2.75" sounds much different than it looks: "two dollars and seventy-five cents." For that matter, as Walsh pointed out to me in a follow-up e-mail, we say "nine-tenths" and not "oh-point-nine" for "0.9."

Indian country

"So far the road has been safe, but tomorrow we get into Indian country," wrote an American soldier before he was killed in Iraq, in a letter published in the summer of 2004 by *The New York Times*. "We had to get the mail through even though it meant riding through Indian country," an army mail carrier told the *Columbus Ledger-Enquirer* after returning from Iraq. "Ramadi [Iraq] is Indian Country—'the wild, wild West,' as the region is called," wrote the *Los Angeles Times* last month.

Comparing the current state of Iraq to the American West before European settlement is unfortunate, says Landon Jones, author of *The Essential Lewis and Clark* and *William Clark and the Shaping of the West*.

"Native Americans serve in the armed forces in remarkably high percentages," Jones says by phone. (According to U.S. Army

Public Affairs, more than 4,000 American Indians and Alaskan Natives served in the Army last year.) "They must find it bizarre that their ancestral homeland has become a synonym today for the land of their enemies."

When Lewis and Clark set off in 1804 for the Pacific coast through the territory of the Louisiana Purchase, "Indian country" was an official term for land outside the borders of U.S. states and territories. "They would put it on maps that way for areas beyond [Louisiana] Territory," Jones said.

But because white settlers often encountered violent resistance to their efforts to displace American Indians, the name "Indian country" also came to connote danger. While Lewis and Clark did not use the term in their expedition journals, each employed it in letters after the trip when Lewis was governor of Louisiana Territory and Clark was superintendent of Indian Affairs for the U.S. government, Jones said. "They used it to talk about where Indians lived, but they also used it to mean threatening place, ominous place," he said.

Since then, however, "Indian country" has been incorporated by American Indians to mean reservations—or, more broadly, anywhere American Indians live. A newspaper devoted to American Indian news and issues calls itself *Indian Country Today*. Its headline over coverage of John Kerry's 2004 campaign speeches to Pueblo and Navajo audiences in the Southwest read: "Kerry courts Indian country." A Colorado-based company called Medicine Root Inc. that offers tours to historical American Indian sites calls its services Indian Country Tourism.

"Indian country" also has technical legal functions, denoting areas where American Indian tribes have sovereignty. A casebook called "Cases and Materials on Federal Indian Law" says the term "defines the geographic area in which tribal and federal laws normally apply and state laws normally do not apply."

These 20th century adaptations of "Indian country," however, have not eliminated the 19th century pejorative use of the term. Some Vietnam soldiers and anti-war protesters used it to refer to the unmanageable jungles of Vietnam. Author Philip Caputo picked up on this usage in his 1987 novel about a U.S. soldier

123

who fights beside an American Indian friend in Vietnam. Caputo called his book *Indian Country*.

But using the term to mean a dangerous place draws on archaic notions of American Indians as savages and presumes a right of Europeans to uproot them to "tame" the wilderness. Says a spokesman for the National Congress of American Indians: "It's not very endearing."

The term "American Indian" itself, incidentally, seems to be regaining some currency, and some consider it preferable to "Native American." "While it is true that the term 'Indian' does not accurately describe the indigenous peoples of the Western Hemisphere, its usage, particularly when incorporated into the term 'American Indian' has been largely (although not universally) accepted by most tribal officials," writes Tim Johnson, executive editor of *Indian Country Today*, by e-mail. "As a matter of style usage the term 'American Indian' seems to be gaining favor over the term 'Native American,' since it carries with it a more specific identification"—after all, he notes, anyone born in the U.S. is technically a native American. The *Chicago Tribune* stylebook lists "Native American" as "an acceptable alternative to 'American Indian' or 'Indian,' if that is what an individual or organization prefers." The Associated Press stylebook says "American Indian" is preferred but advises, "Where possible, be precise and use the name of the tribe."

indirect requests

WOULD YOU mind reading this article?

Linguists have a term for this kind of question, which people use constantly in everyday conversation. They call it a "conventionally indirect" request. It's "indirect" because the meaning of the question doesn't come from the direct meaning of the words. The speaker who asks "Would you mind doing this?" usually doesn't actually mean, "will this inconvenience you?" but rather, "please do this." Someone who asks "can you drive me downtown?" isn't inquiring about your driving ability. They're saying, "Will you take the wheel?"

"It is a request for action rather than for information," explains Rosina Marquez-Reiter, linguist at Britain's University of Surrey, by e-mail. "The beauty of conventionally indirect requests is that the speaker knows that the addressee [a native speaker of the language] will interpret them as requests for action, and also that the speaker will generally be following politeness patterns and will appear non-coercive. That is, he or she will be seen as respecting the freedom of the hearer."

Linguists have long known that conventionally indirect requests are used in different languages, not just English. Spanish, for example, uses phrases such as "te importaria" before a verb. This can serve as an idiom that means "would it matter to you if" followed by the verb.

But little research has been done on how the expectations surrounding these requests differ from language to language. In the current issue of the journal *Applied Linguistics*, Marquez-Reiter and two co-authors compare the indirect requests of English speakers in Britain and Spanish speakers in Spain. They found the expectations behind indirect requests differ considerably from English to Spanish.

The study set up role-playing situations between University of Surrey students who were native speakers of either British English or Peninsular Spanish (Spanish spoken in Spain).

Students were told to talk to a fellow native speaker of their language and make requests to borrow a book, swap bus seats or ask for an advance in pay. Researchers showed them a videotape of their conversations afterward and asked them what they were thinking when they asked indirect questions.

Marquez-Reiter and her colleagues found that although both Spanish speakers and British speakers used indirect requests, the Spanish speakers were more certain that their fellow Spanish students would comply. The British students were less certain that fellow English speakers would cooperate.

For example, in a role-playing situation in which one student was playing a mother riding a bus with a child, the English speaker was more tentative. "Excuse me," the speaker said, "I was wondering, would it be possible if we could sit in these two seats and you could move to another place?" The Spanish student in this situation said simply, "No le importa sentarse en otro lado?" or "Do you mind sitting somewhere else?"

The study concluded that social distance was less of a problem for the Spanish students. They were less intimidated by the lack of familiarity with the other passenger, or, in the case of a student asking a professor to borrow a book, with the imbalance of power.

"The Spanish informants explained that university lecturers are there to help students," the study said, "and that, at least in Spain, they have no problems whatsoever in facilitating materials to students; in fact they are generally 'very friendly' despite social distance."

The British students, on the other hand, were less sure that their professors would lend them the book. With this uncertainty, the students said they were hoping their indirect questions would show how polite and humble they were. "The British always focused on the actual 'imposition' of the request," the study said.

Overall, the Spanish students assumed more familiarity with each other, and expected more helpfulness, than the British students did. Marquez-Reiter attributes these findings to cultural differences between Britain and Spain.

"In my data, the Spanish participants highlighted that a neighbor would have to show 'companerismo' [camaraderie] even if they don't know each other well," she said. "The British, on the other hand, thought that the neighbor didn't need to help even if they knew each other well."

-ing, in newscasting

MILK SALES are up, reported NBC's Peter Alexander on *Nightly News*. What Alexander said was this: "America's favorite drink at home now becoming a popular choice for families on the go." Not "is becoming," but "now becoming."

This strange syntax is getting more common on television news, observes language columnist Geoffrey Nunberg in his 2004 book *Going Nucular: Language, Politics, and Culture in Confron-*

tational Times (PublicAffairs). It was prevalent throughout the 2004 election night and its aftermath.

"For the second election in a row, the long night turning into a long morning in a race that's too close to call for now," said CNN's Bill Hemmer as he signed on the morning following the November 2004 election. He later announced, "The White House declaring that President Bush has won his re-election." Earlier, Wolf Blitzer threw it to analyst Jeff Greenfield by saying, "Jeff, Wisconsin going for Kerry, according to our projection."

Just how common is this style of speaking in broadcast news? In a study of three *NBC Nightly News* broadcasts for a lecture at Oxford University, James Vanden Bosch, English professor at Calvin College in Grand Rapids, Michigan, found that about two out of every five "spoken units" (sentences and fragments) in the broadcasts used this "-ing" form.

Some newscasters have argued this style saves time, but that's seldom true. "Now becoming" takes a little longer to say than "is becoming." Another explanation is that TV is copying newspapers, but newspapers usually prefer to save space by dropping the "-ing" and making a complete sentence: "Wisconsin goes for Kerry."

Grammarians aren't sure what to call this new style (and if talking about grammar causes you to break out in hives, you might want to skip ahead). It looks like an absolute phrase—which modifies an entire sentence, as in, "That being said, I liked the movie overall"—but it doesn't act like one. Absolute phrases are sentence fragments, but when they are joined with a complete sentence, they make sense. When they stand by themselves, they don't. No one says, "That being said."

Sentence fragments are nothing new in TV news; Chevy Chase famously parodied them in the 1970s with his catchphrase "Here now the news." But this new kind of fragment may illustrate the heightened urgency of news in the era of cable and the Web. "It communicates a breathless awareness of immediacy," says Vanden Bosch. "There is an almost manic insistence that this is all late-breaking news, and that I alone have come to tell you."

The problem is that making everything happen in the present can confuse viewers. In the case of Blitzer's statement, "Wisconsin going for Kerry," a viewer could misunderstand whether Wisconsin was leaning toward Kerry ("is going"), had just been awarded to Kerry ("goes"), or went for Kerry earlier ("has gone"). Sometimes a switch in syntax can violate the first rule of language: communicate clearly.

initialism

> The editor in me cannot let pass your reference to ATM and RSVP as "acronyms." They are "initialisms." An acronym has to be a word.
>
> —*Dolores Parker, Tallahassee, Florida*

I SHOULD have mentioned this distinction, although observance of it is declining. *The American Heritage Dictionary* and *The New Oxford American Dictionary* preserve this distinction, but *Merriam-Webster's Collegiate Dictionary* lists an alternate definition of "acronym": "an abbreviation (as 'FBI') formed from initial letters." It defines "initialism" as "an acronym formed from initial letters." So that dictionary recognizes "acronym" and "initialism" as synonyms, as most people do.

interpreting vs. translating

BEFORE YOU make a movie called *The Interpreter*, you have to get one thing straight. An interpreter is not the same as a translator. That's what the makers of the 2005 movie *The Interpreter* learned as they made the first movie ever filmed at the United Nations in New York.

"After they understood the difference between interpreters and translators, they stopped calling us translators," says Brigitte Andreassier-Pearl, the UN's chief of Interpretation Services, who consulted with director Sidney Pollack and actress Nicole Kidman in the making of *The Interpreter*.

Interpreters are in charge of interpreting spoken communication as it happens on the UN floor. Translators work with written documents, under far less time pressure.

"Some of my best friends are translators, so there is no antagonism," Andreassier-Pearl says. "But we're called 'interpreters.' We do a different job. That's one thing I explained to Sidney Pollack, and it's one thing I hope the movie is going to spread around."

To hear interpreters tell it, the difference between interpreting and translating is like the difference between auto racing and a stroll. "Translators work in offices from 9 to 5, with dictionaries, computers and databases. It's a leisurely pace, and if they don't know something, they can go and research," says Andreassier-Pearl. "Interpreters are in the glass booth, in the middle of the action, with no dictionaries and no help. They have to be able to do it right on the spot. It can be kind of scary."

Kidman, cast as a UN interpreter who accidentally overhears a secret threat on an African president's life, had her definitions down when she arrived at UN headquarters to observe interpreters at work. She spent a morning in the glass booth of the Security Council, studying the interpreters and asking them questions. Then she sat down to interview Andreassier-Pearl, a French native with a PhD in French literature who has worked at the UN for 34 years.

"She wanted to know how long you have to wait before you start your sentence," Andreassier-Pearl said. "It's a split second. But it depends how fast the speaker is. And in some languages, you cannot plunge right in—you have to wait for the verb."

Kidman also asked Andreassier-Pearl the most common question interpreters get asked—what do you do if you don't know a word? "We always work in the context [of what's being said]," says Andreassier-Pearl. "You try to understand the meaning and express the idea, you find an idiomatic equivalent right away. Sometimes, I hate to say it, but you skip it."

Idioms can be a linguistic obstacle to diplomacy, but interpreters are ready for them. Andreassier-Pearl recalls one American delegate she was interpreting into French who put her on the spot. "He said, 'Now I'm going to test the interpreter in the booth and see if she knows the idiom,'" Andreassier-Pearl says. "He said, 'You cannot have your cake and eat it too.' In French, you cannot translate that. I said, 'You cannot have it both ways.'"

The UN employs 113 interpreters and nearly as many freelancers. All of them are fluent in at least three languages. Each interpreter has what is called her "active" (or native) language, and two or three "passive" (non-native) languages. Interpreters are assigned, with one day's notice, to interpret from one of their passive languages into their active language. The UN uses six official languages—Arabic, Chinese, English, French, Russian and Spanish.

The job is a paradox—interpreters must remain utterly unnoticeable while serving as a vital link in international diplomacy. To make the job even more challenging, delegates are talking faster, Andreassier-Pearl says, thanks in part to time limits on speeches. "Sometimes interpreters are practically in tears," Andreassier-Pearl says. "They're good, well-prepared, and we do our best, but we're not machines."

Not everyone is satisfied with their efforts. Sometimes as they are speaking, delegates monitor how they are being interpreted. You can tell they're listening to you via their earpieces, says Andreassier-Pearl, when they start to speak more slowly. Occasionally, delegates file complaints with Andreassier-Pearl.

"I always ask them to give precise and specific examples," Andreassier-Pearl says. "I don't [just] want to hear that the interpretation was bad in Room 2 on Wednesday morning. Interpreting is very easy to criticize, but it's very hard to do it."

Update: "Your interview with the Head of Interpretation Services at UNHQ has ruffled some feathers among UN translators," wrote Nigel Lindup from the United Nations Office at Geneva. My comment that interpreters make the difference between interpreting and translating sound like "the difference between auto racing and a stroll" understandably caused particular offense.

"Of course we translators are all fully aware of the 'scary' nature of the interpreter's task and of the sometimes impossible demands placed on them, in particular by speakers who insist on reading very fast from a text they have not had the courtesy to provide; many of us admire them greatly for being willing to expose themselves in a way we translators would not dream of doing," Lindup wrote. But he said that translation is no walk in the park.

"Sure, the words stay put and we can consult colleagues, dictionaries, the Web or specialist glossaries when we need to, but productivity quotas are a reality in the UN and the deadlines are often tight, with last-minute submissions and conference-room papers being required fast, if not yesterday," Lindup wrote. "Even if a document will not be required in the meeting room for another 10 weeks, it still needs to be off our desks on time so as not to hold up the rest of the production process and then be sent out to conference participants in advance.

Lindup added that interpreters consult versions of meeting documents that have been prepared by translators—"documents for which we have often needed to do intensive and thorough research, discussing the most pernickety nuances *ad nauseam* with colleagues, or trawling the Web for the technical references we seek and their equivalents. A good thing for everyone that the words stay put for translators to pore over. Conversely, where we translators are required to attend and write up meetings, we rely on the interpreters if a speaker is using a language we don't cover. When they are fluent and on top of the material we are just so grateful and some of us make it a point to tell them so."

Lindup concluded: "Interpreters and translators alike are part of a vast team, a chain of production that starts with the submission of a document by a Member State several months before a conference and ends with discussion of that document in up to six languages in the meeting room. . . . Ultimately, you see, as colleagues in the same workplace, we depend on each other."

Brigitte Andreassier-Pearl replied to Nigel (and copied me on the reply) that she heartily agreed that interpreters and translators are on the same team, and made it clear that the "auto racing" line was mine, not hers. She ended by writing, "I am sorry if my interview has ruffled some feathers among UN translators. It certainly was not my intention. We depend a great deal on each other as you mention and should you find yourself in NY, please do not hesitate to give me a call and we can talk it over."

I thought my "auto racing" analogy was a reasonably apt—if, I admit, overly cutesy—summary of how Andreassier-Pearl described the differences between the jobs of interpreting and

131

translating—though as I quoted her saying in the article, and as she clarifies above, she wasn't trying to disparage translators. But I take responsibility for a bad analogy, and I'm relieved that despite it, both Andreassier-Pearl and Lindup could—true to their vocations—cordially reach greater understanding of each other.

invented words

See neologisms.

irregardless

> I know that the word "irregardless" is in the dictionary, but I am not sure if it ever has a correct application.
>
> *—Edward Kepuraitis, Frankfort, Illinois*

THE FOUR major dictionaries I checked all include and define "irregardless," but they all label it as "non-standard" and note that the preferred word in Standard English is "regardless." Most dictionaries and usage guides say this word originated nearly 100 years ago, presumably as a blend of the words "irrespective" (which is accepted in Standard English) and "regardless." Some note that "irregardless" is vehemently condemned by users of Standard English, and advise that it's easy to avoid their wrath by simply saying "regardless" instead.

integrity

> What's the adjective form of the word "integrity," when you're referring to someone who displays great integrity? "Integreful"? "Integrated"?
>
> *—Carl Deitrick, Elgin, Illinois*

YOU CAN do one of three things. You can either try to single-handedly revive a word such as "integritive" or "integrious," which English retired centuries ago, according to *The Oxford English Dictionary* (in 1658, Sir Henry Slingsby wrote in his diary, "Such was their integrious candor and intimacy to me . . .").

You can try to get English to adopt the French adjective "integre," meaning "honest, upright"—which some English speakers tried to borrow, without success, back in the 1500s.

Or—my recommendation—you just have to content yourself with describing someone as "a person of great integrity." It's wordy, but it's the only option that other English speakers will recognize.

You might be wondering about "integral," but English has restricted that word to mean "essential to" (or "related to a mathematical integer"). *Merriam-Webster* defines "integrative," meanwhile, as "serving to integrate or . . . directed toward integration."

The word "integrity" comes from the same Latin root as our word "entire," and originally meant "undivided, complete." It can describe both physical soundness of a building, as in "structural integrity," or moral virtue. But for whatever reason, an adjective for the virtue never caught on.

Update: My friend Kristin Bush responded to tell me that, inspired by Jim Vanden Bosch's neological campaign (*see* **presticogitation**), she is trying to gain currency for her word "integruous" as an adjectival form of "integrity." "Not only is it related to the word 'integrity,' but it is also related to the word 'congruous,' which, like 'integrity,' also shows sameness or likeness," she says. "I teach it to my high school English students every year, and most of them learn to use it correctly."

is is

I hear so many people say, "The thing is, is that . . . " Why the double "is"?

—*Noreen Rapp, Chicago, Illinois*

THIS IS a strange case; it sounds ridiculously redundant, and almost never appears in written English, only spoken English. But there's a good explanation for it, according to an article by linguist David Tuggy in a journal on cognitive linguistics. (The article had this title, believe it or not: "The thing is is that people talk that way. The question is is why?").

When you have a clause that starts with "what" and ends with "is" and is followed by the main verb "is," the sentence is perfectly grammatical. An analysis at *Language Log* (www.languagelog. org), based on Tuggy's paper, quotes an example of this from the writer G.K. Chesterton: "What the thing is, is not cowardly, but profoundly and detestably wicked."

You could also say, "What the problem is, is it's not plugged in." (Change the "it's" to "it is," and you have 3 out of 4 words in a row that are identical, and grammatical!) Of course, it's easier to simply say, "The problem is it's not plugged in." But starting with "what the problem is" shows that you're answering a certain question ("what's the problem?")—spoken or unspoken—and not just saying something out of the blue.

Hearing sentences like these, linguists say, probably makes us want to use a double "is" even when it isn't justified by a "what" clause. *Language Log* quotes the uncle of Elizabeth Smart (the nationally known kidnapping victim) as telling CNN in 2003, "And the key thing is, is we have Elizabeth back right now."

issues

When did "issues" become synonymous with "problems"?

—*Tim Adams, Bolingbrook, Illinois*

Author Steve Rushin says he saved a stack of magazines from his youth that featured his hero, Larry Bird, and jokes that when people tell him he "has a lot of issues from his childhood," Rushin wonders, "How did they know?"

The phrase "he has issues" has taken on psychological connotations probably within the last 30 or 40 years. *The Oxford English Dictionary* added a new definition for "issue" in 2003 to its online edition—"emotional or psychological difficulties"—saying this usage is American and often uses a modifying word (as in "attachment issues" or "intimacy issues").

This meaning may have developed from a broader sense of the word "issue": "a vital or unsettled matter," as *Merriam-Webster* defines it (as in "economic issues"). Or it may have started in phrases such as "intimacy issues" that were later shortened to just "issues."

The phrase "have issues with" followed soon after; historian Stephen Goranson sent me this example from a 1983 therapy guidebook: "All family therapists have issues with their own parents, spouses, or children which are unresolved and which predispose them to see situations in a distorted way." When the book said "issues" in that sentence, it wasn't talking about copies of *Psychology Today* magazine.

it, as plural

IN MIDDLE English, the word "it" could refer to a plural, said Kevin Psonak of the University of Texas, in his presentation "The Flourish of the Medieval Plural 'It'" at the Modern Language Association's 2006 convention in Washington, D.C. Psonak gave examples from a collection of 15th century letters, including this sentence: "It are lies all the words that they say." But that usage died out in English almost as quickly as it emerged, Psonak said.

it is what it is

FOX NEWS asked Republican strategist Karl Rove during the 2008 U.S. presidential campaign whether the long Democratic primary race was good or bad for John McCain.

"Well, first of all, it is what it is," Rove said. "You know, sometimes in politics, you can change things, affect things, but other times you just have to deal with it as it is."

Rove employed one of English's fastest-spreading catchphrases: "It is what it is." It's the same phrase Amanda Overmyer used after finishing 11th on "American Idol." "I definitely had hopes of [the top] six or seven," she said. "But it is what it is."

"I'm not going to sit here and dwell on anything, good or bad, that happened in the past," New England Patriots coach Bill Belichick said after his team lost the Super Bowl in January 2008. "It is what it is."

Part regret, part resignation, part defiance and maybe part evasion, "it is what it is" is becoming a catchy motto. It may be a tautology—a redundant definition, like "rules are rules" or "the

135

Cubs will always be the Cubs." But people turn to "it is what it is" to help ease their angst about twists of fate.

The phrase's popularity is too recent to catch the attention of dictionaries or phrase books, but *UrbanDictionary.com* has a definition ready: "a phrase that seems to simply state the obvious but actually implies helplessness . . . as in 'it ain't gonna change, so deal with it or don't.'"

"I think it really means 'take it or leave it' or 'there's nothing I can or want to do about it,'" lexicographer Grant Barrett, co-host of the public radio show *A Way With Words* (www.waywordradio.org), says by e-mail.

The phrase caught the attention of Congress during its 2008 hearings on steroids in baseball. Trainer Brian McNamee testified that when he said to pitcher Roger Clemens, "It is what it is," he meant "the truth is the truth."

Representative Mark Souder reported to the chairman that the phrase was a regional saying. "I asked a New Yorker on the floor, and he said that is a not only Mr. McNamee expression but a New York expression for telling the truth," Souder said.

That's giving New York too much credit for a widespread cliché. If you're going to credit anyone, said the online magazine *Slate* during the hearings, you might have to start with John Locke, the 17th century philosopher who said, "Essence may be taken for the very being of anything, whereby it is what it is."

William Safire pointed to an 1851 edition of *The New York Times* that read, "The *Courier and Enquirer* declares its 'belief' in the Compromise of 1850. Whether it is just what it should have been in all its detail the *Courier* will not say; 'but it is, what it is, and cannot, without destroying it, be made otherwise.' "

Only recently has "it is what it is" vaulted into the realm of ubiquitous catchphrases, perhaps with a boost from popular culture references—a 2001 movie titled *It Is What It Is;* a 2002 song by String Cheese Incident with the same title; a 2004 *USA Today* article naming "it is what it is" as the sports cliché of the year.

Now everyone seems to take it for granted that "it is what it is." Which is strange, because often, things are not what they seem.

Update: Several readers responded to point out the cliché's connections to the philosophy of Buddhism, 14th century mystic Meister Eckhart, and the Spanish song "Que sera sera"—"Whatever will be, will be." That reminded me of Reinhold Niebuhr's "Serenity Prayer": "God, give us grace to accept with serenity the things that cannot be changed, courage to change the things that should be changed, and the wisdom to distinguish the one from the other." And then there's Jesus' prayer in the gospels: "Not my will, but yours be done." I doubt there's a direct connection from the current spread of this cliché to any of these sources, but it's certainly true that a philosophy of accepting difficult and uncontrollable realities has deep roots in ancient wisdom.

-ize

Things about language that puzzle or intrigue me include the phenomenon of making verbs from nouns by adding "-ize" like prioritize (I hate that word!).

—*Judi Zink, Chicago*

Where and why did the noun incentive become the verb "incent" or worse, "incentivize?" We have several perfectly good verbs the users of "incent" apparently have never heard. "Motivate" comes to mind first.

—*Lynn Stevens, Kalamazoo, Michigan*

I DON'T know if "incentivize" is much worse than "hospitalize" and "finalize," which I happen to like, but I would agree that its association with marketing makes it weak in everyday conversation. And yes, three cheers for "motivate"! Although, no doubt someone complained the first time "motivate" was used as a verb form of the noun "motive," don't you think?

Extensive use of "-ize" seems to be restricted to business jargon, but I'll sign a petition to keep it from getting carried away. Still, the suffix itself is as old as its Greek root "-izein," and

English words such as "formalize" and "jeopardize" have been around for centuries.

I wanted to send a follow-up to my question about "-ize" words. On April Fools' Day, two of the college students I work with, having seen that column posted on our bulletin board, Post-It-ized my office with 40 "-ize" words of their own crafty creation ("anesthetize," "motorize," "actualize," etc.). But the students also posted an interesting historical note: "The suffix '-ize' has been productive in English since the time of Thomas Nashe (1567–1601), who claimed credit for introducing it into English to remedy the surplus of monosyllabic words."

—Judi Zink, Chicago

SORRY THAT column led to such verbal vandalism! Nashe did indeed boast of his use of "-ize" as a way to make English more like Greek (which had the suffix "-izein"), and wrote, "Our English tongue of all languages most swarmeth with the single money of monosyllables, which are the only scandal of it."

jean

ONE FALL day at the mall, I saw a sign outside an Express clothing store that read: "Every Single Jean $20 Off." I went inside and asked if that meant I would receive a $40 discount for a pair of jeans. The sales assistant said no, but made no move to change the sign.

A little later, I saw a sign outside Chico's describing its sale as "the perfect pant event."

jewelry

See **February and jewelry**.

journey

IT USED to be that a "journey" was all in a day's work. Now it takes a lifetime.

A Hallmark line of cards called "Journeys" shows that the word "journey," originally a literal unit of time and travel, has become a metaphor for the experience of living life with all its ups and downs.

The word "journey," from the French *la journee*, traces back to the Latin *diurnata*, literally meaning "by day." "The original meaning in French was 'daily,'" says etymologist Anatoly Liberman, author of *Word Origins and How We Know Them* (Oxford University Press). "In Old French the adjective . . . began to function as a noun [and] acquired the vague meaning of 'a day's work, occupation, or trip,' and even 'day.'"

The same meanings carried over into English. A writer in the 1400s, quoted in *The Oxford English Dictionary*, says, "52 journeys from this land . . . there is another land that men call Lamary." That means it took 52 days' worth of travel to get to Lamary. (The verb "to journey" was also in use at that time: A source from 1330 says, "He journeyed then from land to land.")

But writers of the era also were using "journey" as a metaphor for life progression or experiences. Around the year 1440, Bishop Reginald Pecock wrote in his book *The Rule of Christian Religion*, "No man might fulfill his ghostly [spiritual] journey of virtuous living . . . without thy grace."

The meaning of actual travel has not disappeared from our modern use of the word "journey." *The New Oxford American Dictionary* defines it as "an act of traveling from one place to another," and adds that unlike the word "trip," the word "journey" "suggests that a considerable amount of time and distance will be covered, and that the travel will take place over land."

But the metaphorical meaning of "journey" has become one of its most common uses today. It's what lies behind the line of Hallmark cards for people going through difficult life circumstances. "When we started talking to people, they told us they needed cards for events that really do happen in life," Hallmark said in a press release. "Basically, they gave us permission to talk about these specific, sometimes scary life moments"—including a cancer diagnosis, depression, coming out of the closet and caring for an aging parent.

Hallmark is picking up on a familiar metaphor. First daughter Jenna Bush announced in 2007 she is working on a book about a teenage single mother who is HIV positive. The title is *Ana's Story: A Journey of Hope*. A *Baltimore Sun* article about a high school basketball team read, "The situation that accompanies this year's journey to tomorrow's Class 1A game is altogether different from last year."

This use of "journey" has become so common that you can hear its overtones no matter how the word is used. For example, when *The Boston Globe* wrote in a caption that "the aircraft carrier USS John F. Kennedy left Boston Harbor yesterday for its journey to Florida for decommissioning," it was talking about a trip on the ocean, and yet I wondered if the caption used the word "journey" because the trip will mean the end of the ship's life cycle.

Or when the *Globe* wrote about *Well*, which it described as an "autobiographical play [that] traces Lisa Kron's journey away from and back to her suburban Michigan home, bringing together a host of lively characters to tell her story"—it sounds like the "journey" wasn't just a trip to and from her house.

Today, "journey" has become such an abstract idea that you don't even have to leave home to have one. Or to get a Hallmark card.

kind of

See **sort of**.

Latin, legacy in English

THE FIRST irony about the Latin language is that it is often called a dead language, when in fact it is alive and well in other languages—including English. The second irony is that Latin is considered an ancient language, even though, as Swedish linguist Tore Janson writes, "In the last hundred years or so we have taken in more words from this source than ever before."

Janson offers a tidy summary of Latin's nearly three-millennium existence in *A Natural History of Latin* (Oxford University Press). Latin, writes Janson, "was the native language of the Romans in antiquity; it was Europe's international language until two or three hundred years ago; and it is the language from which the modern European languages have drawn the majority of their loanwords. That means there are three good reasons for knowing something about Latin."

Janson's book is a good place to start, although it is a little heavy on history and light on linguistics, and its translation from Janson's original Swedish is clunky at points. Still, *Natural History of Latin* is an authoritative introduction to arguably the most influential language of all time.

Named for the ancient region of Latium, now called Lazio in Italian, Latin emerged in the 8th century B.C. after the settlement of Rome. While it would later become the language of scholarly writing, Latin was probably only a spoken language in its first few centuries, Janson says. And while Latin would come to be associated with the urban vitality of Rome and grandeur of the Roman Empire, its first generations of speakers were farmers, practicing "agricultura," or "cultivation of the field." When Rome overtook Greece and established an empire encompassing the Mediterranean Sea and Europe, it spread Latin far and wide.

This alone would make Latin an important chapter in world history, but the language had a second act after the Roman Empire collapsed. Here lies another irony: Though Latin was the language of an empire that aggressively oppressed Christianity (before adopting it as the empire's official state religion), it was the church that kept Latin alive when Rome fell, using it throughout the Middle Ages for liturgy, theology, and translating the Bible.

After the Renaissance, Latin had a third act as the international language of science and philosophy. In the 20th century, technological innovations made Latin more visible than ever. "Video," for example, is the Latin word for "I see." "Digital" comes from "digit" (digital technology uses code written in ones and zeroes), which derives from the Latin word *digitus* for "finger," because we count with our fingers. The phrase "via satellite" comes from the Latin *via* for "road" or "way" and *satellitis* for "attendant" (which, in a way, describes an orbiting object).

Latin's status as a living language is bolstered by the online encyclopedia *Wikipedia*, which includes Latin as one of the languages into which the encyclopedia is translated (see http://la.wikipedia.org).

A final irony about Latin is that it became the foundation of English despite belonging to a very different language family. Latin spawned the family of Romance languages, including French, Italian, and Spanish, while English belongs to the Germanic family, with such siblings as Dutch and German. But missionaries to England in the first millennium and French conquerors in the second millennium ensured Latin would make its mark on English.

As a result, countless English words—as much as half of the English vocabulary, by some estimates (Janson doesn't weigh in on this)—have Latin roots.

Thus, a primer in Latin—such as Janson's generous appendix of Latin words and phrases—is a primer in etymology. Our word "republic," for example, comes from the Latin phrase *res publica*, or "things of the public." *Aqua*, the Latin word for "water," is the root of "aquatic" and "aquarium." *Frater*, the Latin word for "brother," is behind the English words "fraternal" and "fraternity."

For a supposedly dead language, Latin is having quite an afterlife. Centuries after the fall of the Roman Empire and fade of its language, Latin, three books released in 2007 argue that understanding Latin is crucial to understanding major languages today.

Carpe Diem: Put a Little Latin in Your Life (Hyperion), by Harry Mount, is the most eager to please of the bunch. This relentlessly chatty, self-described "friendly Latin primer" is a fun ride. It's a healthy reminder that Latin was a colorful language, even though students like me learned Latin by rote conjugation and found it rigid and militaristic. "People laughed and cried in Latin," Mount writes. He points to Latin's modern descendant, Italian, and notes, "That most hot-blooded, passionate, and angry of languages is only a small jump from Latin." At times, Mount's book comes off cutesy. His repeated insisting that conjugating verbs isn't pointless only makes it seem all the more tedious. Re-

The word *facere*, for "to make," lies at the root of "factory," "fact" and "defect."

More than 1,500 years after the fall of Rome, Latin isn't going away. "That considerable portion of the world's population who speak a European language," Janson concludes, "will have to use Latin words every day and every hour for as long as one can see into the future."

laughing all the way to the bank

WHEN I'M at the bank, I never hear anybody laughing. Maybe I'm missing something, because lately all kinds of people are reportedly "laughing all the way to the bank."

After Sony's Blu-ray disc was declared the winner over Toshiba in the high definition DVD race in early 2008, the only question left was "how hard Blu-ray backers are laughing all the way to the bank," according to ZDNet.com. A *Wall Street Journal* profile of a woman who paints portraits of dogs said that people used to laugh at her occupation, but now, "with an eight-month waiting list, she's laughing all the way to the bank." The *Toronto Sun* complained that even as the economy struggles, the oil industry

placing the word "subjunctive" with the label "woulda/coulda/shoulda" doesn't seem worth it. And his decision to sugarcoat his run-through of the different declensions of nouns (first through fifth) by hiding them between unrelated anecdotes and trivia is merely disorienting. But, overall, the book is one of the best entry-level introductions to Latin there is.

A more substantive and elegant history of Latin is Nicholas Ostler's *Ad Infinitum: A Biography of Latin* (Walker and Co.). I was impressed with Ostler's restraint in his previous book, *Empires of the Word*, a history of the languages of world empires. In that book, Ostler took us so patiently through forgotten powerhouse languages of world history, such as Akkadian and Sanskrit, that his treatment of Latin was almost an afterthought. But Ostler, chairman of the Foundation for Endangered Languages, has much more to say about Latin, especially its post-Rome legacy in Europe.

is "laughing all the way to the bank."

Where did this cliché come from? Most word buffs credit the entertainer Liberace in the 1950s.

The original phrase Liberace actually used repeatedly—but sarcastically—was "crying all the way to the bank." *The Oxford English Dictionary* quotes Liberace from a 1956 newspaper article about his concert at Madison Square Garden: "The take was terrific but the critics killed me. My brother George cried all the way to the bank." Liberace repeated the quip over the years and wrote in his 1973 autobiography, "When the reviews are bad I tell my staff that they can join me as I cry all the way to the bank."

Liberace's sarcasm implies triumphant defiance, as if to say, "Who cares what you think—I'm rich!" In fact, Fred Shapiro, a librarian at Yale Law School and editor of *The Yale Book of Quotations*, found an early example of Liberace using the phrase with the word "laughing," from the *San Mateo County* (California) *Times* in 1953. The article reported that Liberace wrote to a Chicago critic who had slammed one of his sellout shows and said, "My manager and I laughed all the way to the bank."

Shapiro also found an even older example of the phrase that had nothing to do with Liberace. In 1946, the *Waterloo* (Iowa) *Daily Courier* wrote, "Eddie Walker is perhaps the wealthiest fight manager in the game." After his fighter lost a fight, the article said, Walker "felt so terrible, he cried all the way to the bank." So

"It was the [Roman] Empire that gave Latin its overarching status," Ostler writes. But he adds, "The language was to prove far more enduring than its creator. Its active use [has] lasted three times as long as Rome's dominion."

When you've read these two books, you're ready to graduate to the more hefty *The Blackwell History of the Latin Language* (Wiley-Blackwell) by University of Cambridge professors James Clackson and Geoffrey Horrocks. Though it's been relatively stable in its two-millennia-plus history, that doesn't mean Latin hasn't been subject to the changes and mutations that all lan-

Shapiro says Liberace popularized the phrase but didn't coin it.

However it started, "laughing all the way to the bank" caught on as a cliché for making an unlikely or unworthy profit. The *OED* defines the phrase as "to relish (originally ironically, 'to deplore') the fact that one is making money, especially undeservedly or at the expense of others." When it's said about someone else, the phrase can carry a sense of indignation.

That's what the *Toronto Sun* meant when it accused oil companies of profiting while the economy suffered, and what *The New York Times* meant when it wrote in 2007, "While subprime borrowers try to climb out of the holes they fell into, those who sold and packaged the loans are laughing all the way to the bank."

So far, it seems, online banking has yet to put a dent in this phrase. You no longer have to go to the bank to use its services, but apparently you can still laugh as you cash in.

lay vs. lie

Have you already addressed the problem of the incorrect use of "lie" and "lay"? "Lay" needs an object ("The child will lay down the book"). "Lie" means to assume a horizontal position. This is never used correctly on TV. Now I'm going to lay down my pen and lie down to rest.

—*Margie Watt, Olympia Fields, Illinois*

guages go through. The authors focus on the evolution of the sounds, vocabulary, word, and sentence structure of Latin over the centuries.

Meanwhile, what is probably still my favorite book on the history of Latin, Tore Janson's *A Natural History of Latin: The Story of the World's Most Successful Language* (Oxford University Press), was released in paperback in 2007. All of these books allow you to read up on a language that, even without any surviving native speakers, might just be linguistically immortal.

THE REASON this distinction is so hard to enforce is that "lay" and "lie" are tangled to begin with—"lay" is both its own verb and the past tense of the verb "lie," and "lay" means "lie" in "Now I lay me down to sleep."

It's natural for "lay" to merge with "lie" even more. In fact, *The American Heritage Guide to Contemporary Usage and Style* says, "For many . . . expressions, nonstandard 'lay' is actually more common than standard 'lie,' and in many contexts 'lay' sounds more natural."

But the *Guide* concludes that in published writing, "Copy-editing tradition demands that the two verbs be kept distinct and used according to the prescribed rules."

Update: A couple of readers insisted that "lay" still means "place, deposit" in the child's prayer—"Now I place myself down to sleep." That's technically true, but since the action of "place myself down" in this case is equivalent to the action of lying down, it helps blur the distinction between the two words.

leaps and bounds

I was told by a real estate teacher in the early 1980s that the term "by leaps and bounds" was derived from the real estate term "by metes and bounds." Subsequently anyone I tell this to says I'm nuts. Am I?

—*Dan Stecich, Chicago, Illinois*

NOT NUTS, but probably misinformed. "Metes and bounds" is an old legal term—*The Oxford English Dictionary* traces it to before the year 1400—that means the boundaries of a property. "Leaps and bounds" means large jumps or, figuratively, great amounts of progress, but it was never a legal term.

Plus, the "bounds" of "metes and bounds" means "boundaries," while the "bounds" of "leaps and bounds" means "jumps," as in, "to leap tall buildings in a single bound." There's no evidence of overlap in the history of either phrase.

One similarity these phrases have is that both are redundant—"metes" and "bounds" both mean "boundaries," and "leaps" and "bounds" both mean jumps. The redundancy has survived because of its rhetorical effect.

less vs. fewer

> Why do I hear "less" when it should be "fewer" on radio and TV so often? The example I was given in the third grade was, "Fewer water molecules make less water." Does this still hold true or have the rules changed?
>
> —*Mark Beard-Witherup, Chicago, Illinois*

I LEARNED the same rule: "fewer" means lower in number, "less" means lower in amount. I wasn't told about the exceptions: the phrases "no less than five days" and "less than fifty miles" are usually accepted in Standard English, and the alternatives sound awkward. Checkout aisles for "10 items or less" remain a gray area; I've seen some grocery stores change it to "10 items or fewer."

But it turns out that the merger of "fewer" and "less" has a long history. John Lyly wrote in 1579, according to *The Oxford English Dictionary*, "I think there are few Universities that have less faults than Oxford, many that have more." Dictionaries tend to give both the "number" and "amount" definitions for "less."

If "more" can pull double duty, being used for both number and amount ("more molecules make more water"), why expect any less of "less"?

Lewis and Clark, vocabulary of

A COIN to commemorate the 200-year anniversary of Lewis and Clark's arrival at the Pacific Ocean in 1805 bears the words Clark wrote in his journal when he saw the Pacific: "Ocean in view! O! The Joy!" The coin is actually a correction of a Clark typo. Or a write-o. Clark wrote in his journal, "Ocian in view! O! The Joy!"

One lexicographer who has studied the language of the journals Lewis and Clark kept says the explorers were lexical trailblazers. Their spelling and vocabulary provide a unique linguistic portrait of the English of their era.

"William Clark's masterful cartography and Meriwether Lewis' drawings of flora and fauna are a vital graphic record of the journey to the Pacific Ocean, but it is principally through the captains' words . . . that we see what they saw and feel what they felt," writes Alan Hartley in *Lewis and Clark: Lexicon of Discovery* (Washington State University Press). "It is the aim of this *Lexicon* both to explain the difficult and interesting words in the Corps of Discovery journals and to give the reader a feeling for American English in the first years of the 19th century."

Although Lewis' prose sounds more proper and historically momentous—Hartley contrasts what he calls "the 'backwoods' character of Clark's original writing, and Lewis' more literate style"—it is Clark's creative spelling that is more useful to linguists. Because Clark often spelled words as they sounded to him, his writing gives us a window into early-19th century pronunciation. "His misspellings are an invaluable gift, providing hints of his actual speech," writes Hartley, an independent scholar and lexicographer in Duluth, Minnesota.

For instance, Clark wrote in September 1805, "Great numbers of Indians reside on all those foks as well as the main river," spelling "forks" as "foks." Elsewhere, he spells "board" as "boad" and "horse" as "hose," while Lewis spells "sharp" as "shap" and "shortly" as "shotly." These phonetic spellings suggest the men pronounced the words without an "r"—a phonetic feature of the accent of Virginia, where both men were born.

The expedition, led by Lewis and Clark but joined by dozens of other explorers along the way, was a sampling of 19th century American English dialects, Hartley writes. "The voices of the expedition were many—Virginia drawl, Ohio River backcountry lingo, New Hampshire twang, lilting French Canadian and American Indian," Hartley writes. "The predominant dialects, however, were those of Virginia and the coastal South."

"At times I sat here and read aloud some of those peculiar spellings to get a sense of the sound," Hartley says by phone. "It gives a snapshot of American English at the turn of that century, but it's a very idiosyncratic snapshot."

Lexicon helps shed light on words and expressions that are common today but whose origins are no longer obvious. When Clark wrote, "The Indians were pointing their arrows blank," it means firing at a short distance. This meaning survives in our phrase "point-blank," with the word "blank" bearing its older meaning of "target."

Another shooting-related term is "offhand," meaning to shoot a rifle without resting it on anything to stabilize it. Lewis writes of shooting "at the distance of fifty yards off hand." Today we use the term metaphorically to mean "without an external aid," as in, "I don't know offhand," (that is, without asking someone or looking it up).

Some of the most entertaining entries in *Lexicon* are words that have died out in the 200 years since Lewis and Clark reached the Pacific. Words such as "brickle" (a Scottish-derived version of "brittle"), "chittediddle" (a word for "katydid"), "disembogue" ("to discharge into another body of water"), and "wattle" (to interlace twigs, as in, "wattled together") evoke another era of English.

The explorers' use of the word "slaky," meaning "muddy," is the first written record of the word, according to *The Oxford English Dictionary*. Together with another *Lexicon* term—"thawy," an adjective meaning "in a state of thawing"—Lewis and Clark give us the words to describe the mushy month of March; we can say, "It's thawy out—the ground will be slaky."

Landon Jones, reviewing *Lexicon* in a scholarly journal on the Lewis and Clark expedition titled *We Proceeded On*, praised the book as "richly detailed." "The hundreds of thousands of words published in their journals . . . open a window on a 19th-century American culture that today can seem remote and even baffling," wrote Jones, author of *William Clark and the Shaping of the West* (Hill and Wang). "The vocabularies of Lewis and Clark preserve the ephemera of their culture as faithfully and accurately as chunks of amber can preserve ancient insects."

lexicography, in an online era

THE OFFICIAL Dictionary of Unofficial English (McGraw-Hill) sounds like an oxymoron. If a word is "unofficial," what's it doing in an "official" dictionary?

But to Grant Barrett, author of this dictionary, which is subtitled *A Crunk Omnibus for Thrillionaires and Bampots for the Ecozoic Age*, lexicography—the methods of dictionary-making—can be applied to slang, jargon, neologisms, and other young or obscure words you won't find in a traditional dictionary.

Barrett is a lexicographer for Oxford University Press and the project editor of the *Historical Dictionary of American Slang*. The very existence of his new book makes a bold claim about the relevance of published dictionaries and lexicography in the age of the Internet and open-source reference material.

Online dictionaries such as *Wiktionary* (www.wiktionary.org) and *Urban Dictionary* (www.urbandicitonary.com) are examples of lexicography by democracy: they invite readers to create an entry for any word, new or old, and provide their own definition. At *Wiktionary*, you can edit an existing definition of a word. At *Urban Dictionary*, you can vote for which existing definition best describes a word or phrase from street slang, and the top vote-getter is listed as the first entry. (Another way to use the Web as a dictionary is to go to Google and type "define: dog," for example, and Google will return a list of sentences on the Web that begin, "A dog is . . . ")

"I don't know which words are legit and which words are not," the *Urban Dictionary*'s creator, Aaron Peckham, told the *New York Daily News* in 2004. "I think voting makes it a lot more democratic." Peckham created his website as a computer science student at California Polytechnic State University in the late 1990s. *Urban Dictionary* now has thousands of entries that were created and voted on by visitors. The slogan on the *Urban Dictionary* home page says, "Define your world."

Barrett says he loves the fact that so many people are interested in watching and recording words. *Urban Dictionary* and other Web sources are valuable resources for tracking new words and new meanings of words, he says. "An advantage of online dictionaries is that they can be more up to date," Barrett writes at his website (www.grantbarrett.com). "Because of the theoretically infinite digital space, online dictionaries can include any word they like, words that might never appear in a print dictionary, or might not appear until years later, since most dictionaries have long update cycles, anywhere from a year to decades."

But do-it-yourself dictionaries have their drawbacks, Barrett says. "*The Official Dictionary of Unofficial English* has a couple of beneficial characteristics that *Urban Dictionary* does not," Barrett says by phone. "For one thing, it was compiled by a professional lexicographer. That means that the words have all been substantiated as real, rather than the figment of a 13-year-old's [imagination]."

One purpose of printed dictionaries in a digital age is to measure the staying power and broader influence of words, Barrett says. "It isn't necessarily a good thing that online dictionaries can be more up to date: They are often merely recording those words that won't last and will never spread," he says.

User-edited dictionaries also lack consistency and detail in their entries, Barrett says. One of the first rules of dictionary-making is that you don't use the word you're defining in its own definition.

When you compare entries for the slang word "blaccent" (a combination of "black" and "accent") in *Unofficial English* and *Urban Dictionary*, you can see the difference. Barrett's definition of "blaccent" in *Unofficial English* is "a mode of speech that is said to imitate African American Vernacular English, especially when used by a white person. . . . This term is usually derogatory." The entry is followed by actual examples taken from Web and news sources dating back to 2001.

At *Urban Dictionary*, the top definition for "blaccent" is "whites or anyone besides black folks who speak in the 'urban style of rappers' and such, when they are around black folks, or around others like themselves."

This definition refers to a speaker rather than the speech. It doesn't tell you the word is derogatory. It gives no examples from Web or news sources. And it uses the vague phrase "urban style of rappers," putting it in quotes, while *Unofficial English* uses the more exact linguistic term "African American Vernacular English."

One telling measure of the dictionaries-vs.-the-Web debate

came in 2005, when Peckham published a book version of his *Urban Dictionary* site with the same title. All the entries were cleaned up, and all references to vote tallies were omitted. A user-edited website turned into an author-controlled book. It was a blow against dictionary democracy, struck by one of its strongest supporters.

See also **dictionaries, coexistence with handheld technology.**

like totally

THE PHRASE "like totally" used to belong to the so-called "Valley Girl" dialect. But now, linguists say, "like totally" has entered general informal use in English. And contrary to the stereotypes that this use of "like" is most common among young female speakers, linguists have found that men use "like" this way about as often as women do.

In fact, you can now hear these words coming from a presidential podium: "The impression you get from people who are reporting out of Iraq is that it's like totally dysfunctional," George W. Bush said in a 2007 press conference. In an earlier appearance, the president said, "It just shows how difficult it is to do what some assume can be done, which is, like, totally seal off the border." Both examples are confirmed by transcripts on the White House website (www.whitehouse.gov).

The word "like" often has a grammatical function in a sentence. For instance, "like" can introduce an approximate quotation, as in, "She was like, 'Is there a problem?'" "Like" can also introduce an approximate figure, as in, "I finished in, like, 40th place." And "like" can signal an exaggeration, as in, "He's, like, 100 feet tall."

President Bush seemed to be using "like" in this last way. Is his view, it was overstated to say that Iraq is "totally dysfunctional," and so the word "like" frames this charge as an exaggeration. Similarly, Bush doesn't believe that it's possible to "totally seal off the border" (to immigrants), and "like" helps him make it sound impossible.

But in addition to studying the grammatical function of "like," linguists are interested in knowing who says it. When linguist Mark Liberman of the University of Pennsylvania heard that President Bush had said "like totally," he did an informal search for the phrase "like totally" in a database of transcribed telephone conversations. He found that men and women used "like totally" about equally as often.

Liberman then searched just by age and found that people ages 40–59 said "like totally" roughly as often as people ages 20–39. "It seems that [this use of] 'like' is associated with middle-age as well as young people," he wrote at *Language Log* (www.languagelog. org). Liberman also pointed to a 2005 study by linguist Yoko Iyeiri of Kyoto University that studied transcripts of academic conferences. That study found that men used "like" this way—as a grammatical marker—more often than women did.

So the stereotype that only (or mostly) young women say "like totally" isn't accurate. "I think 'like' is just really contagious," said linguist Carmen Fought. "It's a discourse marker that's very useful."

But Fought noted that despite the growing acceptability of "like," it would probably only come out of President Bush's mouth in a spontaneous setting, not off a teleprompter. "It would be very unlikely in a prepared written speech," she said.

See also Clueless, **linguistic legacy of.**

lost

In 2005, five years after her book on the history of walking, *Wanderlust*, author Rebecca Solnit published a new volume of essays that explore the theme of getting lost and, more broadly, abandoning certainty: *A Field Guide to Getting Lost* (Viking).

Most reviews rave that Solnit, a former recipient of the National Book Critics Circle Award for Criticism (for her book *River of Shadows*) and the Lannan Literary Award, has delivered another elegant work. But some of them—including *The New Yorker* and the *Village Voice*—also praise the way Solnit incorporates what she says is the etymology of the word "lost."

"The word 'lost,'" Solnit says, "comes from the Old Norse 'los,' meaning the disbanding of an army, and this origin suggests soldiers falling out of formation to go home, a truce with the wide world. I worry now that many people never disband their armies, never go beyond what they know."

But ask an etymologist and you'll find that Solnit's literature is better than her linguistics. Like many enticing etymological explanations, this alleged Old Norse origin may make for a good story, but it isn't necessarily true.

"It is not even a theory: it is sheer nonsense," e-mails Anatoly Liberman, professor of German philology at the University of Minnesota and author of *Word Origins and How We Know Them* (Oxford University Press).

I began my etymological query, as I always do, with *The Oxford English Dictionary*. But the *OED* is rather obtuse on this one. It says the verb "lose" (of which "lost" is a participle) came from the Old English "losian"—the verb form of the Old English noun "los," which meant "destruction."

Then the *OED* fudges a bit. It says this Old English word "corresponds" to the Old Norse word "los," which meant "breaking up of the ranks of an army."

Now I'm lost. But I think the case hinges on what the *OED* means by "corresponds." Liberman says I'm right.

"The word 'correspond' is a coy way of hiding one's ignorance," Liberman says. "The story is this. Old English had the noun 'los,' [meaning] 'to come to destruction, perish,'" Liberman explains. "[Old Norse] also had the noun 'los,' which meant 'bringing an army into disarray' (not 'disbanding an army'). Both words were derived from the same root, but neither has to be a borrowing of the other."

Liberman's just getting started with the story of "lost." It turns out the Old English "los" got lost. "The English word 'los' then disappears from texts and surfaces again only in the 14th century. Such cases are not uncommon, and every time something like it happens, one wonders whether we have the continuation of an ancient word or a new formation that has by chance coincided with the old one," he writes.

"The editors of the *OED* did not know the answer, and no one does," Liberman says. "Hence the vague statement about the English [root] 'corresponding' to the Old Norse one (it means that it resembles the O.N. noun). But it was not a case of borrowing.

. . . [The English root] has nothing to do with Old Norse or with the 'disbanding' of armies."

People who are distant relatives often resemble each other despite not knowing each other. Etymologists know the same is true of words. The Old English "los" and the Old Norse "los" do have a common ancestor—the word "leu" in ancient language of Indo-European. But the English and Norse words developed separately.

So Solnit has placed a child with the wrong parent—our modern word "lost" has an English parent, not a Norse one.

meh

WE CAN speak volumes with one-syllable grunts: "nah," "ugh," "blah," "hah!" Now we can add another utterance to our vocabulary: "meh."

"Meh" was popularized on *The Simpsons*—as an expression of apathy. In a 1995 episode, Marge weaves "Hi Bart" on a loom to try to interest him in weaving, but Bart indifferently replies, "meh." (According to an online message board for Simpsons fans, this word was so foreign at the time that closed captioning showed it as "nah.")

In a 2001 episode, Homer tries to talk Bart and Lisa into going to a theme park, and they reply together, "meh." Homer asks if they're sure, and Bart says, "We said 'meh,' " and Lisa adds, "M-E-H. Meh."

"Meh" has yet to enter a major dictionary, but it's listed in the user-edited *Wiktionary* (www.wiktionary.org) as expressing "I don't know (the verbal equivalent of a shrug of the shoulders)" or "I don't care," and in the *Urban Dictionary* (www.urbandictionary. com) as expressing "indifference; to be used when one simply does not care." Ten visitors added "meh" to *Merriam-Webster's Open Dictionary* at www.m-w.com.

A 2007 article on "meh" in the London *Guardian* called it "the word that's sweeping the Internet," and commented, "It means boring. It means not worth the effort, who cares, so-so, whatever. It is the all-purpose dismissive shrug of the blogger and messageboarder."

The Simpsons gets credit for helping "meh" go mainstream, but it did not originate there; the show just brought it out from some hidden corner of the culture. As early as 1992, "meh" shows up on a fan discussion board for the show *Melrose Place*. "Is [he] cute?" one fan asks about a character. Another writes back: "Meh . . . far too Ken-doll for me."

That's one of the earliest available written examples of "meh," but the word probably existed in speech long before. How long? That stumps etymologists.

"Meh" sounds Yiddish to some, because of its similarity to the disapproving Yiddish interjection "feh." A Google search turns up a song from a 1936 Yiddish film with a line that (translated) says, "A goat stands in the meadow, and bleats a sad 'meh!' "

"It's very possible that the 'Simpsons' writers took 'meh' from Yiddish," wrote lexicographer Benjamin Zimmer last year at *Language Log* (www.languagelog.org), but he says he's not convinced. Zimmer concluded, "Whatever Yiddish origins the interjection might have had, they have been lost in post-*Simpsons* usage."

I have my own hunch about the origins of "meh," and I decided to run it past a few linguists. Here it goes.

Like the immortal "d'oh!" invented by *The Simpsons*, "meh" sounds to me like a slight adaptation of a non-verbal utterance. Take "eh"—not the Canadian sentence-ender, but the nasalized "enh" that naturally accompanies the shrug of the shoulders. If you start saying this word before you open your mouth, you naturally add an "M" when you part your lips. For a word that connotes apathy, adding an accidental sound by not opening your mouth in time would make sense.

I thought I should run my theory past someone who actually knows what they're talking about, so I turned to Laura Dickey, phonologist at Northwestern University. "I'd say that what you propose is reasonable phonetically," Dickey said, "but I have no idea if it is true, and I can't think of [another case] when this has happened in English, so there's no precedent."

Lexicographer Grant Barrett, meanwhile, gave me a not-so-ringing endorsement for my theory: "Sure, why not?" he said.

Barrett noted that you can't get too scientific about words such as "meh" and that other *Simpsons* favorite, "d'oh": "I suspect they're both just transcribed versions of oral speech, which has any number of single-syllable sounds that mean a variety of things," he wrote by e-mail.

However it got started, "meh" has given our culture a handy interjection for its default mood of smug indifference. So handy, in fact, that now we're starting to turn it into an adjective. "Nowadays 'meh' has become firmly established in [online] TV fan forums, very often extended to adjectival usage, as in 'that episode was meh' or 'that was a meh performance,' " Zimmer wrote at *Language Log*.

Zimmer has also spotted several instances of "meh-ness," a noun meaning the state of being "meh." He found "meh-ness" in fans' descriptions of the third season of *American Idol:* One singer "started out well but then faded into meh-ness," one fan wrote. "Utter mehness," said another. Last year, an *Idol* fan described a contestant as a "meh-ness to society," a play on the phrase "menace to society."

If you ask me, any word that gives English speakers more fodder for puns is a welcome addition to our language.

Update: Reader Beverly Feldt supports the theory of Yiddish origination. "When I first heard the use of 'meh' on *The Simpsons*, I took it to be a variant of the Yiddish 'mnyeh,' a non-word vocalization (like 'oy!') used to express skepticism, indifference, etc. I had grown up hearing and using this sound—like "meh," only with nasal and glide sounds added to increase the scorn and expressiveness. In his wonderful book *Hooray for Yiddish*, the late Leo Rosten devotes more than a page to "mnyeh," giving it twelve definitions and as many examples. Rosten writes, "A master of intonation can make 'mnyeh' jump through hoops of deft sarcasm, polite dubiety, heartless deflation, ironic dismissal or icy derision."

merry

A 2004 White House announcement addressed a matter of urgent national concern, when First Lady Laura Bush revealed that the theme of the White House Christmas decorations this year would be "A Season of Merriment and Melody." The decorations incorporate classic Christmas songs such as "Rudolph the Red-Nosed Reindeer" and "White Christmas."

The "merriment" theme gave a boost to a word that has been lagging lately in the English language: "merry." As with our Christmas ornaments, we pick "merry" out of our closets this time of year, blow the dust off it, and put it on prominent display in anticipation of December 25. After that, we put it back in a box and keep it in storage for the next 11 months.

In fact, about the only places "merry" turns up nowadays, other than "Merry Christmas," are in phrases such as "the more the merrier," "to make merry" and the biblical quote "Eat, drink, and be merry, for tomorrow we die."

"Words do tend to stick around in these fixed phrases after they've lost general currency, often precisely because they evoke a bygone world," says linguist Geoffrey Nunberg, author of *Going Nucular: Language, Politics and Culture in Confrontational Times* (PublicAffairs). "'Merry Christmas' wears its status as a traditional greeting on its sleeve and brings with it all kinds of Dickensian stereotypes of old-fashioned Christmas."

A search for "merry" on LexisNexis turns up few results that aren't Christmas greetings, the word "merry-go-round," or the female name, Merry. One of the rare sightings of the adjective appearing on its own comes in a report filed last week from Warsaw for Copley News Service by Judith Morgan. "Cafes are full and merry; windows of traditional restaurants are still-life paintings: lace curtains, brass candlesticks, burnished bowls of ripe apples and pomegranates."

But even this example sounds deliberately quaint. The word has so much Victorian residue that it's rare to hear it as a serious reference to the present, says Erin McKean, Chicago-based lexicographer. "No one says, unironically, 'Have yourself a merry old time' or, 'It was a merry party,'" she says.

When people do use the word this way, it's often with a wink and a reference to eggnog. That's the other main surviving sense of "merry": intoxication. Reporting on one of singer Brian McFadden's nights out, the *London Daily Mirror* (which wishes its readers "a Mirror Christmas") wrote, "Brian was very merry and had topped up a bottle of vodka with Red Bull." *The Oxford English Dictionary* says this definition dates back at least as far as John Wycliffe's 14th century translation of 1 Samuel 25:36: "Nabal's heart was merry within him, for he was very drunken."

"Merry" can also mean playful mischief. *People* magazine's 2004 profile of George Clooney called him "Hollywood's merry prankster." Shakespeare used the phrase "a merry jest," (though he also wrote "merry cheer.")

"'Merry' has had a long ride in English, with a much broader range of meanings than it has now," Nunberg writes by e-mail. "At one point or another it has meant 'brightly colored,' 'bright,' 'attractive,' 'pleasant' (as in 'a merry day'), 'fragrant,' and 'happy' (which is probably what was meant by Robin Hood's 'merry men')."

"Merry," which comes from the Old English word "mirige" for "pleasant," as does "mirth," is not entirely obsolete. *USA Today* referred to Lindsay Lohan's "merry, raspy laugh," without reference to alcohol, pranks, or the holidays.

But the word's days are numbered, even in the phrase "Merry Christmas," McKean says. "I think 'Merry Christmas' is on its way to becoming a fossilized phrase, almost idiomatic. Think how it's funny or cute to say 'Happy Christmas!' instead," she says.

It's becoming increasingly common to hear people use the phrase "Happy Holidays." Not only does it sound less archaic, it's also the safest option when you don't know which holiday someone is celebrating.

Laura Bush stuck with "Happy Holidays" in her greeting to reporters in 2004, even as she discussed the theme "Merriment and Melody." In closing, she repeated, "Happy Holidays, everybody." But one reporter responded, "Merry Christmas."

"Merry Christmas," she replied.

Another word, incidentally, that has shed its Victorian skin is "gay," as we know whenever we sing about "gay apparel" in "Deck the Halls." Author Richard Lederer addressed this in his 1994 book *Adventures of a Verbivore* (Pocket Books). "Many of my readers have written to complain that a perfectly wonderful word has been lost to general usage," Lederer wrote. "But as much

as you and I may need 'gay,' the gay community needs it more,"
for self-esteem and a sense of cultural identity, he said. Lederer
suggested that if you're looking for a synonym for the former
"gay," you might as well use "merry."

meta

TOO MUCH meta. That's what Sam McManis wrote earlier this year
in *The Sacramento Bee*, talking about the movie *Tristram Shandy:
A Cock and Bull Story*. The movie, he explains, is "a movie about
making a movie of an 18th century comic novel that was about
the conventions of novel writing," McManis explained.

"How very meta it all is," he added.

That's right: "meta." The prefix has now taken its place as a
separate word in the English language.

The Oxford English Dictionary defines "meta" as an adjective
that describes "something that is self-parodying and self-referential in reflecting or representing the characteristics it alludes to
or depicts."

The *OED*'s entry cites a 1993 article in *The Boston Globe*,
which also complained about meta in pop culture. *The Globe* said,
"When anchorwoman Connie Chung made a guest appearance
on the sitcom 'Murphy Brown' to advise anchorwoman Murphy
not to sacrifice her journalistic integrity by making a guest appearance on a sitcom, that was just plain meta."

Ironically—or maybe it's meta—the *OED*'s earliest example
of "meta" in print, a 1988 article in *The New Republic*, reports that
Merriam-Webster lexicographer David Justice predicted "meta"
would become a word.

"He predicts that, like 'retro'—whose use solely as a prefix
is so, well, retro—'meta' could become independent from other
words, as in, 'Wow, this sentence is so meta,'" wrote *The New
Republic*. "If so, you heard it [here] first."

Nearly two decades later, the prediction has come true. "Meta
has become the new irony these days," McManis observed in *The
Sacramento Bee*. "It's the trendy—albeit far from new—pop-cul-
ture device perfect for a navel-gazing, self-referential populace
that wants its entertainment in a continuous loop."

And McManis was writing before the release of the 2006 movies *A Prairie Home Companion*—a movie portraying a fictional radio program, based on an actual radio program—and *Lady in the Water*, which has a character named "Story," and features a fictional critic's commentary on some scenes as they are taking place.

Maybe because we feel inundated by meta, the word often appears today in phrases such as "too meta" and "so meta." The phrase "so meta it hurts" is a category at Flickr, the picture-sharing website. Many pictures in that category are pictures of people taking pictures.

I considered writing an article about writing this article, but I thought that would just be too meta.

This usage is a new twist in the millennia-long history of "meta." The word began in ancient Greek as a preposition meaning "after." The word "metamorphosis" literally means "after transformation." "Meta" is also buried in the word "method," which comes from the Greek word "methodos," a compound of "meta-hodos"—literally meaning "journey after."

Aristotle's book *Metaphysics* discusses subjects that Aristotle thought should be taught "after physics"—after the natural, empirical sciences—such as philosophical questions about existence.

After "meta" was adopted into Latin, and then into English, the prefix came to mean "above" or "beyond," possibly because of the heady contents of Aristotle's *Metaphysics*.

"I think that the Greek 'meta' was indeed taken and extended [in English], probably beyond recognition for a native speaker of ancient Greek," says Helma Dik, a classics professor at the University of Chicago who specializes in Greek linguistics. "But then, the ancient Greeks stretched prepositions themselves all the time, so after a quick immersion course in present-day English I'm sure they would be fine with it."

In the late 20th century, computers gave "meta" new life. Early computer keyboards had a Meta key, which controlled the function of other keys (the equivalent of the Alt key on a Windows computer today, or Command key on a Mac). Most Web pages include "meta tags"—hidden lines of code that describe what the page is about and include key words for search engines to find.

But only in the last decade or so has "meta" become a word of its own. It's usually used to describe movies about movies, journalism about journalism or blogs about blogs.

This sense of "meta" probably began with the word "metafiction"—self-referential fiction, which *The Oxford English Dictionary* traces to 1960. (The *OED* and *The New Oxford American Dictionary* are the only major dictionaries to include a separate entry for "meta" as a word.)

"'Meta' is . . . creeping more and more into everyday conversations, even if it's not nearly as widespread as, say, 'irony,'" wrote Laura Miller in *The New York Times Book Review* in late 2002.

One opponent of the spread of the word "meta" posted a comment anonymously at the website called (what else?) *MetaFilter* (www.metafilter.com).

"The word [should be] either 'circular' or 'reflexive' or 'redundant' or 'ironic,'" the visitor wrote. "Self-referential isn't remarkable anymore, so let's not pretend we have to invent a new word for it."

Too late.

most vs almost

When I was in school, we were taught that proper grammar would be "almost all" and "almost every." But these days the *[Chicago] Tribune* uses "most all" and "most every." Please let me know when this new use of the word "most" became interchangeable with the word "almost."

—*Patricia Makowski, Des Plaines, Illinois*

THAT HAPPENED at least as early as the 16th century, according to *Fowler's Modern English Usage* (third edition). "Most" used this way probably started as an abbreviation of "almost"—in fact, it used to be written with an apostrophe before the word to show that letters had been dropped, according to *The Oxford English Dictionary*. These days, Fowler's says, using "most" instead of "almost" is "effectively limited to some U.K. dialects and to American English."

As I hear it, "most every" is more likely to be used as a rhetorical flourish; the debut album of the Chicago-based band Lying in States was called *Most Every Night*, which packs more poetic punch than "Almost Every Night."

mouses

SEE THAT mouse next to your computer? Pretend there are two of them. What would you call them: "mice" or "mouses"?

In the first 15 years or so of its mainstream life, the computer mouse has had an uncertain plural, word watchers say. But in the current issue of *English Today*, linguist Alan Kaye argues that "computer mouses" is starting to win out.

Kaye takes issue with the 1999 book *Words and Rules: The Ingredients of Language* (Harper Perennial) by Steven Pinker, which stated that most English speakers either avoid the plural of computer mouse or reluctantly choose "mice." (Most dictionaries list both "mice" and "mouses" as possible plurals for the computer instrument.)

Kaye surveyed more than 1,000 students at California State University at Fullerton, where he teaches linguistics, and he found that about 90 percent opt for "mouses" as the plural of the clicking device. "Insofar as my own California dialect is concerned, 'mouses' is the correct form and 'mice' refers exclusively to rodents," Kaye writes.

Bill Walsh, chief copy editor at the national desk at *The Washington Post* and author of *The Elephants of Style* (McGraw-Hill), says he is inclined to agree—even though most authoritative advice he's seen recommends "mice." "I think 'mice' is an irregular plural unique to the animal," Walsh writes by e-mail. "Once we've coined a new sense of it, we go by modern processes and eschew the irregular." (Maybe some of the confusion comes from the fact that the computer mouse usually exists in solitude; you only need one to work your computer.)

"Computer mice" gets about six times as many results as "computer mouses" in Google searches, but "computer mouses" gets about six times as many results as "computer mice" in a search of newspaper articles in the LexisNexis database.

This phenomenon isn't unusual in English, as Pinker observed in *Words and Rules*. A baseball player may fly out, but an announcer says the player "flied out," not "flew out." You have one "silly goose" and multiple "silly gooses." When the Walkman debuted, stores advertised that they sold "Walkmans." And get two people in Mickey Mouse costumes together, and you have Mickey Mouses, not Mickey Mice. Kaye calls this phenomenon "semantic bifurcation": The same word can have different forms when it has different meanings.

You might be wondering how English got into this "mouse" mess to begin with—why does one mouse plus one mouse equal two "mice"? The problem is that in Old English, some words were made plural by changing the middle of the word rather the end. So the singular "fot" and plural "fet" in Old English became our "foot" and "feet," and the singular "mus" and plural "mys" became "mouse" and "mice."

The term "computer mouse" comes from somebody thinking the device resembled a rodent. It's the same association behind the word "muscle," which comes from the same root word as "mouse"—due to "the resemblance of a flexing muscle to the movements of a mouse," according to *The American Heritage Dictionary*.

Of course, some of us would have to start working out to get our muscles looking more like mice.

muggle

See **Harry Potter, language of.**

multifaceted

THERE'S ONE thing it seems everyone can agree on about U.S. policy in Iraq: It should be "multifaceted."

"The solution lies in a multifaceted strategy that brings together all the vested interests and backs them up with credible force," wrote James A. Lyons Jr. in *The Washington Times* in late 2006. "Our best strategy for protecting ourselves will always be a nuanced and multifaceted approach," wrote Cynthia Tucker in *The Atlanta Journal-Constitution*. A report from the National

Intelligence Estimate called for "sustained, multifaceted programs targeting the vulnerabilities of the jihadist movement."

"Multifaceted," basically meaning "having many parts or functions" or just "versatile," is a multifaceted word. In a Lexis-Nexis search of newspaper articles from last month, "multifaceted" shows up next to words such as "appeal," "backfield," "career," "delights," "India," "law," "presentation," "poem," "store," and even "pencil."

You have to ask—if a pencil can be called "multifaceted," is there anything that can't? Does the word carry much weight anymore, or is it one of those words that sounds sophisticated but actually has more style than substance?

"Multifaceted has been around since the mid-1800s, and is a perfectly good word," says John Walston, author of *The Buzzword Dictionary* (Marion Street Press). "But it also fits my base definition of a buzzword: a usually important-sounding word or phrase used primarily to impress laypersons."

It's a quirk of the English language that "two-faced" (meaning "deceitful") is a bad thing but "multifaceted"—literally meaning "many-faced"—is a good thing, especially when it's the opposite of "simplistic."

"Facet" comes from the French word "facette," meaning "little face." English first used it to describe a jewel, which sparkles when light bounces off its many facets, or surfaces.

Since then, "multifaceted" has more figuratively come to mean "complex." *The Oxford English Dictionary*'s first example of this meaning is an 1892 reference to "the multi-faceted mind of the German Aristophanes." It then quotes a 1965 book on business: "The nature of decisions is multifaceted and continually variable." (The *OED* even found a few examples of the cumbersome noun "multifacetedness," the earliest coming in a 1979 article that talked about "the intensity and multi-facetedness of human relationships.")

The literal use of "multifaceted" as "many-sided" clung to life throughout the 20th century—the *OED* lists a 1965 article describing disco balls, and later ones on artistic sculptures, for example.

But today, unless you are talking about jewelry or geometry, the "having many faces or surfaces" meaning of "multifaceted" seems to have given way to "versatile, having different parts."

Now it's hard to tell if the original meaning is ever intended, even when it works. For example, author Caroline Weber wrote this in *The New York Times* about Marie Antoinette: "With her glittering rise and shattering fall, her ambiguous political allegiances and unmistakable personal style, the queen has proven multifaceted enough to accommodate most any interpretation, any ideology, any cultural bias."

Here, the sense of the queen having different faces, one for each different interpretation of her, would make sense. But this meaning was either lost on many readers, or it isn't what Weber meant.

Noor Quek of the Singapore Breast Cancer Foundation told the Singapore *Straits Times* last month, "I love a multi-faceted life—being a mother, wife, daughter, friend, helping with charitable causes, a career woman and being plain old me." Again, the idea of having different faces or roles combined in one person fits the original meaning of "multifaceted." But "having different parts" is probably what Quek was saying.

"Probably for most people the metaphor is now dead," says Arnold Zwicky, a linguist at Stanford University. "The shift is a natural one . . . and provides a very useful word."

myself

THE PRONOUNS "me," "myself," and "I" look like a tidy trio. "I" is a subject, "me" is an object, and "myself" is reflexive, usually paired with "I" for reference —"I'll get myself a new coat"—or emphasis—"I did it myself."

But now "myself" seems to be working overtime. Here's an example: "The decision to take action was an operational matter, but was taken with the full knowledge of the prime minister, the deputy prime minister and the secretary of state for transport, as well as myself," Homeland Security Secretary Michael Chertoff assured the public in 2006.

Chertoff should have said "and me," according to those who

believe the use of "myself" is getting out of control. In a survey of its Usage Panel, a handpicked group of authors, *The American Heritage Dictionary* found that 75 percent of the panel rejected replacing "me" with "myself" in the phrase "like me." A resounding 88 percent frowned on "myself" in a compound object—"he asked John and myself"—instead of "John and me."

Yet *The American Heritage Dictionary* notes using "myself" in place of "I" or "me" is common in the history of English literature. In the 19th century, Emily Dickinson wrote, "to wonder what myself will say," and fellow poet John Ruskin wrote, "To myself, mountains are the beginning and the end of all natural scenery." In the 14th century, Chaucer wrote in his prologue to "The Canterbury Tales," "There was also a reeve and a miller . . . a manciple, and myself."

Apart from literature, "Such uses almost always occur when the speaker or writer is referring to himself or herself as an object of discourse rather than as a participant in discourse," according to *Merriam-Webster's Collegiate Dictionary*. In other words, the speaker uses "myself" to become a character in the story she's telling.

Like it or not, *Merriam-Webster* concludes flatly, "These uses are standard." How did this happen? There are at least four theories.

- **Formality.** Saying "as well as myself" rather than "and me," as Chertoff did, may seem more authoritative and businesslike—qualities we want in a homeland security secretary.

- **Modesty.** "Myself" can defer attention away from the speaker and avoids saying the seemingly self-centered word "me." This is Katie Wales' conclusion in her 1996 book *Personal Pronouns in Present-Day English* (Cambridge University Press), a survey of English pronouns. "The 'self' forms appear more polite and deferential than the simple pronouns," Wales writes, "and it may well be that the physical 'length' of them, however 'inelegant' they may be appear in such contexts . . . is symbolic here of a degree of indirectness."

167

- **Hypercorrection.** English speakers are afraid of grammatical constructions such as "John and I" and "John and me." One is a subject ("John and I"); the other is an object ("John and me")—but we aren't confident we'll get it right so we fudge it by saying "John and myself." This suggestion comes from *The Cambridge Grammar of the English Language* by Rodney D. Huddleston and Geoffrey K. Pullum (Cambridge University Press), which calls this use of "myself" an "override reflexive," where "myself" is overriding the usual pronoun.

- **Shorthand.** What used to be an emphatic, "He said it to me, myself," has over time become: "He said it to myself." "There's a model for the structure in emphatic reflexive constructions," Pullum writes by e-mail. "It's not just a random choice from the wrong part of the paradigm to try and look polite or modest."

naked as a jaybird

What are the origins of the phrase "naked as a jaybird?" Is "jaybird" related to "jailbird"?

—*Dave Huyser, Grand Rapids, Mich.*

"THIS PHRASE, and its British counterpart 'naked as a robin,' do not have clear origins," write Mike and Melanie Crowley at their website, *Take Our Word for It* (www.takeourword.com). "The only plausible, yet undocumented, reason that a simile about nakedness might refer to these birds is the fact that bluejays and robins, when they first hatch, look quite naked, even though they do have a small amount of down [feathers] on them."

I found your "jailbird" suggestion compelling, because prisoners are stripped of nearly everything they own, although they do tend to get clothes. But the Crowleys say the British were saying "naked as a robin" before Americans started saying "jaybird," so the phrase's origin probably has to do with birds and their adornment—or lack thereof.

National Grammar Day

I WILL have mixed feelings on the upcoming National Grammar Day.

I confess: I'm one of those people who cares about the difference between a gerund and a participle, between a restrictive and non-restrictive relative clause. This puts me in a tiny minority of deranged grammatical eccentrics—people you should generally try to avoid.

But I have converted from my former life as a grammar prosecutor.

Only now do I know the truth: Sometimes it is best to follow the conventions of standard written English, as quirky, arbitrary and illogical as they often are (explain to me why "aren't I?" is considered grammatically correct?).

But most of the time—when we're among friends, family, or anyone we feel comfortable with—we should simply let our hair down and allow our unpolished emissions of language to burst out of us in all their untidy splendor.

Try to talk to your friend on the phone the way you would write for an English teacher in a classroom, and you'll sound ridiculous, not to mention unfriendly.

So I can't join the witch hunt of the Society for the Promotion of Good Grammar (which goes by the unappetizing acronym of SPOGG), which is sponsoring National Grammar Day as a chance to flag any violation of standard English usage in any situation.

"If you see a sign with a catastrophic apostrophe, send a kind note to the storekeeper," urges SPOGG at www.nationalgrammarday.com. "If your local newscaster says 'Between you and I,' set him straight with a friendly e-mail." Such corrections are seldom friendly, welcome, or necessary. They are usually self-righteous, irritating, and misinformed.

The policewoman behind National Grammar Day and SPOGG is Martha Brockenbrough, who serves as grammar guru for Microsoft's *Encarta* website (encarta.msn.com), where she writes a column called "Grumpy Martha's Guide to Grammar and Usage."

There she urges readers to avoid using an adverb with a word like "unique" (too bad for our founding fathers, who dreamed of "a more perfect union"), and to avoid saying "decimate" unless you mean "reduce by one tenth" (if 10 percent of educated English speakers know and care about that distinction, I'll give Grumpy Martha one tenth of my candy bar).

Brockenbrough reprimands pop stars for grammar gaffes in song lyrics, including Bryan Adams for singing "if she ever found out about you and I" (it should be "you and me," she says)—even though that's the best way to rhyme with the line before it: "She says her love for me could never die." And she takes Elvis to task—is no one sacred?—for singing "I'm all shook up" instead of the proper "all shaken up."

Raise your hand if you prefer this correction. That's what I thought.

A more level-headed grammatical authority is Mignon Fogarty—known to her Web visitors and podcast listeners as Grammar Girl (grammar.quickanddirtytips.com). She told me by e-mail that she likes the idea of having a day set aside for civil discussions about grammar and usage, as long as they stay civil.

"I hope that instead of getting caught up in the wicked glee of attacking signs with misplaced apostrophes or sending nasty notes about typos to editors, participants focus on spreading the word about the style points and grammar myths that many people latch on to as truth," Fogarty said. "For example, some publications use serial commas and some don't; it's OK to split infinitives; and sometimes it's acceptable—even preferable—to end a sentence with a preposition. It's shocking, but true!"

And please, leave Elvis alone!

Update: Martha Brockenbrough responded on her website by saying that I was taking the whole thing too seriously—that she's just pretending to be grumpy, and that people can complain to their TV stations all in good fun: "Nathan Bierma of the *Chicago Tribune* called it a witch hunt. We aren't sure what he thinks we have against witches, but we are certain he should launch a sense-of-humor hunt." The problem is that insincere grumpiness is very rare. Even if Brockenbrough herself can pull off good-natured grammar policing, few other Americans can (as I know from reading countless—and utterly earnest—e-mails alleging the decline of the English language), since "good-natured grammar policing" is nearly a contradiction in terms, like "enjoyable tax audit."

Brockenbrough also points out that elsewhere at *Encarta* she wrote that despite her earlier condemnation of Elvis (which she now claims was just kidding), she was "tempted to give Elvis a hall pass" on his bad grammar, since it's just a rock song. But she added that she "could make a case for [replacing the song's title with] 'All Mixed Up,' because it keeps the same meter as the original song"—and doesn't break any rules. She concludes that "All Shook Up" works in part because it "contributes to the feeling of chaos that Elvis is feeling. He's so mixed up he can't get the grammar right."

But hedging on whether or not to exonerate Elvis in the name of artistic license is worse than not acknowledging artistic license at all—the whole point is that artistic license can and should, without any deliberating, exempt poets and singers from worrying about the conventions of standard usage. If they didn't break standard conventions, they wouldn't be very artistic (or regionally authentic, which is crucial to Elvis' music). (And yes, both Martha and I know that Elvis just sang this song; he didn't write it—Otis Blackwell did. But if you sing a song on a recorded album, you can presumably be held responsible for its syntax.) My advice: don't try to enjoy "All Shook Up" on the basis of its supposedly bad grammar as a symptom of disorientation. And beware people who try to excuse their pickiness as merely insincere grumpiness.

See also **correctness; grammar, descriptive; pedantry, history and misguidedness of; prepositions, ending sentences with;** and **usage.**

nauseous vs. nauseated

I am bothered by the use of "nauseous" by someone to claim that they are sick to their stomach, rather than "nauseated."

—*John Grove, Chicago, Illinois*

Since the "-ous" ending in English so often means "state of" (as in "joyous" and "zealous"), I've always thought this prescription for "nauseous"—causing, not having, nausea—was a strange one, although I usually try to follow it out of deference to picky people.

It's true that saying "I am nauseous" will get a giggle from those who insist you're saying you make other people to want to vomit. But this amusement is the only purpose I can think of for this distinction. It's a classic case of a rule whose violation doesn't cause any confusion; everyone knows what you mean if you say, "The roller-coaster made me nauseous." And they did back in the 17th century, when a medical manual quoted by *The Oxford English Dictionary* stated, "It may be given . . . to children or those that are of a nauseous stomack."

next weekend vs. this weekend

I have a question for you that has bothered us for years. If it's Wednesday, and I tell my husband we have plans "next

NEOLOGISMS

A list of words that readers invented for a contest in *The Washington Post* in 1998 has been kept alive by an e-mail hoax. An e-mail forward that has been circulating and posted on blogs claims to give the results of the "*Washington Post* Mensa Invitational" for 2005. Most of the invented words listed in this e-mail appeared in the *Post*'s "Style Invitational" on Aug. 2, 1998, following the *Post*'s announcement of a word-inventing contest. "There is no Mensa Invitational, only the Style Invitational," says Deborah Howell, ombudsman for *The Washington Post*.

The original "Style Invitational" submissions deserve proper credit. The *Post* asked readers to take an existing word and make a new one by adding, subtracting or changing a single letter, and then provide a possible definition. The winning word was "sarchasm," defined as "the gulf between the author of sarcastic wit and the recipient who doesn't get it," credited to reader Tom Witte. Other submissions included "inoculatte: to take coffee

weekend," he assumes I mean in three days, when I mean in a week and three days.

If I'm referring to an event in three days, I call it "this weekend." For me, "next weekend" means the weekend after "this weekend," whereas for my husband they have the same meaning. What is the proper meaning of these terms? We've resorted to using dates; "we have plans Saturday the 14th."

—*Kathy Ables, Willowbrook, Illinois*

I'VE ALWAYS tried to call the upcoming weekend "this weekend" and the weekend after that "next weekend." But the third edition of *Fowler's Modern English Usage* says this usage is not standard. "In normal use, if said or written early in a given week, 'next Friday' means the immediately following Friday in the same week," *Fowler's* says.

Fowler's suggests your solution: "it is advisable to add the date of the Friday that is meant," or, in the case of individual days, to say "a week from Friday."

intravenously when you are running late" (Chuck Smith), "vaseball: a game of catch played by children in the living room" (Russ Beland), and "intaxication: euphoria at getting a refund from the IRS, which lasts until you realized it was your money to start with" (Greg Oetjen).

I thought the *Post*'s game was worth reviving, so in March 2006 (after debunking the "Mensa" myth) I invited readers to submit their own neologisms, or invented words, following (more or less) the *Post*'s original guidelines of changing one letter. In April 2006 I printed some of the best in my column. The winner was Don Marsch of Homewood, Illinois, who earned top honors for both best overall word—"gladually"—and overall achievement, with seven winsome inventions, no doubt coming to a dictionary near you.

Angle-Saxon: a trigonometrically gifted English native.

Bobility: royal line of people all named "Robert."

173

candemonium: the sound of early morning garbage pickup.

cansternation: frustrated feeling when soup can lid falls into the soup.

gladually: describing happiness arriving slowly.

malindrome: evil curse that's the same spelled forward or backward.

slimmering: reducing fat in food by slow boiling.

For his winning efforts, Don received a copy of *Ballyhoo, Buckaroo, and Spuds: Ingenious Tales of Words and Their Origins* by Michael Quinion (Smithsonian Books). Here are some of the best of the rest.

clueier: having a better grasp on a situation

—*Tracy Shields, Chicago, Illinois*

cruspy: crisp and crunchy texture (as in foods). My daughter was about 10 years old when she came up with this word to describe an apple pie's crust. She said, "This taste cruspy."

—*Mel Hopkins, Naperville, Illinois*

niche

Why do people say the word "niche" as if it rhymes with "itch," instead of as if it rhymes with "quiche"?

—*Marilyn Rottman, Grand Rapids, Michigan*

OF THE four dictionaries I checked, two list both the "nitch" and "neesh" pronunciations, one lists both "neesh" and "nish," and one lists only "nitch." For what it's worth, "neesh" is the pronunciation provided in Yvette Reche's book *French for Le Snob: Adding Panache to Your Everyday Conversations* (Santa Monica Press).

nickname

See **etymology**.

drismal: for years I've been using the word "drismal" (or "drizmal") to describe a dreary, drizzly, dismal day.

—*Rebecca Moskowitz, Lincolnwood, Illinois*

extry: one more. We often heard my dad at the dinner table use the phrase, "Can I have an extry slice of bread with the pot roast?"

—Ken Mottet, Berwyn, Illinois

iPody: Taking your music with you to the throne!

—*Kurt Westbrook, Poynette, Wisconsin*

maddering: One of my favorite invented words is one my son David coined when he was about four: "maddering"—as in, "What are you maddering about?" or, "Mom! He is maddering again!" A wonderfully descriptive blend of the words "mad" and "muttering."

—*Trudy Mc Vicker, Libertyville, Illinois*

maleable: A 18–34-year-old male who is easily shaped, controlled or influenced by the media or retailers.

—*Margo Rife, Western Springs, Illinois*

nor

Here's a question for you about the use of the word "nor" in a real estate document regarding lot restrictions:

"No residential structure shall be erected or placed on any lot hereof which has an area of less than 5,000 square feet nor a width of less than 50 feet at the front building set back line."

My question is whether "nor" here indicates segregatory meaning or combinatory meaning—at least that's as far as I've gotten by consulting Quirk and Greenbaum's *Comprehensive Grammar of the English Language*.

— *Mimi Rosenbush, Chicago, Illinois*

175

pertneart: When we traveled by car, it was my job to ask Dad, "Are we there yet?" And his answer was always the same. "Pertneart." English translation—"We are pretty near it (our destination)." And, yes, "pertneartly" is the adverb version.

—*Ken Mottet, Berwyn, Illinois*

residebt: costs incurred by the resident of any domicile (home, apartment, condominium, trailer, etc.), that may include but are not limited to mortgage payments, rent, fees, taxes, upkeep and the like. Origin: a typographical error (once recognized, had greater meaning than first intended).

—*Barry Klor, Des Plaines, Illinois*

"I'D READ it as equivalent to 'or' here," writes linguist Geoff Nunberg by e-mail. "It's clearly disjunctive—"either A or B.'" I'm no lawyer, and neither is Nunberg. But just in terms of language, it seems that even if B is true but A isn't, you can't build that house.

Northern Cities Shift

THE MIDWEST'S linguistic terrain is often assumed to be as flat and stable as its actual terrain. But linguists taking a closer look at the upper Midwest—the inland North, as they call it—have found this isn't true. The inland North, they say, is home to a series of inexplicable pronunciation changes they call the Northern Cities Shift.

In the cities surrounding the Great Lakes, a region that includes western New York, southern Michigan and northern portions of Ohio, Indiana and Illinois, many speakers have changed the way they say short vowels. They have come to form the vowel sounds from a different point in their mouths than speakers in their region once did—a pronunciation shift that apparently has happened within the last 50 years.

"It's an extraordinary rotation of the short vowels," says William Labov, a linguist at the University of Pennsylvania who

stragedy: a detailed plan for handling a catastrophe.

—*Ted Mellow, Buffalo Grove, Illinois*

typicritical: I made this word up to describe politicians who make statements that are hypocritical. Everyone I say it to knows exactly what I mean.

—*Patrick McGarry, Springfield, Illinois*

pioneered the study of the Northern Cities Shift. "People don't know it, but Syracuse, Rochester, Buffalo, Detroit and Chicago all have the same local accent."

The first vowel to move was the short "a" of "apple." The "a" moved forward in the mouth, resulting in a short sound that resembles the sound made by the last two syllables of the word "idea."

In his book *How We Talk: American Regional English Today* (Houghton Mifflin), Allan Metcalf tells the story of British linguist Ian Catford who moved to the University of Michigan. Catford thought he heard a student calling his name. It turned out the student was calling to her friend Ann—but her pronunciation made "Ann" sound like "Ian."

The second vowel to move in inland North pronunciation was the short "o" of "block." The sound moved forward in the mouth, toward the vacated position of the "a" of "apple," until "block" began to sound a little like "black."

More recently, other vowels have been in flux in the inland North. Linguists say the Northern Cities Shift is a chain reaction. When speakers change the way they produce one vowel sound, another moves in to take its place—otherwise, vowels would begin to sound alike.

The so-called "open oh" of "caught" and "ought" has moved

177

toward the previous position in the mouth of the "o" of "cot," so "caught" imitates the former pronunciation of "cot." Taking the place of the "open oh" is the "u" of "but," so "bus" has begun to sound like "boss." The "e" of "bet" has been moving farther back in the mouth so that "bet" resembles "but."

"The mouth's only got so much room in it," says Dennis Preston, a dialectologist at Michigan State University who has spent years studying the Northern Cities Shift. "English has a notorious number of low vowels. We're crowded in the bottom of the mouth. When one moved a little bit forward, another one would move to be distinct."

No one knows how the Northern Cities Shift got started. Labov traces it to the western part of New York state, where he says vowels were set in motion by patterns of immigrant settlement.

"My guess is that all of these various dialects of western and eastern New England mixed together and created a common dialect by simplifying all of these diverse patterns," Labov says.

But other linguists aren't convinced.

"It's shrouded in mystery," Preston says. Preston has devoted his research to how the shift spread, and how it was resisted by certain groups. For example, African-Americans have not adopted the pronunciations of the Northern Cities Shift, and rural areas have been slower to adopt it than urban centers.

"As it moved westward, it moved from large urban area to large urban area," Preston says of the shift. "It didn't move through the countryside. It was like a pebble skipping across a pond, and each time the pebble hits, it forms waves that spread out."

Yet the shift happened so subtly and gradually that no one could tell their vowels were changing.

Now Preston has turned his attention to how different ethnic groups in Michigan—including Mexican-Americans, Arab-Americans and Polish-Americans—have adopted or resisted the Northern Cities Shift.

"People think of the Midwest as being more of the standard than other dialects," says Laura Dickey, linguistics professor at Northwestern University. "But the Midwest has its own peculiarities, just like other regions."

often

When did the pronunciation of "often" become "off-ten?" I was taught in grammar school that the word is pronounced "off-ihn." Everybody from movie stars to political candidates now mispronounces the word. After all, you wouldn't "soften" your clothes, right?

Also, I am personally going to interrupt the next person to add a "-th" sound to the word "height." I almost never hear it pronounced properly, without the "-th" at the end.

— *Mike Sullivan, Huntley, Illinois*

PRONOUNCING THE "t" in "often" has historical basis, but by now it may be a relic. *The American Heritage Guide to Contemporary Usage and Style* explains the history. "During the 16th and 17th centuries, English experienced an especially widespread loss of consonants, among them the "d" in 'handsome' and 'handkerchief,' the "p" in 'raspberry,' and the "t" in 'chestnut' and 'often,'" the *Guide* says. "Because of the influence of spelling, however, there is sometimes a tendency to restore sounds that have become silent. This is the case with 'often,' which is now commonly pronounced with the 't.'"

"Heighth" is also a throwback to an older pronunciation. The third edition of *Fowler's Modern English Usage* acknowledges this history—and the natural association of the "-th" pronunciation with the words "width" and "length"—but sternly condemns this pronunciation in current use. It says the "-th" alternative "was common in the 17th century and was the spelling used by Milton, [but] is now used only by the poorly educated."

on the lam

I am interested in finding out more about the phrase "on the lam," as I think I know how it is used, but not necessarily what it means or its origin.

— *Jim DeGroot, South Holland, Illinois*

If you're "on the lam," you're running from the law. I was surprised to learn that "lam" originally meant "beat" or "strike." It comes from the same Old English root word as the word "lame," and so the verb "to lam" meant to give someone a crippling beating. Etymologist Dave Wilton of www.wordorigins.org says "on the lam" developed alongside the phrase "beat it" in the late 1800s, and that both meant to avoid getting clobbered. "I think it's likely that the semantic change was from a beating to fleeing a beating," Wilton writes by e-mail. So you would go "on the lam," or become a "lamster," to keep from getting lammed.

Why the word "on" in "on the lam"? It's not clear, although *The Oxford English Dictionary* says that an early version of the phrase was "take it on the lam." I hear "on the lam" as parallel to the phrase "on the run."

In any case, while the verb "lam" has left the language, the phrase "on the lam" remains in our custody.

Oxford English Dictionary, Shorter

Yes, *The Shorter Oxford English Dictionary* really is shorter. It may be two big volumes, nearly 2,000 pages each, with a total price tag of $175. But that's tiny compared with the full *Oxford English Dictionary*, the magisterial, comprehensive record of the English language that spans 20 big blue books and weighs 142 pounds.

"The complete *OED* is a formidable thing," says Jesse Sheidlower, the dictionary's New York–based editor, by phone. "It's not necessarily the one that you want to use if you just want to get straightforward information out of a dictionary. You don't always need what's in the full *OED*."

So the 2007 edition of the *Shorter OED*, released by Oxford University Press, is as efficient as it is bulky. Gone are most of the *OED*'s quotations—the examples of each word, laboriously collected from famous lines from literature and other sources—that make the full *OED* indispensable but expensive. (The complete set of the *OED* retails for just under $1,000, though I notice it's a bargain at $670 through Amazon.com.)

"The quotations are part of the great appeal of the *OED*," Sheidlower says. "On the other hand, they do take up a large amount of space. What makes the full *OED* as large as it is, is not that it has more entries; it's large because of the quotations."

Also gone is every word that the full *OED* has labeled "obsolete" as of the year 1700, unless that word appears in the King James Bible or the writings of Shakespeare, Milton, or Spenser. So *Shorter* says goodbye to "babion" (an insult meaning "baboon," last recorded in the year 1624) and "spatch" ("kill," last seen in 1616), among other antiques.

Shorter still covers the historical basics: Each entry includes the century of the first known written example of the word, along with a handful of quotations for major words. And as with the full *OED*, definitions are listed from oldest to most recent, so the first definition of "silly," for example, is its meaning in the 1400s: "deserving of pity, compassion, or sympathy."

But *Shorter OED* is also longer—at least longer than the last edition of *Shorter OED*, which was released in 2002. The new edition features more than 2,000 new words and phrases, including "blogroll," "carbon-neutral," "onesie," and "splitsville."

Shorter OED might be the only version of the *OED* that ever gets published in book form again. The *OED* editors have completed a revision of the full *OED* (which was last published in 1989) for the letters A through P (the revisions show up in the online edition of the full *OED*). Sheidlower says they haven't decided yet whether or not to publish another 20-plus-volume edition of the entire *OED*; they'll know by the time they get to Z.

In the meantime, the best way to use the full *OED* is the *OED*'s website (www.*OED*.com), which offers monthly and yearly subscriptions and is accessible at most libraries.

Update: Sheidlower wrote me afterwards to say that the *OED* team's revision has actually gone from M through P, so they have much farther to go, and won't be done when they finish Z. In May 2008, *The New York Times* Magazine wrote, "As of now, Oxford University Press has no official plans to publish a new print edition of *The Oxford English Dictionary*." It quoted Sheidlower as saying, "We have about 20 years' more work to do revising and adding entries. Who knows what will happen with technology in 20 years?"

pagan

HINDU READER and Chicago resident Vanamali Thotapalli e-mailed me to suggest that dictionaries revisit their definitions for "pagan" and "heathen." "Pagan" is defined in *The American Heritage Dictionary* first as a polytheistic believer, but its fourth definition is "a hedonist." "Heathen"'s second definition is "one who is regarded as irreligious, uncivilized, or unenlightened." "This shows an obvious Christian bias and hatred towards other religions," Thotapalli wrote.

Responding to this concern by e-mail, Joseph Pickett, editor of *AHD*, said he would flag the word in the *AHD*'s database for further review. "Pagan is derogatory in some uses, and heathen probably in all of them, so we should probably indicate this somehow," he said.

Update: The revised fourth edition of *AHD* released in 2006 now labels the objectionable definitions for "heathen" and "pagan" as "Offensive."

parmesan

I cringe every time I hear the word "Parmesan" (cheese) on TV, which is often, because I love to cook and I like watching cooking shows. Every single time I hear the word, it is, without exception, mispronounced as though the S were like the Z in "azure." My *Webster*'s dictionary shows that "Parmesan" is to be pronounced as though the S were like the Z in "daze."

—*Gloria Kaplan Sulkin, Chicago, Illinois*

OF THE half-dozen dictionaries I checked, only *Merriam-Webster's Collegiate* recognizes the "ZH" pronunciation in the third syllable of "parmesan." But all of them have a "ZH" pronunciation for the word immediately after it: "parmigiana," the Italian root of "parmesan." It means "of Parma" but entered English to mean "with Parmesan cheese" (as in "chicken parmigiana"). People probably conflate the pronunciation of "parmesan" and "parmigiana," and with good reason.

The Passion, English subtitles of

OBSCURED BY the controversy surrounding Mel Gibson's *The Passion of the Christ* was one relatively mundane bit of trivia: the movie's debut marked the widest release ever of a film with English subtitles.

The subtitles were actually Plan B. Gibson originally intended to show the movie without them, letting the sound of the Aramaic, Hebrew, and Latin—not to mention the spattering blood—speak for itself. "He was real hard-set against them," said Alan Nierob, Gibson's publicist. "He initially thought they would be a distraction. . . . It's a very visual movie." Gibson also wanted to avoid the phony air of British English that has plagued so many film renditions of the life of Jesus Christ, Nierob said.

But after early screenings of the film without subtitles, Gibson decided to insert them for the sake of clarity. "I'm glad he did," Nierob said. "It is a better movie with them. I've seen it both ways, and it's great [either way], but it's much better with subtitles, I felt."

The task of achieving linguistic authenticity fell to William Fulco, a Jesuit priest and professor of ancient Mediterranean studies at Loyola Marymount University in Los Angeles. Gibson got Fulco's name from Yale University, where Fulco received a doctorate and taught Aramaic.

"I got a call while I was in Jerusalem: 'Hey, Padre, It's Mel, I got a job for you,'" Fulco said. "I said, 'Mel who?' We talked for about an hour. He told me about the project, and I couldn't pass it up."

In 2002, Gibson gave Fulco the script written by Benedict Fitzgerald, mostly derived from the Gospels, and asked Fulco to translate it into Aramaic, Hebrew, and Latin. Fulco then translated the script back into English subtitles.

The use of multiple languages in the film reflects the linguistic diversity of Palestine during Jesus' life. Most people spoke Aramaic, which the Jews adopted while exiled in Babylon in the 6th century before Jesus' birth.

Hebrew, their language before the exile, was retained in religious writings and liturgy (and is spoken by Jesus in prayer in *The Passion*). Latin was spoken by the Roman soldiers occupying the region. Greek was spoken throughout the Roman Empire, thanks to Alexander the Great, but was seen as a sign of secularization and thus resisted by many Jews.

Fulco left Greek out of *The Passion,* substituting Latin in occasional cases where Greek might have been used. He also made mostly imperceptible distinctions between the elegant Latin of Pilate and the crude Latin of soldiers, thanks to an X-rated source he found on his shelf.

"I tracked down some obscene graffiti from Roman army camps," Fulco said. "Somebody who knows Latin really well, their ears will fall off. We didn't subtitle those words."

Fulco even confessed to some linguistic mischief. "Here and there I put in playful things which nobody will know. There's one scene where Caiaphas turns to his cohorts and says something in Aramaic. The subtitle says, 'You take care of it.' He's actually saying, 'Take care of my laundry.'"

Other linguistic tricks of Fulco's serve a function in the script. For example, he incorporated deliberate dialogue errors in the scenes where the Roman soldiers, speaking Aramaic, are shouting to Jewish crowds, who respond in Latin. To illustrate the groups' inability to communicate with each other, each side speaks with incorrect pronunciations and word endings.

Later, "there's an exchange where Pilate addresses Jesus in Aramaic, and Jesus answers in Latin. It's kind of a nifty little symbolic thing: Jesus is going to beat him at his own game," Fulco said. "One line [in that exchange] I kind of enjoyed is when Jesus says, 'My power is given from above, otherwise my followers would not have allowed this.' That's [spoken in] the pluperfect subjunctive." It may take a linguist to appreciate that feat of Latin grammar as remarkable for being uttered by a Palestinian Jew who mostly spoke Aramaic and Greek.

For the relatively few Middle Eastern Christians who still speak Aramaic, *The Passion* may sound riddled with mistakes, but as Fulco points out, "modern Aramaic dialects are as different [from ancient ones] as Chaucer and modern English."

Still, now that the movie is in general release, Fulco fully expects to get an earful about his use of languages. "We linguists are a crazy bunch," he said. "The more obscure the language, the more people try to prove their territory worthwhile and say, by God, we're going to sniff out errors."

pay your respects

HERE IN my hometown of Grand Rapids, Michigan, I lined up along the motorcade route to pay my respects as President Gerald R. Ford's funeral procession passed by.

Then I wondered, how do you "pay your respects"? What exactly are "respects," and how do you "pay" them?

It got me thinking about the elevated, ceremonial language we use around the death of public figures, such as the former president and soul music icon James Brown, who died within a day of each other and whose funerals dominated news coverage. For those occasions, out come such expressions as "pay respects," "pay homage," "lie in state," "lie in repose," "final farewell."

According to a search of LexisNexis, newspapers used the phrase "pay their respects" nearly as many times during the week after Brown's and Ford's deaths as they did the entire month before. On the day of Ford's funeral in Grand Rapids, a search of Google News found more than 1,000 headlines containing the phrase "pay respects" or "pay their respects." The phrase was also spilling out of the mouths of television commentators.

So what are "respects"? Curiously, most dictionaries describe this sense of "respects" as gestures of honor or politeness but say nothing about death or funerals.

The Oxford English Dictionary defines "respects" as "deferential or courteous attentions; actions expressive of respect for a person; politenesses, courtesies." It labels this entry "Obs.," meaning this meaning is now "obsolete." The *OED* quotes Jonathan Swift writing in a 1729 letter, "You are the first to present my most humble respects to the duchess of Queensberry," and another writer in 1782 saying, "Pray give my respects to him." ("Respect" comes from the Latin "respectus," meaning "to look back at" or "regard.")

In the *OED*'s entry for the phrase "to pay one's respects," the definition is "to show polite attention to a person by presenting oneself or by making a call." A line from a 1688 play by Sir George Etherege reads, "If I can I will slip away, and pay my respects to your lady."

So how did "paying respects" come to be associated specifically (or at least primarily) with mourning? The answer may lie in a subtle variation of the phrase that was also in use last week: "paying one's last respects" or "final respects." (Google News found 83 headlines containing "last respects" and more than 200 with "final respects" from the week after the deaths of Brown and Ford.)

The best guess is that "to pay one's last respects" began, either by euphemism or by eloquence, as a phrase describing honoring the deceased (and comforting the bereaved family) by making a final visit. Funeral visitation is the last time we can show "polite attention to a person by presenting oneself or by making a call," in the *OED*'s words.

But now that the phrase "paying respects" is all but obsolete except when it is used in the context of funerals, the qualifier "last" or "final" is no longer necessary. "Paying one's respects" does all the linguistic work that "paying one's last respects" used to do.

I found some support for my theory from John Ayto, British etymologist and editor of *The Oxford Dictionary of Slang*. "I'd be surprised if it weren't a euphemistic extension of the notion of paying one's respects to a living person, which seems to go back to the 17th century. It became simply a polite way of saying 'pay a visit to someone,' with the implication of presenting them with expressions of one's esteem, regard, etc. for them," Ayto writes by e-mail. "So I think that what the transfer to the deceased brings with it is the notion of 'visiting'—being personally present at the obsequies, as a sign of respect."

Other ceremonial words of mourning are showing their age: "Repose," as in "lying in repose," was originally a verb meaning "rest," and comes from the French word *reposer*, which the *OED* says is simply a French combination of "re-" and "pause."

The word "homage" (which showed up in 167 headlines following Ford's death, according to Google News), is literally "allegiance to a man" (with "hom-" meaning "human," as in "homo sapiens"). It originally meant political or religious loyalty, but drifted to today's sense of showing honor or respect, especially after a person's death.

One other word I noticed popping up everywhere in posthumous reference to Gerald Ford was "decent." "The press applied the word 'decent' to [Ford] so often that it stopped sounding like praise and started to sound like an insult," wrote Jack Shafer at *Slate*. Shafer based his view that "decent" is a weak word on its meaning of "'adequate' and 'just enough to meet the purpose,'" in his words.

But Shafer didn't acknowledge that "decent" (from the Latin "decens," meaning "appropriate" or "fitting") has different meanings that can be used separately. "Decent" can mean "free from immodesty or obscenity," as *Merriam-Webster* defines it—the opposite of "indecent." And there's the way the media was using "decent"—*Merriam-Webster*'s fifth definition: "marked by moral integrity, kindness, and goodwill."

The fact that "decent" can sometimes mean "adequate" might weaken its overall impact, but it's not exactly faint praise.

pedantry, history and misguidedness of

A FEW years back, linguist David Crystal was talking with Lynne Truss after she interviewed him on a British radio show. She said she was thinking of writing a book about punctuation.

"I wouldn't bother," Crystal told Truss. "Books on punctuation never sell."

Lo and behold, Truss' eventual book, *Eats, Shoots, and Leaves: A Zero-Tolerance Approach to Punctuation* (Gotham) became a best seller in Britain, and then in the United States.

Crystal says he's surprised and happy for Truss, but one part of her book's title bothered him: the term "zero-tolerance." He bristles at the suggestion that language has to be policed. So Crystal wrote a book of his own: *The Fight for English: How Language Pundits Ate, Shot, and Left* (Oxford University Press). It's a history of pedantry, or pickiness about language usage.

At first, Crystal's book seems to be an overreaction. Yes, Truss' book sold millions of copies, but it only talked about punctuation, not spelling, grammar, new words and other things that bug today's language pedants. Besides, Crystal says that unlike many pedants, Truss is interesting and good-humored. But the fact that Truss struck such a chord with her call to be a "stickler" with "zero-tolerance," he says, calls for a calmer, alternative approach.

Crystal's approach is based on two realizations—the fact that language pedants have been complaining about English usage for centuries, and the fact that variation and change in language are, in Crystal's words, "as natural as breathing." Realizing these truths, Crystal argues, would calm the grammar rage and improve public debates about English usage.

Crystal's history of pedantry runs a little long on pre-Truss pedants and a little short on present-day pedants. Without a chapter on recent and current language scolds, he doesn't satisfactorily connect Truss to her historical forerunners. But the length of his history is part of his point: You can pick just about any time in the history of the English language and find someone criticizing someone else's English.

Back in 1387, Crystal says, one historian in Britain wrote, "All the language of the Northumbrians, and especially at York, is so harsh, piercing, and grating, and formless, that we Southern men may hardly understand it."

In 1589, George Puttenham urged poets not to "follow the speech of a craftsman . . . or other of the inferior sort . . . for such persons do abuse good speeches by strange accents or ill-shapen sounds, and false orthography [spelling]."

In 1754, Philip Stanhope made the dire declaration, "It must be owned that our language is at present in a state of anarchy."

Whether it was "bad" spelling, pronunciation, grammar, or the influence of foreign words, many pedants have been worried that English would not survive. Either all those worriers were wrong, and English continued to do just fine, or they were right, and English has declined so severely that it's no longer worth trying to save. Either way, Crystal shows, the complaints of today's pedants are, historically speaking, pointless.

Worst of all, Crystal argues, is the legacy of pedants from the 1700s, the self-appointed language authorities who put nonsensical bans on split infinitives and sentence-ending prepositions that somehow caught on among English teachers and are still taught today. (I was surprised to learn that some of these pundits dared to criticize Chaucer, Shakespeare, and the translators of the King James Bible for making these "errors.") If you believe these practices are somehow wrong, Crystal says, "you have been taken in by the big con"—namely, "insisting that one person's personal taste . . . should be the yardstick for everyone."

Crystal says critics dismiss him as "Mr. Anything Goes," as trying to abolish all rules. But he maintains it's not true. The opposite of pickiness, he argues, is not permissiveness, but perspective—the historical perspective that language always changes and pedants are forgotten, and the social perspective of "appropriateness." Common sense tells us that different kinds of English are called for in a business and in a bar. We speak differently to bosses, spouses, and friends—and we should, because we have different relationships with them. So hard-and-fast rules don't help.

But the pedants continue to press on, under the illusion that they are heroes of language preservation. In reality, Crystal states flatly, "The only languages that do not change are dead ones."

See also **correctness; grammar, descriptive; National Grammar Day; prepositions, ending sentences with;** and **usage.**

pesky

When did the accepted adjectival form of the noun "pest" morph into "pesky"?

—*Paul O'Toole, Orland Park, Illinois*

ETYMOLOGISTS DON'T have much evidence that an adjective "pesty" ever existed, so they look elsewhere for an explanation, according to Anatoly Liberman, author of *Word Origins and How We Know Them* (Oxford University Press), and writer of *The Oxford Etymologist* at blogs.oup.com.

"The Swedish linguist S.B. Liljegren noted . . . that a peascod had formerly been believed to possess magical powers," Liberman writes by e-mail. "In some parts of the North of England, 'peascod' is pronounced as 'peskit.' There the curse 'A peascod on you' sounds 'A peskit on you.' Liljegren suggested that 'pesky' . . . goes back to 'peskit.'"

Liberman isn't sold on this story. "This is an ingenious though a rather far-fetched derivation," he says, but adds, "If neither of the two hypotheses ('pesty' or 'peascod') is accepted, we will be left with a verdict 'plaguing' every student of slang: 'Origin unknown.'"

podium vs. lectern

A speaker's stand, or desk, is not a podium. It is a lectern. One stands on a podium. One stands at a lectern. This is a common error made by experienced professionals in all media, as well as by educators and, it seems, linguists.

—*Bill Gershon, Skokie, Illinois*

IT'S TRUE that the word "podium" comes from the Greek *pod* for "foot," as does the word "podiatrist," and originally meant a platform for your feet. But a word's history can't enforce its meaning. "Lectern" comes from a Latin root meaning "read," so by the same logic the only thing you'd be allowed to do behind a lectern is read.

The first test for English usage must always be this: What will communicate clearly, and what will confuse? Telling someone to stand behind the podium will be understood by nearly every educated English speaker alive. Telling someone to stand on the podium might get you strange looks.

politeness

POLITENESS CAN mean phoniness. "I was just being polite" is a way of saying, "I didn't really mean it." We often associate politeness with insincerity or softening the truth.

But politeness can play a crucial role in professional and personal relationships, says Chris Christie, linguist at Loughborough University and founding member of the Linguistic Politeness

Research Group, an organization of academic researchers who study polite speech and behavior.

In 2005 Christie and her colleagues launched the *Journal of Politeness Research*, planning to publish two issues per year, with Christie as editor. "Understanding the wide range of politeness behavior that is expected in a culture, and the way this is influenced by the context of an institution or the social relationship between speakers, is very complex, and far from self-evident," Christie writes by e-mail. "Misjudging the effect of what you say can be extremely important—for communicating ideas and for fostering personal relationships."

Christie says researchers have begun to rethink their definition of politeness. For years, they assumed politeness was basically a way to avoid conflict and preserve social image. Now, Christie says, researchers view politeness as speech and behavior that goes "beyond what is normally expected in a situation." Politeness, she says, is more than just manners; it's the extra work a person puts into building a relationship through communication.

Christie says linguists researching politeness have looked at its relationship to domestic violence, managerial communication in business, and the apologies of politicians, but there hasn't been a way for researchers to keep track of each other's work.

The purpose of the journal, she says, is to collect articles on politeness from different academic fields, including anthropology, communication studies, political science and psychology, and put them in one place. "One of the problems with politeness research in the past has been that it is useful in so many different fields that important findings and applications have not always fed back into a development of the theories," Christie says. "We hope that the launch of the *Journal of Politeness Research* will ensure that this doesn't happen in the future."

The first issue included articles on the relationship between psychology and linguistics in the study of politeness, and on politeness and gender in the workplace. Perhaps the most intriguing topic in the inaugural issue is "Impoliteness and 'The Weakest Link,'" written by Jonathan Culpeper, linguist at Lancaster University in the U.K. Culpeper analyzes the intonation and context of Anne Robinson's cross remarks on her show (which still airs on

191

the BBC). Anne Robinson's trademark dismissal—"You are the weakest link, goodbye!" —according to Culpeper, "fits the vocal characteristics of 'anger/frustration,' such as slightly faster tempo, tense articulation and much higher pitch average."

Culpeper defines impoliteness as either intentional offense by the speaker, perceived offense by the hearer, or both. He observes that Robinson's curt catchphrase is a formulaic trademark of the show, not intended to offend the contestant. But since the verbal responses of contestants suggest that they do take personal offense, Culpeper says, Robinson's rudeness, however staged, qualifies as impoliteness.

pomma point

PUNCTUATION IS too emotional, says a marketing firm that created a new punctuation mark it calls the "pomma point."

"No punctuation mark currently exists in the English language that connotes a feeling of mild joy, vague happiness or heightened indifference," according to Torque Market Intelligence, the Toronto firm behind the website www.pommapoint.com. "If you want to congratulate a colleague that you do not interact with closely on the birth of a child, which you are genuinely sort of

POLITICAL SLANG

Political language is often stuffy and dull, but it can also be clever, creative and cruel. Here are some of the clichés and coinages that have spiced up American politics, from the 2004 book *Hatchet Jobs and Hardball: The Oxford Dictionary of American Political Slang* (Oxford University Press) by Grant Barrett.

also-ran: from horse racing, a candidate that also ran in the race but did not win (*see also* **horse racing clichés**).

bafflegab: confusing rhetoric.

barnstormer: a politician who makes several campaign stops in succession, especially in rural areas.

bigwig: a powerful person (coined in Colonial times for the large wigs worn by people of importance).

happy about, there is no appropriate punctuation."

So use a pomma point, Torque urges, and send an e-mail like this: 'Congratulations on the birth of George __. '" The horizontal line with a period at the end (type underscore and then period) is meant to be a punctuation mark that's halfway between a period and an exclamation point. Its name, pomma, is a combination of "period" and "comma" because "pexclamation" didn't have the right ring to it, according to Mark Healy, the Torque marketer who created it.

Healy calls the pomma point an experiment in viral market-ing—marketing that relies on word-of-mouth rather than tradi-tional advertising. He says his pomma point website has gotten some modest traffic from blogs. "It wasn't bad for something so obscure, with no dollars behind it," Healy says by phone. "I don't know that we're really going to push it," Healy said. "It should take off on its own accord if it's going to."

But Healy says the pomma point is not just a marketing stunt: It is meant to remedy something he and his colleagues frequently see in e-mails—the excessive use of exclamation points.

Language watchers doubt the pomma point will catch on. "It reminds me of those flash-in-the-pan neologisms that are too

---

boondoggle: May have originally referred to an ornamental leather strap. In politics, it came to be used to describe a pointless expen-diture or project—especially one using public money.

clothespin vote: a vote made without enthusiasm, for a candi-date who is negligibly less objectionable (or odiferous) than his opponent.

dirty tricks: secret operations carried out against political oppo-nents. The expression was made popular during the presidency of Richard Nixon.

fat cat: a rich person, especially a contributor to a campaign.

gag rule: a rule prohibiting discussion of a certain issue on the floor of Congress.

self-conscious and cute to survive," says Martha Barnette, host of *A Way With Words* (www.waywordradio.org). "It's gratuitous, like adding 'as it were' to an already perfectly good sentence. . . . I can't imagine reaching the end of a sentence that expresses mild joy, vague happiness, or heightened indifference and feeling a pressing need for anything but a plain, old period."

Invented punctuation tends to have a shorter life expectancy than invented words, partly because invented words usually require little or no explanation. If I tell you I'm a golf-aholic, you can probably guess I'm addicted to golf. A pomma point, on the other hand, will strike most people as a typo, or gibberish—obscuring rather than clarifying your tone.

The only notable new punctuation mark to make any kind of impact last century was the "interrobang"—a 1962 ad executive's idea for a combination of a question mark and exclamation point (the top of the exclamation point goes through the curve of the question mark; they share the dot at the bottom). By now, hardly anyone has heard of it, nobody uses it, and ending a sentence with alternating question marks and exclamation points remains the standard way to note disbelief.

In our computing culture, the closest cousins to the pomma

-gate: a suffix used in the naming of a scandal, in reference to the Nixon administration's Watergate.

gerrymander: the manipulative redrawing of congressional districts, named in 1812 for Massachusetts Governor Elbridge Gerry, who redrew his state's districts.

gladhander: a politician who engages in feigned or forced friendly greetings. This term seems to have cropped up early in the 20th century.

hardball: aggressive tactics; cited in 1972 in Carl Bernstein and Bob Woodward's classic book on Watergate, *All the President's Men*.

hatchet job: an attack on a politician's reputation.

point are emoticons, symbols developed to add some emotional nuance to instant messages. One of the best known is the smiley combination of colon-hyphen-parenthesis meant to give a cheerful tone to a message like "Congratulations on the birth of George :-)" If you look at it correctly, :-) looks like a smiling face tipped on its side. The pomma point doesn't really look like anything. But in either case, if you don't recognize the symbol, you won't understand the emotion conveyed with the message.

As linguists know, the best way to add or subtract emotion in a message is to do it with your voice.

pom-pon

> My dictionary says that a "pom-pom" is an anti-aircraft gun used on ships during World War II. A "pom-pon" is an ornamental tuft or ball of yarn. (Such as used by cheerleaders.) Every recent reference to cheerleading that I have seen has used the word "pom-pom." I would appreciate your comments.
>
> —*Carol Natke, LaGrange Park, Illinois*

jawbone: to attempt to persuade by oral argument.

John Q. Public: average citizen; dates to the early 1920s; "Jane Q. Public" didn't show up until the mid-'70s.

kangaroo ticket: a combination of nominees in which the running mate is more appealing than the presidential candidate (possibly coined to refer to a kangaroo's propulsion from its hind legs, or to the weight it carries in its bottom half).

leak: to release restricted information.

lobby: to attempt to persuade legislators. The Willard Hotel in Washington, D.C., maintains President Ulysses S. Grant, who frequented the place, used the term "damned lobbyists" in reference to men who staked out the hotel lobby hoping to buttonhole him.

MOST OF the dictionaries I checked say that "pom-pom" and "pom-pon" are interchangeable (in addition to the "anti-aircraft gun" definition for "pom-pom," for which "pom-pon" is not an alternative).

Even if there was a distinction, the similarity of the "M" and "N" sounds would all but ensure that it wouldn't last. "The interchangeability of 'm' and 'n' sounds is common in many languages," Grant Barrett, author of *The Official Dictionary of Unofficial English*, writes by e-mail. Barrett says it's conceivable "that the changes in the way English is spoken have made 'pom-pom' more common than 'pom-pon' because it feels more right on the tongue or is easier to say."

prepositions, ending sentences with

It seems to be more often that I want to use a preposition at the end of a phrase ("that's what we came for"), which I have

mugwump: politician who withholds support from his or her party (from an American Indian term for "chief").

neverendum: referendums introduced repeatedly until they succeed. Dates back only to the 1990s.

play in Peoria: as in "That will play in Peoria"; to resonate with the common American.

pork barrel: federal legislation that specifically benefits the district of a certain constituent. It's apparently a long-lived tradition; the term crops up after the Civil War.

prebuttal: statement or argument presented in anticipation of an opponent's argument.

pundit: political commentator, from the Sanskrit "pandita" for "a learned man."

tried not to do at the orders of my English teachers. But the alternatives, which I sometimes use just to feel like I've written properly, can be so awkward ("it is that for which we came"). Any advice for using this device appropriately without ending every sentence in a preposition?

—*Emily Varner, Wheaton, Illinois*

YOUR INSTINCTS are right: joining a verb with a preposition to form a "phrasal verb" is perfectly natural in English and always has been (Shakespeare wrote in *The Tempest*, for example, "We are such stuff as dreams are made on.")

According to *The American Heritage Guide to Contemporary Usage*, it was 17th century poet John Dryden who started the successful campaign to have this practice frowned upon. But as the *Guide* says, "English syntax not only allows but sometimes even requires final placement of a preposition"—indeed, just try to move "upon" in the previous sentence. It doesn't work.

scalawag: a white Southern supporter of Reconstruction in the Civil War era; origin unknown.

snollygoster: an unscrupulous politician.

stump: to give a campaign speech, coined for the use of tree stumps as outdoor platforms for speakers.

timber: a politician who is capable of running for president, as in "presidential timber."

watchdog: a person or organization dedicated to monitoring government corruption.

Yellow-dog Democrat: a Democrat so loyal that he'd vote for a yellow dog if it were his party's nominee.

zoo plane: an airplane of journalists covering a traveling politician. The term goes back to the early '70s.

For sanity's sake, unless you're writing a book or business report or giving a Nobel Prize acceptance speech, you can probably ignore this and many other picky grammatical commands of your English teachers. Few of them are helpful or sensible for informal, everyday communication.

See also correctness; grammar, descriptive; National Grammar Day; pedantry; and usage.

prepositions, poetry about

Now THIS is inspired poetry: In her 2006 collection titled *After* (HarperCollins), poet Jane Hirshfield includes her odes to the prepositions "of" and "to."

Of "of," she writes, "Its chain link can be delicate or massive. . . . Though one thing also connects to another through 'and,' this is not the same."

To "to," she writes, "Your work requires both transience and transformation: night changes to day, snow to rain, the shoulder of the living pig to meat."

presticogitation

JAMES VANDEN Bosch has been on a one-man lexicographical campaign for 20 years.

In the mid-1980s, Vanden Bosch—my English professor and now my colleague at Calvin College in Grand Rapids, Michigan—coined the word "presticogitation." It's a spin-off of the word "prestidigitation," which means "sleight of hand" and is used to describe magicians (derived from the French *preste*, meaning "nimble, quick," and the Latin *digitus* for "finger.")

"Presticogitation" is the cerebral equivalent—"rapid mental processing that commands compliance because of its speed and beauty," as Vanden Bosch defines it.

"Since the mid-1980s, I've been asking students to try to find room for it in their writing," he says. But Vanden Bosch says his campaign is more than a personal indulgence; it has a teaching purpose.

"I wanted my students in English 101 and Linguistics to

start thinking about new words being added to the language," he says. "I was trying to get them interested in paying attention to new words—noticing when they saw them or heard them, and being willing to be a little more playful about the fact that language changes."

Vanden Bosch first published the word "presticogitation" in 1988 in Calvin's alumni magazine, and started inserting it in letters to the campus newspaper. He spread the word—literally—wherever he could.

"I might drop it into a conversation, and students of mine would use it every now and then in a student evaluation," Vanden Bosch said. "It had limited but real currency here on campus already by the late 1980s."

By the time I had him as an instructor, Vanden Bosch was telling students he wanted his word to earn the highest lexicographical honor there was—an entry in the esteemed *Oxford English Dictionary*. In 2001, after speaking at a conference at Oxford University, Vanden Bosch had a golden opportunity to plead his case with John Simpson, chief editor of the *OED*.

Simpson did an electronic search for "presticogitation" and found a handful of results, most of them in the writings of students of Vanden Bosch. "He could not believe that I had conned that many Calvin College students into putting that word into print," Vanden Bosch says. "He was greatly amused."

But that didn't bring Simpson much closer to putting "presticogitation" in the *OED*. "He looked at me with a kind of charitable sympathy and pity when I told him I wanted to get this word in the *OED*," Vanden Bosch recalls. "He said, 'Everybody wants to get a word in the *OED*.'"

Last fall, "presticogitation" took another step toward popularity when syndicated columnist Dale Dauten wrote about Vanden Bosch's lexicographical campaign. Dauten's column ran in newspapers such as the *St. Louis Post-Dispatch* and *Arizona Republic*, prompting lexicographer and slang watcher Grant Barrett to list "presticogitation" at his slang website (www.doubletongued.org).

"It's the very first step in making [it into] any dictionary: just

199

getting the term on the record," Barrett writes by e-mail. But Barrett emphasizes that "presticogitation" still has a long way to go.

"All it means is that I found it and recorded it. Nothing more. [My site] is all about recording terms that are undocumented or under-documented, especially those from the Internet. Being recorded by [my site] is not a vote by me in favor of a word, nor evidence of its success, nor a prediction about its future."

Other lexicographers also voice caution about the future of "presticogitation." "The fact that 'presticogitation' is a blend tends to make its long-term success less likely," says Joseph Pickett, executive editor of *The American Heritage Dictionary*.

Pickett points out that new words tend to grow naturally, not as the result of personal campaigns. "Unless your professor takes it undercover, his campaign is doomed," Pickett says.

Of course, "presticogitation" doesn't lend itself to casual use; the only times I've used it without explanation have been in e-mails to Vanden Bosch or other students of his. I've written about the word and Vanden Bosch's campaign at my personal blog, which earned the word a few more search results at Google. But up until now, I've never used the word in print.

Jesse Sheidlower, the North American editor of the *OED*, says published articles about the origins of "presticogitation" are of little help. "The criteria for including this in any general dictionary, including the *OED*, are more or less the same," Sheidlower writes by e-mail. "We'd need to see substantial evidence of its genuine use. . . . These examples would need to be unconnected to the word's coiner and should not make any kind of explicit comment on the word's newness or meaning. And there would need to be a great many such examples."

Sheidlower concludes: "I don't see this word being successful. However useful the word may be, it's too self-conscious, and its need is too small."

Vanden Bosch acknowledges the tall odds against his word ever ending up in the *OED*. "I have no illusions about my chances," Vanden Bosch says. "It's the quixotic nature of the enterprise that pleases me."

See also **Andrea-ese, neologisms.**

preventive vs. preventative

> What is the accepted usage for the words "preventive" and "preventative"? I used to have to type veterinary reports that referred to "preventative medicine" and felt odd about it, especially since the vets who insisted it was correct were not very good at grammar.
>
> —*Mary Erickson, Lynwood, Illinois*

THE USUALLY fussy *Fowler's Modern English Usage* (third edition) shrugs its shoulders on this one: "Both words entered the language in the 17th century and they have been fighting it out ever since," *Fowler's* says. "Both are acceptable formations, and the most that can be said is that the shorter form is the more frequent of the two, and is the one recommended here for most contexts."

The Oxford English Dictionary gives early examples of both words that makes them appear interchangeable. Thomas Fuller wrote in 1639, "A preventive war grounded on a just fear of an invasion is lawful." Roger Boyle wrote in 1655, "All preventative thoughts of hostility were silenced."

The American Heritage Medical Dictionary lists "preventive" with "preventative" as an alternate form. But then it gives a separate entry only for "preventive medicine," not "preventative medicine."

props

YOU HAVE to give the website *Xanga* a prop or two for taking the plural word "props" and making it singular. But mad props go to queen of soul Aretha Franklin, the original expression's queen.

"Props" means "proper recognition," according to the *Urban Dictionary*, a user-edited online dictionary of slang (www.urbandictionary.com). The word often appears with the intensifier "mad."

Lexicographer Grant Barrett says the first known example of "props" in print comes in a 1990 profile of rapper Roxanne Shante in the *Chicago Tribune*. "I was one of the first female rappers, but I've always gotten my props," Shante, then 19, told the *Tribune*.

She added, "That means I get respect."

Around this time, the word "exploded on the scene as part of the hip-hop revolution," says Barrett, author of *The Official Dictionary of Unofficial English* and project editor of the *Historical Dictionary of American Slang*, whose "P" section is in progress.

But so far, "props" has been a plural. No one says, "I give him a prop." So "prop" would be considered a "false singular"—an unused singular form of a plural word.

John Ayto, British etymologist and editor of *The Oxford Dictionary of Slang*, says this isn't unusual. "It's not uncommon to refer to what is essentially a single, unified concept by means of a plural noun (such as 'congratulations'), at least part of the purpose of which often seems to be to make the reference sound larger, more encompassing, more impressive (and expressive)," Ayto writes by e-mail. "I think 'props' could be part of that phenomenon."

But log onto a blog hosted by *Xanga* (www.xanga.com), and you'll see that "props" is now living single.

Xanga invites readers to award "eProps" to bloggers who write worthy entries. It gives readers these choices: "2 eProps," "1 eProp," "0 eProps." Bloggers who collect the most eProps are ranked and featured at *Xanga's* home page—a coveted spotlight in the world of blogging. (It usually takes about 200 and 300 eProps to earn this distinction.) "Eprops are a way to give 'props' to another member," *Xanga's* website explains. "It's really just a way to let someone know you enjoyed their post."

Word watchers say the word "eProp"—and the concept of giving someone a single "prop"—is a new wrinkle in the history of "props." "I do not know 'prop' as a singular," Wayne Glowka, chair of the American Dialect Society Committee on New Words, writes by e-mail. Ayto agrees, saying "props" exists "only in the plural, as far as I know."

The singular of "props" may be just the latest stage in a lexical life cycle that has spanned nearly four decades. Back in 2001, the question of the origins of "props" was posted at the American Dialect Society's message board. Linguist Margaret Lee gave some props to the queen of soul. "In her 1967 hit, 'R-E-S-P-E-C-T,' Aretha Franklin says, 'All I want you to do for me is give me my propers when you get home,'" Lee wrote. "The hip-hop generation shortened it to props."

Some listeners hear the word "profits" in that line, instead of "propers" (two lines earlier, Franklin sings, "I'm about to give you all of my money"). But Franklin tried to set the record straight in a column by William Safire in *The New York Times* in 2002. "I do say propers," Franklin said. "I got it from the Detroit street. It was common street slang in the 1960s."

"It seems very likely that 'propers' came first and 'props' later," Barrett says. His research has turned up two relevant citations of "propers" in the wake of Franklin's song: a 1972 article by a linguist in the *English Journal*, pledging "to give the rest of you your propers," and a 1981 quotation from a boxer in *The New York Times*: "The least they could have done was give me my propers." Barrett intends to create a paper trail of these citations leading from Aretha Franklin's "propers" in 1967 up to Roxanne Shante's "props" in 1990.

The word "prop" has older, mainstream meanings that are unrelated in origin. "Prop" meaning an item used on stage for a play is an abbreviation of "property." A "prop" on an airplane is a "propeller," from the Latin *propellere*, meaning "to push forward." The oldest sense of "prop" in English means something that is used to support, or "prop up" (or "prop open") something else. It probably comes from the Dutch noun *proppe*, meaning a "support." The slang sense of "props" is now common in informal English, though it has yet to enter a major dictionary.

"'Props' is pretty well near a colloquialism in American English," Barrett says. "It's been so often used that it no longer really requires explanation. . . . 'Propers,' on the other hand, is still slangy."

Proust's English

WHAT STANDS out in this phrase from novelist Marcel Proust: *mes snow-boots que j'avais pris?*

It means "my snow-boots which I had brought." You don't need to know French to see the word "snow-boots" sticking out.

The phrase, from Proust's masterpiece seven-volume novel, translated into English as *Remembrance of Things Past*, is just one example of an eye-catching English loan word in the midst of Proust's French prose, says Daniel Karlin, author of *Proust's English* (Oxford University Press).

Other examples from *Remembrance* include *les films, les cocktails, le revolver, le golf,* and more than a hundred others. One character even says "le five o'clock tea." That's a lot of English for a French author who, Karlin writes, "never traveled to England, never learned English, and confessed his inability to either speak the language or understand it when it was spoken." ("I don't claim to know English," Proust once said in French. "I do claim to know Ruskin"—the English writer Proust translated into French.)

But Karlin says Proust's use of English was no accident. "Proust's use of such words was almost never dictated by necessity; if he had wanted to avoid the word 'snow-boots' here he could easily have done so, as the phrase *caoutchoucs americains* demonstrates," Karlin writes in his introduction. That phrase means "American rubbers" and appears later in the same paragraph.

"He chose it, I think, because it made a small but distinct contribution to the theme of snobbery and social embarrassment which is being developed in this episode," Karlin continues. "The shame that [the character] feels at his footwear *faux pas* is transposed to the word itself."

It was seeing that word "snow-boots," Karlin reflects, that spurred his interest over a decade ago in Proust's use of English. He started keeping a list of all of the English words and phrases that Proust used.

Karlin's book is more than a literary analysis of what the use of English reveals about the author and the characters in *Remembrance*—it is a window into the cultural tension of 19th century France. France was always uneasy about the influence of English, from the time of the Norman Conquest in 1066 to the present day—as English replaces French as the language of diplomacy and becomes the lingua franca of technology.

In the 19th century, Karlin says, France had just coined the derogative term *anglomanie*, meaning "anglomania," which Karlin defines as "an excessive adoration for Englishness, whether in politics, social behavior, philosophy, or literature." Yet many French people associated English with social prestige and sophistication (the way, ironically, many Americans today revere French words and French food). Proust's characters, Karlin says, illustrate this tension between admiration and fear of Englishness in the way they use English.

"I'm a literary critic by training, but I've always been interested in language use, particularly in its historical context," Karlin writes by e-mail from Boston University, where he teaches English. "The book grew out of my noticing all these English words and phrases, and then realizing that they weren't accidental but meaningful. So the book is literary criticism, but founded on observation of language use, both that of Proust and others."

quote, as a noun

Is the use of "quote" as a noun rather than a verb acceptable? I was taught that "quote" is only a verb, as in "Can I quote you on that?" and "quotation" is the appropriate noun form. Has "quote" just become an abbreviation that insurance companies started using to save time?

—*Kathryn Gaglione, Salt Lake City, Utah*

T.S. Eliot wasn't an insurance agent, as far as I know, and he wrote in a 1922 letter, according to *The Oxford English Dictionary*, "Do you mean not use the Conrad quote or simply not put Conrad's name to it?"

The noun "quote" meaning "quotation mark" is probably even older. It appeared in print in a 1888 book called *Printer's Vocabulary*.

Recency Illusion

Stanford's Arnold Zwicky spotted a "Dr. Language" column at www.yourdictionary.com claiming that the phrase "between you and I" (instead of "between you and me") is a "linguistic virus" that started to spread "about 20 years ago."

205

Zwicky wrote at the *Language Log* (www.languagelog.org) that this is "wrong, pretty spectacularly." Zwicky said Dr. Language should check *The Oxford English Dictionary*, where one can see that Shakespeare himself used this phrase. In *The Merchant of Venice*, Bassanio reads a letter that says, "All debts are cleerd betweene you and I." In *As You Like It*, Celia says, "My father hath no childe but I." The *OED* says this usage of "I" as an object as well as a subject was "very frequent" in Shakespeare's time.

Zwicky calls this "another instance of the Recency Illusion, the belief that things YOU have noticed only recently are in fact recent." He explains: "This is a selective attention effect. Your impressions are simply not to be trusted; you have to check the facts. Again and again—retro *not*, double *is*, speaker-oriented *hopefully*, split infinitives, etc. —the phenomena turn out to have been around, with some frequency, for very much longer than you think. It's not just Kids These Days." Zwicky says related mistakes include the Frequency Illusion—"once you notice a phenomenon, you believe that it happens a whole lot"—and the Adolescent Illusion—"the consequence of selective attention paid to the language of adolescents ("those kids") by adults."

reincarnation and language

A COLLEAGUE handed Sarah Thomason a 2005 article from *The Daily Yomiuri*, an English-language newspaper in Japan, titled "Recalling Past Languages from Past Lives." The article, written by a Japanese professor of psychology and English in a column called "The Practical Linguist," said studies have shown that some people can speak a language from a previous life.

Thomason, a linguist at the University of Michigan, sighed and logged onto *Language Log*, a blog written by linguists (www.languagelog.org). Calling these claims "linguistic pseudoscience," Thomason wrote that studies of supposedly reincarnated speakers show that they do not know "more than a handful of isolated words" of languages from their supposed previous lives, and that they "had both opportunity and motivation to learn these words" in their current lives.

Thomason has published critiques in the journals *American*

Speech and *Skeptical Inquirer* of these linguistic claims about rein-carnation, especially the findings of Ian Stevenson, a psychiatrist at the University of Virginia. Beginning in the 1970s, Stevenson studied subjects such as a West Virginia woman who, under hypnosis, conversed in German and claimed to be a 19th century German teenager named Gretchen.

Thomason studied Stevenson's transcripts of conversations with "Gretchen" and concluded the woman couldn't have been a native of Germany in a former life. "Gretchen usually answers with just a word or two rather than in full sentences," Thomason wrote in the *Skeptical Inquirer*. "All she seems to know, either for speaking or for understanding, is a handful of words." Many of Gretchen's words, Thomason added, closely resemble their English equivalents—*braun*, for example, is the German word for "brown."

Of Gretchen's responses to questions she was asked in Ger-man, many were either repetitions of the question or *ja* or *nein* ("yes" or "no"). Of Gretchen's other 102 responses, Thomason said, only 28 were "appropriate" or sensible answers, while 45 did not make sense and 29 were "cop-out" answers such as "I don't understand" or "I don't know."

Thomason says that in one telling exchange, the interviewer asks, *Was gibt es nach dem Schlafen?* This literally translates "What is there after sleeping?" but is intended to mean "What do you eat for breakfast?" Gretchen answers, *Schlafen, Bettzimmer*, mean-ing "Sleep, bedroom." Thomason points out that not only did Gretchen misunderstand the question, she uses the word *Bet-tzimmer*, while a native German speaker would say *Schlafzimmer*, literally "sleep room."

"Do we need a paranormal explanation for her knowledge of some German words and phrases? Surely not," Thomason wrote. Stevenson found that the woman never studied German in school nor was she spoken to in German during her childhood, but Thomason says so-called "passive exposure," such as watching a subtitled movie or reading a German textbook, would be enough to explain her minimal vocabulary.

Similar studies of supposed reincarnated speakers have similar results—subjects have such little grasp of the vocabulary and sentence structure of their supposed former native languages that it is unlikely they were ever fluent in those languages, she says.

Thomason doesn't suspect Stevenson or his subjects are trying to perpetrate a hoax, but she asserts any linguist can spot these flaws in vocabulary and grammar.

Stevenson is still at the University of Virginia School of Medicine, in the division of personality studies. Citing sensational and scornful treatment of its research in the past, the department's researchers do not grant media interviews.

But one ardent defender of Stevenson's work thinks Thomason is dismissing it too easily. Robert Almeder, philosophy professor at Georgia State, responded to Thomason in his 1994 book *Death and Personal Survival: The Evidence for Life After Death*, and made his case in a telephone interview.

"If I bumped into you and spoke in French, you would conclude that I know French. Even if I only respond to you 28 times and don't understand you the other times, it doesn't follow that I don't know French, only that I know French imperfectly," Almeder said by phone.

So while Thomason wants an explanation for why a supposed native speaker of a language has trouble speaking and understanding it, Almeder wants an explanation for how a non-speaker of a language could speak it at all. He says "passive exposure" can't account for the phenomenon, because hearing words and phrases in one context wouldn't enable subjects to use them in another setting to answer questions. "If someone is speaking in well-formed sentences in a foreign language, and has never used the language before, we have something that really needs to be explained," Almeder said.

Thomason believes any combination of passive exposure, memorization, and guesswork is enough to explain Gretchen's version of German. "It is very easy to guess, under appropriate circumstances, what someone has said to you in a language you don't know well, and to deploy very limited knowledge of some words and set phrases in answer to questions you've guessed," she says by phone. "The subject's wrong guesses show clearly that that's what she was doing."

Almeder says Stevenson's studies are just some of the scientific evidence for reincarnation he lays out in *Death and Personal Survival*. "Reincarnation has occurred, I believe that," Almeder says, and adds that his evidence for reincarnation is so strong, "it would be irrational not to believe."

restaurateur

> Why does the word "restaurateur" not have an "n" in it?
>
> —*Paula Castleton, Highland Park, Illinois*

I NEVER noticed that "restaurateur" was missing the "N"! With language, as with so many things, we often see what we expect to see.

Both "restaurant" and "restaurateur" come from the French word *restaurer*, literally meaning "to restore." *The Oxford English Dictionary* says that "restaurant" comes from the present participle form of this verb, which ends in "-nt."

In English, we add "-ator" to a verb stem to mean "one who does this," as in "terminate" and "terminator." In French, you add *-ateur*. Add that to the verb stem "restaur-" and you get "restaurateur."

-s, as a transforming ending

> A question popped into my head while I was sleeping/dreaming last night. I wondered if you might know. Are there any other words in the English language besides "new" wherein when an "s" is added, it changes the entire meaning of the word?
>
> —*Marian Taylor, East Dundee, Illinois*

MY COLLEGE English professor, James Vanden Bosch of Calvin College in Grand Rapids, Michigan, has some suggestions. His answers fall into two categories: words that can change to another part of speech when "s" is added—"heroic" (adjective to noun), "ruin" (verb to noun), "wrap" (verb to noun), and "chill" (verb to noun); and words that change their meaning with an added "S" as you requested: "spectacle," "glass" (taking an "-es" ending), and "dropping." I would place "new" in the first category, since "news" turns the adjective into a plural noun, but retains the meaning of the word.

Update: As I revisit these examples I wonder if "new" could go in the second category, since the "new" in "news" actually means "report." I chuckled when reader Louis Altman of Northbrook, Illinois, related this story: "When I was a student at Cornell in the 1950s, I tutored foreign students in English. One day a student walked into my room reading a letter he had recently received. I asked, 'Any news from home?' He answered, in all seriousness: 'Only one new.'"

Reader Bob Stigger wrote, "Adding a letter to a word so as to completely change its meaning is a staple technique in cryptic crossword puzzles, which as it happens I construct. Probably the classic example of adding an S at the end to completely change meaning is 'needles' → 'needless.' A fun example is 'princes' → 'princess', because you *add* the letter S to change a plural into a singular, exactly the opposite of what usually happens." Craig Bloomfield of Arlington Heights, Illinois, added the examples of "asses," "bras," "discus," and "posses" (the plural of "posse," which changes to "possess").

Nancy Spector posted this query to her *Wordcraft* message board (wordcraft.infopop.cc) and got an impressive resulting list, including "cares," "drawer," "due," "ha," "I," "saw," "sweat," and "sweet"—and two special words that can do the "add S" trick twice in a row: "a" becomes "as," then becomes "ass"; and "hi" becomes "his," then becomes "hiss."

-s, necessity of in double possessives

I often see the use of the possessive with the "'s" after the use of the possessive "of." For example: "A friend of my sister's." Is the "'s" necessary because the word "of" already conveys the possessive form?

—*Murad Meneshian, Glenview, Illinois*

ETYMOLOGIST MICHAEL Quinion tackled this at *World Wide Words* (www.worldwidewords.org).

"The technical name for this construction is double genitive or double possessive," Quinion wrote. He said this form has a long history; Dickens used it, for example, when he wrote "an aunt of my father's" in David Copperfield.

The double possessive often occurs naturally to English speakers—especially with pronouns: we say "a friend of mine" but not "a friend of me."

While "of" does indicate possession, it's such a vague and versatile word that the double possessive is often needed for clarification.

Quinion's examples are "a bone of the dog"—which could be taken to mean either a bone the dog is chewing on or a bone in the dog's own skeleton—and "a picture of Jane," which means that Jane appears in the photo, not that she owns it.

However, Quinion also points out we tend to use the double possessive only in cases where the owner is a human or animal, and not, for instance, an organization. We say "Friends of the Library" but not "Friends of the Library's." Why do English speakers make this distinction naturally in our speech, without being taught it? It's a linguistic mystery.

seasonable

Something about our language has been bugging me for some time. Whenever newspapers refer to sales of homes, automobiles or just about anything that has a cyclical nature they use the word "seasonal." When they talk about the weather they use the word "seasonable." Is there an explanation why?

—*Jack Patterson, Glenwood, Illinois*

IT'S TRUE that "seasonable" is used to describe weather that is characteristic of the season, though usually only for pleasant weather—we don't call a blizzard "seasonable." But "seasonable" is also used interchangeably with "seasonal." A police dispatcher told the *Sun Journal* in New Bern, North Carolina, that there are "seasonable differences" in the number of calls he gets (things pick up in the summer months). A resident of Port Orchard, Washington, quoted by the Associated Press this month, defended her school district's use of the term "winter break" instead of "Christmas break" by saying, "It's a seasonable description."

The Oxford English Dictionary shows that the word "seasonable" dates to the 14th century, while "seasonal" didn't appear until the 19th century. Because it's so much older, "seasonable" has always been more versatile; over time, it has meant "in season," "temporary," "mature" and even "savory when used as seasoning."

serial comma

When listing things, do you put a comma between the second to last item and the "and"? For instance: "We bought eggs, milk, and fabric softener." My students debated it. Many do not do it, saying they've been taught that way in English 100. I've been taught to include the last comma.

—Nicholas Dekker, Columbus, Ohio

LIKE YOU, I was also taught to include what is called the "serial comma" (because it follows the second-to-last item in a series), and so I'm in that habit. I also use it because I don't want to suggest a special relationship between the second and third item if there's no comma to separate them.

But you probably won't see a serial comma in my column in the *Chicago Tribune*, which doesn't doesn't use it; in fact, most newspaper, wire service, and magazine stylebooks follow a no-serial-comma rule. No one is absolutely sure how the convention got started, but it's widespread in American journalism and if I forget and put in a serial comma, my *Tribune* editors remove it.

The *Oxford Style Manual*, the guidebook for Oxford University Press (and the namesake for the alternate label for the serial comma: the "Oxford comma") sees it my way: "If the last item in a list has emphasis equal to the previous ones, it needs a comma to create a pause of equal weight to those that came before." And

The Chicago Manual of Style says it "strongly recommends" the serial comma, "since it prevents ambiguity." (It adds that you don't need any commas when all the items in the list are joined by conjunctions: "eggs and milk and fabric softener.")

Opinion is so divided on the serial comma that I don't think anyone can look down on you for doing it one way or the other. The best rule is to follow the textbook or stylebook your school or organization uses. If it doesn't have one, I'd say go with *The Chicago Manual of Style*.

shambles

"WITH BACK-TO-BACK losses in Iowa and New Hampshire, [former presidential contender Mitt] Romney's expensive win-it-early strategy is a shambles," reported *U.S. News and World Report* in early 2008. "If you leave your company a shambles," asked *Newsweek*, "do you deserve a gold-plated send-off?" "Public records show that his financial life was a shambles," wrote *The Philadelphia Inquirer* about a disgraced local politician.

Shouldn't that be "in shambles," not "a shambles"? And if so, what is a "shamble"?

"Shambles" is weird because of that final 's,'" Martha Barnette, co-host of the public radio show *A Way With Words* (www.waywordradio.org), writes by e-mail. "Especially if you don't know the word's origin, it's tempting to understand it as a plural, the same way you might say that someone's campaign is 'in tatters.'"

The root of "shambles" is the Latin *scamnum*, meaning bench or stool, which entered Old English as "sceamol" and morphed into the Middle English "shamel." Here it adopted the meaning of "vendor's table," and soon specifically meant "table for selling meat."

This is where the strange-sounding singular usage may have started: "a shamels" could mean "a meat market," since it was a single place with multiple tables for selling meat. Before long, the definition included "butcher shop," and since a butcher doesn't just sell meat but also kills it, "shambles" eventually took on the overtone of "slaughterhouse."

"Shambles" has done double duty as both a singular and

a plural throughout its lifetime. *The Oxford English Dictionary* quotes this line of dialogue from a 1623 play: "I stink like a fish shambles . . ." with "shambles" clearly singular. The plural usage has always hung on: William Drummond wrote in a political essay in 1638, "The bodies of commonwealths are already turned into skeletons, the cities into sepulchres, the fields into shambles." A history book from 1885 reads, "Nobles, priests, and women were slaughtered like sheep in a shamble" (the plural of which would be simply "shambles," not "a shambles").

"Shambles is a good illustration of what happens with so many words when their meaning gets watered down over time," Barnette says. "I doubt many people see the bloody poetry in the word 'shambles' when they hear it."

By now, "shambles" can mean any situation of deterioration, and it can still be singular or plural. The examples above show that "a shambles" still has currency. But saying that something is "in shambles" also is common. "If her campaign was in shambles, it was her job to fix it or take the consequences," *The New York Times* wrote of Hillary Clinton's presidential campaign. The Associated Press described Kentucky's state economy as "in shambles." *The Boston Globe* quoted the owner of a renovated historic inn in rural Vermont, "When we [first] saw this old inn, it was completely dilapidated, ceilings collapsing, bathrooms in shambles."

So what is it, singular or plural? Dictionaries don't clear things up. *Merriam-Webster's Collegiate Dictionary* says "shambles" is "plural but singular or plural in construction." *The American Heritage Dictionary* says the word is "plural . . . used with a singular verb." *The Oxford English Dictionary*'s entry is for the singular "shamble," but it marks the modern usage as "plural" and then gives a singular definition: "a scene of disorder or devastation."

The parallel to the phrase "in ruins" or "in tatters" is so strong that "in shambles" sounds right—it sounds like a pile of fragments. And the etymology is so remote that hardly anyone thinks "a slaughterhouse" when they hear "a shambles." So it's usually safe to say "in shambles." Or, to be extra safe, you could try to have it both ways, as a *Boston Globe* columnist did last month when he wrote that the U.S. strategy for dealing with Pakistan is "in a shambles."

shiver me timbers

"Shiver me timbers!" What the heck does that mean, anyway?

—*Delia Rellis, Dyer, Indiana*

THE FIRST place I looked was the website of the annual "Talk Like a Pirate Day" (www.talklikeapirateday.com). The site's glossary says "shiver me timbers" is "like saying, 'Oh, My!' like my legs are shaking." By this thinking, "timbers" is either a slang word for legs, or a literal reference to wooden legs.

But *The Oxford English Dictionary* says "timbers" could be "applied to any object" that was "composed wholly or chiefly of wood." It defines "shiver my timbers" as "a mock oath attributed in comic fiction to sailors." Its earliest example is from Captain Frederick Marryat's 1835 novel *Jacob Faithful*, in which a character says, "I won't thrash you Tom. Shiver my timbers if I do."

I contacted Fred Shapiro, the workhorse behind the massive new *Yale Book of Quotations* (Yale University Press). He searched a database of 18th century texts and found a 1786 book in which a sailor returns from a voyage and arrives at the wedding of his fiancée—to someone else—and exclaims, "Shiver my timbers!"

"From looking at other occurrences in [this database], it appears to me that the phrase originated in comic literature," Shapiro writes by e-mail.

My guess is a novel or movie about pirates helped associate the phrase with pirates. I did a search of the text of *Robinson Crusoe* and didn't find it, but I suspect a pirate movie at some point made this the signature catchphrase of the stereotypical pirate.

Update: Several readers pointed out that I had looked in the wrong book. In Robert Louis Stevenson's *Treasure Island*, the pirate Long John Silver repeatedly says "shiver my timbers," launching the phrase into timelessness.

skin of your teeth, by the

I am asking whether you can recommend a good resource for the origin of phrases, such as "by the skin of your teeth." I've heard there is a book or website for such phrases.

—Chuck Mepyans, Aurora, Illinois

PHRASES ARE notoriously difficult to document reliably, and urban legends often substitute for history. But a compilation by the late Charles Earle Funk titled *2107 Curious Word Origins, Sayings and Expressions* is useful, as are the websites *The Phrase Finder* (www.phrases.org.uk) and Michael Quinion's *World Wide Words* (www.worldwidewords.org/qa). The full text of E. Cobham Brewer's *19th century Dictionary of Phrase and Fable* is online (www.bartleby.com) (**update**: a revised and expanded edition of *Brewer's* by John Ayto has since been released by Collins), although its comments on origins are spare. More helpful is the *Morris Dictionary of Word and Phrase Origins* (Collins). *The Oxford English Dictionary* gives historical examples of select phrases as part of its entries for individual words—for example, "mad as a hatter" is listed under "mad."

As for "by the skin of one's teeth," the phrase comes from English translations of the Hebrew Bible, but its meaning is uncertain. The phrase is first cited by *The Oxford English Dictionary* in the Geneva Bible of the 16th century, which translated Job 19:20 from Hebrew as "I have escaped with the skin of my teeth."

Despite the odd imagery, the phrase caught on as an idiom. Biblical commentators speculate that the phrase either refers to the gums, or that it means "nothing," because skin does not exist on teeth.

so, as intensifier

DEPENDING ON your opinion of the TV show *Friends*, Chris Roberts has had either a fun or a cruel task. Roberts, a student in anthropology and linguistics at the University of Toronto, was assigned to watch every episode of the first eight seasons of the show.

Roberts had a linguistic reason for the marathon. He was listening to the way *Friends* used intensifiers—words like "very," "really" and "so." Roberts and his professor, sociolinguist Sali Tagliamonte, co-authored a study of *Friends* that appears in the current issue of the journal *American Speech*.

Sociolinguists study not only the way people speak but also the social judgments and perceptions we make based on the way people speak. Tagliamonte says she's interested in intensifiers because they occur naturally—speakers don't tend to give them a lot of thought—and they vary among cultures and generations.

The study for *American Speech* focuses on intensifiers that accompany adjectives, as in "really hot" and "so happy." Roberts documented every adjective uttered on *Friends* through 2002. He found that about one out of every five adjectives appeared with an intensifier.

The next step was to see which intensifier was being used the most. When Tagliamonte co-authored a study of British English intensifiers for the journal *Language and Society* in 2003, she reported that "very" makes up nearly 40 percent of all intensifiers in British English, followed by 30 percent for "really," 10 percent for "so" and around 3 percent each for "absolutely" and "pretty."

The *Friends* data turned out to be different—so different. On *Friends*, the word "so" made up 45 percent of all intensifiers, followed by "really" at 25 percent, "very" at 15 percent, "pretty" at 6 percent and "totally" at 2 percent.

This suggests that "so" is on the rise in American English, Tagliamonte says.

"I think the movement is towards a new intensifier," Tagliamonte says. "Either the *Friends* actors pushed it, or maybe they just picked up on it in vernacular culture and used it. This is just speculation. If they can influence how everybody wore their hair, why not intensifiers?"

Tagliamonte cautions against the simplistic conclusion that *Friends* or any television show leads to copycat language use. Linguists have consistently found that although people may watch the same television shows, they still retain their regional ways of speaking, especially their pronunciation. But Tagliamonte says linguists need to take a new look at whether the media affect our grammar—in this case, our intensifiers.

"As the media's influence becomes more profound in our lives, we have to say to ourselves, perhaps its influence [on our language] will increase," Tagliamonte says. "That's an open question."

But one thing is clear: the rise of "so" is just another phase in the life cycle of English. Since the 12th century, popularity among English intensifiers has shifted from the now extinct "swithe" to "well" and "right," and more recently to "pretty," "very" and "really." While "very" is considered the most formal and proper, all of these words have similar literal meanings—"truly" or "to a great extent."

Friends took its share of heat from critics for dumbing down the culture, but Tagliamonte says there's nothing inherently unintelligent about "so." It's just the latest intensifier to come of age.

"In what sense is the use of 'so' as an intensifier a dumb thing?" Tagliamonte asks. "It's one of the perfectly good adverbs of English that have been conscripted into the intensifier system. How we judge these features socially is a completely different thing."

solecism

THE WORD of the Day that turned up in my e-mail inbox was "solecism," meaning a breach of grammar or etiquette. It comes from the Greek word "soloikismos," for "speaking incorrectly."

I learned this from Merriam-Webster's free service for word buffs—you can sign up at www.m-w.com, but I warn you, it launches endless etymological expeditions. Here's how it happens.

"According to historians," my Word of the Day e-mail continued, the ancient city of Soloi in Asia Minor "had a reputation for bad grammar," thanks to settlers from Athens who let their proper Greek deteriorate in their new surroundings.

Come on, I thought. A city known for its bad grammar? Doesn't that sound like an etymological tall tale, a fable told by English teachers to scare students into diagramming sentences?

So I e-mailed my college classics professor, Ken Bratt of Calvin College in Grand Rapids, Michigan, to test the city-of-bad-grammar theory of "solecism."

He said the Greek root was a general term for speech and acts deemed barbarous. He hadn't heard the theory about the settlers at Soloi, but he pulled up some apparent evidence for it at the Perseus Digital Library, a magnificent digital repository of ancient texts (www.perseus.tufts.edu).

Perseus serves up some early examples of "solecism," including Aristotle's use of "soloikizo" in his classic text *On Rhetoric* to refer to an error of syntax, and Roman historian Aulus Gellius' use of the Latin derivative "soloecismus" to mean "misprint."

The Perseus library also delivers sources that corroborate the story of Soloi. The influential Greek-English Lexicon of Liddell and Scott, for example, renders "soloikos" as "speaking incorrectly" and adds, "Derived from the corruption of the Attic [Athenian] dialect among the Athenian colonists of Soloi in Cilicia." I followed my finger to "solecism" in one of the big blue volumes of *The Oxford English Dictionary* at the Harold Washington Library and read the same story, attributed to "ancient writers."

There you have it. Case closed.

Except for one reference at Perseus that gave me pause. The entry for "Soloi" in *The Princeton Encyclopedia of Classical Sites* contains one sentence of caution: "That 'solecisms' are derived from the atrocious Greek spoken in Soloi is perhaps untrue, for the poets Philemon and Aratus . . . were natives."

How, indeed, could it be that a city known empire-wide for its sloppy speech also produced renowned poets? I called Jonathan Hall, chair of the classics department and Committee on the Ancient Mediterranean World at the University of Chicago. Turns out he was in Rome, so I e-mailed him my questions.

The problem with the story of Soloi, Hall replied, is not Philemon and Aratus. Aside from the fact that their birthplaces can be disputed, "There's a world of difference between 'high' literary prose and daily vernacular," he writes, adding that many Greek poets were fluent in both.

The real problem, Hall says, is that evidence for Soloi's reputation for bad Athenian Greek is scarce and may have been embellished by ancient historians. "The ancients constantly engaged in somewhat amateurish attempts to identify etymology," Hall writes by e-mail.

The earliest available usage of "solecism," Hall says, is by the 6th century B.C. poet Anakreon, in which he beseeches Zeus, as Hall translates, "to silence the solecian speech lest you utter barbarisms."

Whose speech Anakreon wants Zeus to silence, and why he calls it "solecian," is not known. Anakreon's poetry survives mostly in fragments whose context is forever lost, Hall says. "It is certainly possible that Anakreon had Cilician Soloi in mind," he adds, "but without more of his original verses we cannot be sure that [this] was not the product of a later writer's imagination."

Strangely, one century after Anakreon, the historian Herodotus uses "soloikizo" to mean "to speak bad Scythian"—another ancient language spoken clear across Asia Minor in what is now Iran.

Hall also writes that he doesn't know of any official Athenian settlement at Soloi. "While they did embark on disastrous expeditions to Egypt and Cyprus in the 5th century," he says, "the Athenians didn't really have an interest in southern Asia Minor." To make matters worse, Hall says some Greek historians seem to confuse the Soloi in Cilicia (near Mersin in present-day Turkey) with the city of Soloi in Cyprus, an island in the Mediterranean Sea.

In short, it's not clear who settled Soloi in Cilicia, what they spoke there, or how well. So how did the city-of-bad-grammar story about Soloi get started?

"I have no idea, but I wouldn't take it too seriously," Hall writes. Since Greek morphed into various dialects throughout its ancient empire, he observed, "it's difficult to understand why, objectively speaking, Soloi should have been deemed so infamous in this respect."

Even Strabo, a reputable Roman historian, wrote in the first century that he didn't know whether the Latin word "solecise" was "derived from [the city of] Soli, or made up in some other way."

This is where many word history expeditions end up: some

tempting theories, many tidbits and tangents, few solid conclusions.

As I console myself with this realization, I savor the irony of poor Joe Shepherd, age 12, who was ousted from the 2004 National Spelling Bee on the word "solecism." Joe started out "S-O-L-I"—which, alas, is the Latin name for Soloi—and was gone. It was a misspelling about misspeaking.

sort of

> I've been noticing "sort of," a meaningless phrase (related to "like"?) that I thought was a Britishism and is common in the parlance of academics, but I now hear everyone using it.
>
> —*Ellen Rosen, Chicago, Illinois*

THE PHRASE "sort of" started as "of a sort"—in other words, "of that kind" ("sort" is Latin for "lot, share, or category," according to *Merriam-Webster*). We still use this original meaning when we say, "Tom is the sort of person who takes his Christmas lights down in March." There is a group of people who leave their lights up till springtime, and Tom is one of them.

So "sort of" originally meant "one of those," but eventually took on the meaning of "somewhat similar to those," and today it can simply mean "somewhat."

"Tom is sort of lazy about taking down his Christmas lights." Tom is somewhat lazy, but not as lazy as the people who leave their lights up till May.

I assumed this use of "sort of" was informal—and I try to avoid it in published writing—but *The Oxford English Dictionary* finds "sort of" in Standard English as early as 1858, when William Pirie wrote this sentence in his book *An Inquiry Into the Constitution, Powers, and Processes of the Human Mind*: "One is a sort of bewildered in attempting to discover what it really is which constitutes the obligation."

This progression of the meaning of "sort of"—from "one of" to "somewhat similar" to "somewhat"—seems pretty natural to me. In fact, the same thing happened to "kind of."

The word "kind" started out meaning something like its cognate "kin"—family or group. Over time, "of a kind" morphed into "kind of," then "kind of" became "somewhat," and by 1804, according to the *OED*, one poet was writing, "I kind of love you, Sal—I vow."

Spanish and English use among Latin-American U.S. immigrants

MEXICAN-AMERICANS WERE the largest group of immigrants to the United States in the 1990s, according to the latest census. But even as their presence grows, Mexican-Americans do not represent a long-term challenge to the status of English as the primary language of the United States, says a 2005 study by researchers at the State University of New York at Albany.

In fact, if any language is losing ground in the United States, that language is Spanish, the study said. Most descendants of Latino immigrants speak only English.

"English is almost universally accepted by the children and grandchildren of the immigrants who have come to the U.S. in great numbers since the 1960s," said the study, which was conducted by the Lewis Mumford Center for Comparative Urban Research at SUNY-Albany. In the case of Mexican immigrants, the study said, "The very high immigration level of the 1990s does not appear to have weakened the forces of linguistic assimilation."

The study comes in the wake of Harvard political scientist Samuel Huntington's controversial book, *Who Are We? The Challenges to America's National Identity* (Simon & Schuster). The book asserts that immigration from Latin America, especially from Mexico, will divide the United States into two nations, one of them English-speaking, the other Spanish-speaking.

"This report makes that seem quite unlikely, at least in the near future," said Richard Alba, director of the Lewis Mumford Center, in an interview by telephone. "There would have to be radical changes in patterns of language assimilation for [Huntington's] predictions to come true."

The study found that while 85 percent of the children of Latino immigrants speak at least some Spanish at home, 92 percent of them speak English "well" or "very well." By the third generation or later, 72 percent of Latino Americans speak only English—up from 64 percent in the 1990 census.

The census data suggest that Latino immigration is following patterns evident throughout American history: Immigrant groups settle in ethnic neighborhoods and retain their native tongue, but their children begin to drop their parents' language and use English exclusively.

Compared with other current immigrant groups, the number of bilingual children of Spanish-speaking immigrants is somewhat higher. In the latest census, 85 percent of Latino immigrants' children are bilingual, compared with 61 percent of Asian immigrants' children. But the report also found that most Latinos who remain bilingual in the third generation and beyond live in communities along the Mexican border, in areas where Spanish was spoken long before settlement by English speakers.

So, Alba said, the warnings of Huntington—and of U.S. English, a Washington lobbying group that says English must be named the official language of the U.S. in order to encourage immigrants to learn it—are off the mark.

"It's the immigration phenomenon that is misleading people here," Alba said. "The pace of immigration has been increasing for the last 35 years, therefore Spanish speakers are becoming more and more prevalent. But this does not at all address whether or not [speaking Spanish] continues across generations. . . . [Latinos] recognize the need to be proficient in English, and proficiency levels are very high."

speed

See etymology.

spelling

PSYCHOLOGIST GREG Simpson was studying Korean with the help of a graduate student, a Korean native, when a thought struck him.

"You don't have spelling bees, do you?" Simpson asked her. He had to explain what they were.

"She kind of laughed and said, 'No, we wouldn't have that,'" Simpson recalls. "Then she paused and said, 'But I know why you have them.'"

Korean has a simple correspondence between spelling and sounds. English, with its many foreign influences and irregularities, does not.

"Spelling bees are largely an American phenomenon, something that is unique to the English language," says Paige Kimble, 1981 champion and director of the Scripps Howard National Spelling Bee. "We are simply not aware of any long-standing spelling bee programs in other languages."

Indeed, the major spelling bees that do exist around the world—everywhere from Mexico to Japan to Saudi Arabia—use English words, Kimble said.

"In almost every other language, spelling is phonetic. There are very few rules, and once you know those rules, spelling is straightforward," Kimble said. "English is this beautiful mess of words collected over centuries from languages all over the world. To become good spellers, English speakers have to learn a little bit about these languages and their patterns."

Simpson, who chairs the psychology department at Kansas,

SPANISH WORDS IN ENGLISH

Other than Old English, Latin, and French, which language has contributed the most words to the English language?

It's Spanish. And it's not just names for foods, such as "nacho" and "salsa," or names for dances such as "mambo" and "tango." For more than 500 years, the language of Spain has made its mark on English, as you can see in the 2007 book *Spanish Word Histories and Mysteries: English Words That Come From Spanish* (Houghton Mifflin), from American Heritage Dictionaries. Here are a few English words this book says descended from Spanish:

aficionado: from the Spanish word *aficionar*, meaning "to inspire affection"—which itself came from the Latin word "affectio," the same root word of the English word "affection." Originally referred in English to bullfighting fans.

has devised a way to study how the brain connects spelling to pronunciation. "There are two ways of getting to the pronunciation of a word," Simpson says. "One is to look the whole word up in your mental dictionary. The other way is to translate the letters into sounds and basically construct the pronunciation."

He has concluded that the more common the word, the more people tend to use the whole-word—or "lexical"—method to pronounce it. The rarer the word, the more people rely on the partial-word or "sub-lexical" method, mentally sounding it out.

Simpson found that English speakers take longer to react to rare words than Korean speakers react to rare Korean words. English speakers, he concludes, are fumbling around for the whole word; Korean speakers save time by using phonetics and sounding the word out.

Because their spelling rules are more consistent, Koreans are more likely to use them to pronounce a word, Simpson says.

"The degree to which fluent adult readers seem to be using their knowledge of the sound system varies among languages," Simpson said. "When the spelling of a word is a more reliable cue to how it can be pronounced, a reader might use that information more."

---

alligator: from *el lagarto*, meaning "the lizard," as the creature was called by 16th century Spanish explorers of Florida.

barbecue: from the Spanish word *barbecoa*, meaning a wooden rack used either to roast meat or as a makeshift platform for sleeping outside over wet ground.

cafeteria: Spanish word meaning "small restaurant," or literally, "coffee shop"—with *cafe* meaning "coffee" and the suffix *-eria* meaning "shop."

chocolate: Spanish word derived from the word *chicolatl* in Nahuatl, the language of the Aztec empire. That word was probably a compound of the Nahuatl words *chicolli*, meaning "long hooked stick," and *atl*, meaning "water," and referred to the Aztecs' stirring process for producing their chocolate beverage.

Not only does Korean have a more consistent sound system, but its alphabet actually provides visual clues to how to produce a sound, Simpson said.

"Look at our letters N, D, and T. Although their sounds are related—if you feel where your tongue is, you'll see it's in the same place for all of them—the letters don't look at all similar," Simpson said. "In Korean, sounds that are related are represented by letters that are visually similar to each other."

In a spelling bee, whole-word and partial-word recognition may both come into play, Simpson said. Contestants may recognize an entire word from the word lists they study beforehand, or they may try to take it syllable by syllable or ask for the word's

guerrilla: Spanish word meaning "little war," from the Spanish word "guerra" for "war."

guitar: Spanish word for the stringed instrument, from the Arabic word *qitara*, originally from the Greek *kithara*, for an ancient stringed instrument.

hurricane: from the Spanish *huracan*, for "tropical storm."

intransigent: from the Spanish *los intransigentes*, meaning "the uncompromising ones," originally the name for the 19th century opponents of the monarchy in Spain, ultimately derived from the Latin *transigere*, meaning "to settle, to make an agreement"—the same root word of our English word "transaction."

jalapeno: named for Xalapa, the capital of the Mexican state of Veracruz, known for the pepper with this name.

jerky: from the Spanish word *charqui*, likely from the word "ch'arki" ("dried meat") in Quechua, the language of the Inca empire.

macho: Spanish word for either a male animal or a man with qualities that are considered masculine. From the Latin *masculus*, meaning "male."

moment of truth: Hemingway probably introduced this phrase to English in his book *Death in the Afternoon* about bullfighting. The

language of origin, which the rules allow, in hopes of distinguishing between, say "-us" and "-ous."

Spelling bee contestants may lament English's opaque orthography when asked to spell words such as "euonym" or "succedaneum" (two winning words in recent years). But Simpson said we shouldn't necessarily disparage English spelling for its complexity.

"English starts taking a bad rap after a while," he said. "There are some characteristics of English spelling that suit it very well. For example, were we to start our spelling from scratch, we would not spell sign, S-I-G-N. However, if we change it, then the connection between the words 'sign' and 'signature' would be lost."

Spanish phrase for the decisive moment of a bullfight, he wrote, is *hora de la verdad*, literally meaning "hour of truth."

mosquito: Spanish word for "little fly," from the Spanish *mosca* for "fly."

rodeo: from the Spanish word *rodear*, meaning "to round up" or simply "to surround."

salsa: Spanish word for "sauce," from the Latin *salsus*, literally meaning "salted."

ten gallon hat: not a hat that stores water, but a hat that is decorated with *galons*, the Spanish word for decorative braids on a sombrero.

tornado: not from the Spanish word *tornar*, meaning "turn"—whose participle form is *tornado*—but actually from the Spanish word *tronada*, meaning "thunderstorm," related to the Spanish word *tronar* for "thunder." English explorers in the 16th century misspelled the word *tronada* as "ternado."

volcano: from the Spanish *volcan*, from the Latin name of the Roman god of fire, Vulcanus, who was believed to cause volcanic explosions.

spinster

THE WORD "spinster" was retired in 2005 by the British Government after centuries of use as the official term for a woman who has never been married. The male counterpart, "bachelor," also has been shelved. The Registrar General had used these terms on marriage certificates to describe the previous status of newlyweds. But now that homosexual couples can enter into what the Government calls "civil partnerships," the Registrar General wanted terminology that could apply to gay couples. From now on, an unmarried Brit, regardless of sexual orientation, will officially be called a "single."

"Spinster" was first recorded in the 14th century as the name for the occupation of spinning wool—a job usually done by a woman. Eventually both the job and the name became so associated with unmarried women that the British Government adopted it in the 17th century as the official title of an unmarried woman, according to *The Oxford English Dictionary*.

The word has never lost its connotations of social inadequacy that came, in centuries past, with being an unmarried woman beyond marrying age. "I can't feel the word is much of a loss," wrote British etymologist Michael Quinion at *World Wide Words* (www.worldwidewords.org), adding, it has been "a very long time since an unmarried woman referred to herself by this title in seriousness."

statistically improbable phrases

"CILICE BELT." "Sweater pocket." "Corporal mortification."

If you're reading those two-word phrases in a book, chances are the book is Dan Brown's *The Da Vinci Code*, according to a search feature from Amazon.com. In 2005, Amazon rolled out "statistically improbable phrases," or "SIPS," a feature that finds word pairs that are unusually common in a book compared with other books.

The feature only works for "Search Inside" books, whose publishers have granted Amazon permission to include their text in a searchable database. (Amazon won't say how many "Search

Inside" titles it has, only that the number "is in the hundreds of thousands.")

"SIPs are a fun discovery mechanism," says Bill Carr, vice president of digital media for Amazon. "It's a fun way for the customer to get a sense of key phrases and key concepts in a book. It's an unusual, unique wxay to get a flavor of the book."

The payoff for Amazon is that when you click on the SIP, you get a list of other books that have the same SIP, and you might want to buy them. Click on "electoral count," an SIP for David MacCullough's *John Adams*, and up pops a list of 14 books containing this SIP, such as Lloyd Robinson's *The Stolen Election: Hayes Versus Tilden 1876*.

Some SIPs are revealing ("old sport" in F. Scott Fitzgerald's *The Great Gatsby*), while others are numbing ("fossiliferous formations" in Charles Darwin's *Origin of Species;* "linearized fluctuations" in the book *Artificial Black Holes*).

But others aren't phrases at all. The one glitch in Amazon's algorithm appears to be that it doesn't take punctuation into account. So some of its word pairs aren't actually word pairs—they're words separated by commas, periods or even prepositions.

For example, "failed civilization" is an SIP in *Imperial Hubris* by Anonymous. Clicking on it leads to a reference to this phrase from John Entelis' *Islam, Democracy and the State in North Africa:* "The Ottomans failed as a civilization . . ."

That split at least yields a similar meaning, but others do not. Select "approval points" under Jon Stewart's *America (The Book)* (in which a pretend presidential board game tells players, "Lose three approval points"), and you find this sentence from Edmund Morris' *Theodore Rex:* "An occasional curt nod indicated his approval of points made in Taft's subsequent speech."

Amazon won't say what's in its algorithm. Carr says SIPs aren't subjective; Amazon doesn't have anyone double-checking the "improbable phrases." "It's not necessarily designed to have a human check element to verify whether a phrase is key to the book," Carr said. "The aim of the feature is to use mathematical, algorithm-derived phrases that occur more frequently in some books than in other books, and that will be interesting to customers. It's derived by math, not humans."

Two other Amazon features for "Search Inside" books are "Concordance," which lists the 100 most common words in a book, and "Text Stats," which lists several word statistics, including "words per sentence," "words per dollar" and the percentage of "complex words," defined as words with three or more syllables. "Text Stats" also lists the "Fog Index," a formula that uses the average sentence length and the number of complex words to generate an approximate grade level for the reading.

tawdry

See **etymology**.

than her

We had a friend who would stop people in midsentence to correct them on this, and I would like to know if she was right. She would correct people who said, "Anne is taller than her," telling them it should be, "Anne is taller than she." This doesn't sound right to me, but maybe it is because I have heard the common contracted form too many times. Was our friend right?

—*Ron Coates, Aurora, Illinois*

YOUR FRIEND has a case, but the basis of her case is so strange to me that her zeal seems out of place.

Standard English has indeed traditionally required "than she" because "she" is a subject of an imaginary clause—"than she is tall." But what person in her right mind would ever say, "Anne is taller than she is tall"? Who hears "You won't find a better woman than her," and understands it as, "You won't find a woman better than she is good"?

Because a clause such as "than she is tall" is usually imaginary and rather convoluted, people tend to prefer "than her." There's good grammatical reason for this; some linguists call "than" a preposition rather than a conjunction in this case, and a preposition takes an object rather than a subject.

The Cambridge Grammar of the English Language comes to the same conclusion with different terminology. It calls "than" a conjunction and "her" an "immediate complement." So next time someone says "Anne is taller than her," give them an immediate compliment.

that, as a demonstrative pronoun

Is it just me or does the Metra [passenger train service] announcement asking us to "add your eyes and ears to that of our own" sound odd? Or does Metra only have one ear and or eye?

—*Mary Beth Riley, Willowbrook, Illinois*

Dictionaries say the demonstrative pronoun "that" takes singular antecedents, while "those" takes plural ones—leading Metra passengers to imagine the speaker of this message as a cyclops.

Our language does allow comparisons of singular and plural noun phrases using the phrase "that of our own." NASA's website speaks of "stars of masses similar to that of our own Sun." But even when it follows a plural, the phrase "that of our own" points to a singular noun. The sun has one mass.

that, necessity of in relative clauses

As a copy editor, this issue has been driving me nuts. Is the use of the word "that" necessary in phrases such as "I found out recently that he crashed the car," or can one simply say "I found out recently he crashed the car"?

—*Kathryn Neumeister, Washington, D.C.*

This one bugs me all the time. As far as I know, there's no clear guideline. It's a matter of feel.

In most cases, "'that' is grammatically optional," according to *The Cambridge Grammar of the English Language*, which adds, "It is somewhat more likely to be omitted in informal than formal style, and when the [sentence is] short."

But the *Cambridge Grammar* says there are some relative clauses that can't live without "that." For example, if you change your sentence to "The car that crashed was his," then cutting "that" will make it sound strange. Or take the sentence, "I'll tell him that tomorrow things will get better." Without "that," we don't know whether "tomorrow" is when you'll tell him, or when things will get better.

these kind

More often than not, talking heads on TV, especially football color announcers, say "these kind of plays." Please make them stop.

—*David Smith, Glencoe, Illinois*

YOU VASTLY overestimate my power over TV announcers. But it's not just sportscasters who say "these type of things" or "these kind of things."

A search at Google Scholar, which searches academic articles, turns up thousands of examples like this one from the International Society for Optical Engineering: "Two places where these type of data sets can be found are. . ."

An article in the *Journal of Agricultural and Food Chemistry* reads, "However, reliable quantitative data . . . needed for these kind of studies are lacking."

The expected phrases would be similar to "these types of things" or "this kind of thing," with "this" matching "type" as a singular, or "these" matching "types" as a plural.

People who say "these type of things" are instead matching "these" and "things." They treat "type" as a modifier of "things" instead of the object of "these."

Another explanation is that this started with speakers dropping the "S" in "types" to avoid saying three of them in a row: "these type of things" rolls off the tongue a little more easily than "these types of things."

It doesn't stop there. The blogging linguists at *Language Log* have heard "these type things"—without the "of."

Paul Baker of the Celtic trio Brigid's Cross explained his band's eclectic musical style to the *Cleveland Plain Dealer* in May 2006 by saying, "It's a high-energy vibe type thing."

Theresa

I am doing genealogy. Another member of my family thinks that "Therese" or "Theresa" is an anglicized version of "Esther." Could you and would you shed some light on this for me or direct me to a good basic source book?

— *Mary Ann Lawson, Vernon Hills, Illinois*

AUTHOR GEORGE Thompson looked this up for me in *The Oxford Dictionary of English Christian Names*, a 1977 reference book that says the origin of the name "Theresa" is probably either the Greek verb "therizo," meaning "reap," or the Greek name "Therasia," for an island near Crete. The book says "Esther" is "the Persian equivalent of the Hebrew 'Hadassah,'" though it adds that others claim "Esther" is from the Persian "stara" for "star."

Thompson then found a more recent and comprehensive guide for names: the *Oxford Dictionary of First Names* by Patrick Hanks, Kate Hardcastle, and Flavia Hodges (Oxford University Press). It gives the same story for "Esther," but hedges on "Theresa," saying the name is "of problematic origin," but might have a connection to the Greek name for the island "Thera."

In any case, there doesn't seem to be any etymological connection between "Esther" and "Theresa."

they, singular

EVERYONE KNOWS he or she should mind his or her grammar.

Everyone also knows that saying "he or she" and "his or her" makes a simple sentence somewhat tedious and self-consciously politically correct, but that using only masculine pronouns is archaic and sexist.

Saying "everyone knows that they should mind" is widely considered a grammatical error because "everyone" is singular and "they" is plural—they don't match. Saying "one should mind one's grammar" is considered stuffy and impersonal. Saying "all people know that they" is overstating the case—"everyone knows" usually means conventional wisdom, not universal knowledge.

Enter Richard Neal, author of the book *The Definitive Solution to the Problem of Sexist Language: How and Why It Is Solved* (Sense & Reason). In 2003, Neal applied for a patent for his plan to replace the words "him," "his," and "her" with the word "hir" (which he pronounces as "here"), as well as "hesh" (pronounced "heesh") for "he" and "she" and "wan" for "man" and "woman." Neal's application was posted at the website of the U.S. patent office (www.uspto.gov).

"My patent primarily involves the transcription of texts," Neal says by phone. "I have an algorithm by which [these words] would be selected out. What I have in mind is to go back and modify texts, such as the Bible and other classical texts."

But getting computers to automatically extract sexism is no simple task, wrote Mark Liberman, professor of linguistics and computer science at the University of Pennsylvania, at *Language Log* (www.languagelog.org). There's no foolproof way, he said, for a computer to know how English pronouns are functioning in a sentence and when to replace them. Take the ambiguous phrase "gave her dog food": it could mean somebody gave dog food to a female or it could mean somebody gave food to a female owner's dog. As Liberman wrote, there are "problems in automatic text understanding that can't now be solved."

Even if the patent is approved, "hir" and company face an uphill battle. Contrived words thrive in slang and in reference to technology, but English speakers have been resisting innovations to our language's system of pronouns and possession for more than a century.

Several proposals for "epicene" (gender neutral) pronouns have been launched and crashed: Lawyer Charles Converse proposed the word "thon" in 1884. Twentieth century feminists submitted "tey" and "et," among more than a dozen others. None caught on. Even Neal's "hir" has been tried before; the online encyclopedia *Wikipedia* traces it back to 1981.

The simplest solution to the problem of finding an epicene

singular pronoun, linguists say, is already in the language—use "they." A singular "they" is nothing new. Writing at the *Random House* website, Jesse Sheidlower, North American editor of *The Oxford English Dictionary*, pointed out that many reputable writers used the singular "they." Shakespeare wrote in *Much Ado About Nothing*, "God send every one their heart's desire!" The King James Bible translated Matthew 18:35 as, "If ye from your hearts forgive not every one his brother their trespasses . . . "

Linguist Henry Churchyard lists these and other samples on his website (www.crossmyt.com/hc), including 75 citations from the works of Jane Austen. "Singular 'their' (etc.) is not an innovation, but old established good usage," Churchyard writes. "So here anti-sexism and traditional English usage go hand-in-hand."

Sheidlower adds that the singular "they" should be no more objectionable than the singular "you." English used to reserve "you" and "your" for plurals, and used "thou," "thy" and "thee" for the singular. But "thou" and the others dropped out, and "you" started pulling double duty. Eventually, "they" could, too, and "he or she" will be as old-fashioned as "thou."

through thick and thin

THE CHICAGO Bulls' slogan for their 2004–2005 season-ticket campaign was "Through Thick and Thin!"

The implication is clear: If you're a true fan, you stand by your team in good times and bad (and buy season tickets either way).

The slogan may seem to concede the team's prospects that year were not that good; there's little need, after all, to appeal to fans' endurance, patience, and loyalty if you anticipate a successful season. But the team has said the slogan is meant as a token of appreciation for Bulls fans, who have supported the team through recent losing seasons. It is not meant as a warning of things to come.

"In the last six years, we've compiled the worst six-year record in NBA history, in terms of wins and losses, and yet our attendance cumulatively has ranked No. 1 in the NBA," says Steve Schanwald, the Bulls' executive vice president of business operations, who helped come up with the slogan.

"The fans have supported us in good times and bad. We thought [the slogan] was a good tribute to our fans to illustrate how they have stuck with us no matter what."

But is the team worried the slogan suggests fans should prepare for another rocky year? "People can interpret things any way they want," Schanwald says. "The intention of the campaign is to say that Bulls fans have stuck with us in spite of our record."

One of the biggest questions about the phrase "through thick and thin" is exactly what "thick" and "thin" mean. "Most people, when they hear the phrase applied to anything, the word 'thick' means good times, and the word 'thin' means bad times," Schanwald says. Under this interpretation, a "thin" year is like a "lean year" (which *WordReference.com* defines as "not profitable or prosperous").

But *The Oxford English Dictionary* suggests the opposite is true. Its first citing of "thick and thin" is from Geoffrey Chaucer's *The Canterbury Tales* in 1386. When the horse runs away in "The Reeve's Tale," Chaucer writes, in his Middle English, "And forth with wehee, thurgh thikke and thurgh thenne" ("And with a 'whinny' he went, through thick and through thin").

The *OED* says the phrase can be interpreted to mean "through thicket and thin wood." So "thick" is the bad part—the dense portions of the woods where progress is most difficult. (This aligns with the meaning of the phrase "in the thick of it," meaning "the worst of it.")

"THICK and THIN are substantivized adjectives [adjectives that function as nouns] that apparently referred to a narrow passage and a clearing," e-mails Anatoly Liberman, linguist at the University of Minnesota. "When horse riders of chivalric romances

THOU, REPLACEMENT BY YOU
The 16th century was a tumultuous time for the pronoun "you," according to a 2005 article in the journal *Language Variation and Change*. The pronoun "ye" used to serve as a subject in English ("ye must"), while "you" was only used as an object ("for you"). But then "you" began pulling double duty, wrote Helena Raumolin-Brunberg of the University of Helsinki, in a study of written documents from the era. She found that in the early 16th century,

and knights errant had vanished, the origin of the metaphor was forgotten."

The phrase's staying power, Liberman says, owes in part to its consecutive "th"'s and single syllables. "The phrase joined a host of alliterating binomials like SPICK AND SPAN and SAFE AND SOUND," he writes.

The tidy pairing of opposites in "thick and thin," Liberman added, ensures the phrase communicates its meaning of "no matter what," even when its original references to good and bad, or "thicket and thin wood," have faded from view.

Still, maybe the medieval meaning could work just as well on a billboard. The Bulls could say: "We may not be out of the woods, but we hope you'll stay in the saddle."

throw for a loop

What are the origins of "it threw me for a loop"?

—*Kathy Kaiser, Joliet, Illinois*

THIS ONE threw me for a loop.

The Oxford English Dictionary's explanation doesn't satisfy me. The *OED* says that "loop" refers to the centrifugal (or "centripetal," to be exact) force exerted by a train, plane, or roller coaster when it travels in a loop, causing your head to spin. As *Aeroplane* magazine wrote in 1913, "Pegoud succeeded in looping the loop completely."

But that explanation strikes me as too specific. Could such an all-purpose phrase really have come from the laws of physics in air travel? Especially at a time—early in the 20th century—when

"you" served as a second-person subject less than 10 percent of the time, with "ye" making up the other 90 percent. But "you" pulled even with "ye" in the mid-1500s, and almost completely replaced it by the early 1600s. Raumolin-Brunberg says the change started in the middle social classes, then eventually became accepted as Standard English.

"aeroplanes" and roller coasters were in their infancy?

I would be less surprised if the "loop" we're wondering about is related to the word "looped," an early-20th century slang word for "drunk," but there's no evidence of that. (It's not clear, either, what's behind the word "loopy," meaning "crazy.")

Then there's "throw." The original phrase was "knock for a loop," and often referred to boxing. Most sources say "throw for a loop" emerged only in the last 30 years or so.

But when I asked Fred Shapiro, editor of the new *Yale Book of Quotations* (Yale University Press), about this phrase, he found some much older examples of "throw for a loop." The earliest he found was from the *Kingsport* (Tennessee) *Times* in 1937: "It isn't surprising that so many mothers are thrown for a loop when they discover that their little girls are beginning to be boy-conscious."

Air shows, boxing or intoxication? "Knock" or "throw"? My head is spinning.

till

Recently you used the phrase "people who leave their lights up till May" (*see* **sort of**). I have been under the impression that the word "till" may be used as a verb ("till the soil") or a noun ("put the money into the till") but that when one really means "until" one should use the shortened form, 'til.

—*James Wilson, Chicago, Illinois*

I USED to think so too, till (there it is again) linguist Geoffrey Pullum corrected this myth last year at *Language Log* (www.languagelog.org). "'Until' is actually an early 15th century embellishment of 'till,' made by adding 'on' before it (as in 'Keep right on till the end of the road')," he wrote. "Eventually the two merged into one word, and the two synonyms lived alongside each other happily ever after. The word 'till' is older, and has always been correct. It has never been a contraction or shortening."

Pullum said the same is true of "though" and "although."

titular line

> Just like "denouement" describes the point in a book where all the different plot lines are resolved, there is a term that describes where the title is first used, or where the reason for the title first becomes clear. I remember learning this in an advanced high school English Lit course but cannot recall the term. An example is in Chapter 10 of *To Kill a Mockingbird*, (with the first statement of the proverb), "It's a sin to kill a mockingbird."
>
> — *David Knutson, Gurnee, Illinois*

YOU STUMPED me and every literature professor and word expert I asked! If the term does exist, I trust a reader to supply it by e-mail.

Update: Mike Beran of Chicago was the only reader to supply the term "titular line," adding, "A good example is from the 1993 movie written by Quentin Tarantino, *True Romance:* 'To remain loyal when it's easier, even excusable, not to. . . . That's a true romance.'"

to hospital vs. to the hospital

> Why do Brits and Canadians go "to hospital" and Americans "to the hospital"?
>
> —*Candace Drimmer, Chicago, Illinois*

THIS CASE is interesting, because Americans do "go to school," "go to church," and "go to jail" (though seldom in one day). On the other hand, we "go to the airport," "go to the mall," and "go to the movies."

Essayist Lionel Deimel examines these examples at his website (www.deimel.org) and says he sees a pattern in how "the" is used. He compares the phrase "go to college"—which refers to the process of getting an education, with "go to the college," which means traveling to a particular school.

"In the absence of the article, 'go to' emphasizes not a physical destination, but participation in some process that takes place at such a destination, which is often an abstract 'place,' "Deimel concludes. "We go to school to learn, to church to worship, to jail to be punished, to court to obtain (or avoid) justice, and to town to experience urban life."

By this logic, Deimel says, "perhaps Americans should speak of 'going to hospital' if, for example, they are checking in to have an operation. If they are just visiting, on the other hand, they are surely 'going to the hospital.'"

I doubt that distinction will catch on, and I wonder about other cases where it doesn't apply. "Going to the mall," for instance, says more about beginning the process of shopping than it does about identifying a specific destination. Same with "going to the country." But Deimel might be on to something in looking at the difference between process and place.

But now it's late, and I'm going to the bed.

treason

"'TREASON' HAS been much in the news of late," wrote Dave Wilton in his *A Way With Words* newsletter (www.wordorigins.org). In fall 2006 the United States brought treason charges against an American citizen for allegedly working in al-Qaeda training camps. A month earlier, Iva Toguri, also known as "Tokyo Rose," died in Chicago; she was convicted of treason in 1949 but pardoned in 1977.

"The early sense of 'treason' means simply betrayal and does not have the specific meaning of betrayal of the state," Wilton wrote. Medieval law divided treason into "high treason"—crime against the state—and "petty treason,"—crime against a citizen—Wilton explained. Only "high treason" lasted, and became exclusively associated with the basic word "treason."

triennial

Is there a word for "three times a year?" I know that semiyearly means twice a year. I've heard the word "triannual" or "triennial" to mean three times a year, but "triennial" means every third year, right? I need to title a chart that shows students' scores on [reading tests] taken three times a year.

—Anita Koszyk, Northfield, Illinois

I LOOKED up "triennial" in *Merriam-Webster's Collegiate Dictionary* and *The American Heritage Dictionary*. Both define "triennial" as occurring once every three years or lasting three years. So "triannual" (three times a year) and "triennial" (every three years) can follow the same distinction as "biannual" (twice a year) and "biennial" (once every two years). But the distinction is so obscure that it's best to simply say either "three times a year" or "every three years."

troop

Recently, the media's use of the word "troop" has left me confused. I always thought that the word was a plural, like "bunch" is. However, glaring headlines have begun declaring facts such as "65 troops killed in Iraq."

— Julie Stone, Darien, Illinois

"TROOP" HAS always meant more than one, from its origins in the French "troupe"—a word that we still use in English for a group of actors. Some sources even suggest a link between "troop" and the archaic English word "thorp," meaning "village."

The informal use of "troop" to mean "one soldier" may have been popularized in the Vietnam era. *The Oxford English Dictionary*, which added the definition for "troop" of "a soldier, a trooper" in 1993, labeling it "colloquial," quotes Tim O'Brien's 1973 book *If I Die in Combat Zone:* "You don't smoke dope, do you, troop?" ("No, no sir!")

This new wrinkle might have been picked up by journalists from the military. Or it might have arisen out of necessity; technically, "soldiers" only serve in the Army, not the Navy, Marines, or Air Force, and the generic "servicemen" is sexist.

Or this might be a case of what linguists call "back-formation": Because the plural "troops" means "a lot of soldiers (or military personnel)," people go on to assume the singular form must mean "one."

Whatever the source, the new use of "troop" made possible a 2006 headline in the satirical newspaper, *The Onion*, under a picture of a single soldier: "Kuwait deploys troop."

truthiness

IN ITS 16th annual vote on the words of the year, the American Dialect Society voted "truthiness" as the word of the year for 2005. The ADS defined "truthiness," which was coined on the satirical "Colbert Report" on Comedy Central, as "the quality of stating concepts or facts one wishes or believes to be true, rather than concepts or facts known to be true." Colbert defines "truthiness" as "truth that comes from the gut, not books." The Associated Press' report on the ADS voting failed to credit host Stephen Colbert with the coinage, leading him to pretend to fume on air, "I'm not mentioned, despite the fact 'truthiness' is a word I pulled right out of my keister," and accuse the AP reporter of a "sleaz[y] piece of yellow journalism."

"Truthiness" was voted the word of the year for 2006 by visitors to the website of Merriam-Webster. Michael Quinion wrote at *World Wide Words* (www.worldwidewords.org) that the word "triumphed by such a large [ratio], 5 to 1, that an unbiased observer must wonder about the possibility of ballot-stuffing. That would be fitting for a word that means the quality of stating concepts or facts that one wishes or believes to be true rather than those known to be true."

Despite its apparent popularity, "truthiness" doesn't yet meet Merriam-Webster's requirements to get into the dictionary. The word hasn't graduated to general use on its own; it mostly pops up in conjunction with Colbert.

By the way, Colbert wasn't the first to use the word. *The Oxford English Dictionary* cites this quote from 1824: "Everyone who knows her is aware of her truthiness." But here, "truthiness" simply meant "truthfulness."

try and vs try to

See **could care less vs. couldn't care less.**

uber

IT TOOK less than three years for advertisers to shelve the word "metrosexual." Advertising executive Marian Salzman and two co-authors popularized the word in a 2003 book about marketing to a new kind of male customer, the "metrosexual"—a man who is straight but sensitive and fashion-conscious, traits that popular culture stereotypically considers feminine or homosexual.

In 2007 Salzman and her co-authors published *The Future of Men* (Palgrave Macmillan), and a new term—"ubersexual." Their top three ubersexuals are Bono, George Clooney and Bill Clinton—guys who feel your pain but whose heterosexual orientation is unambiguous.

Ubersexual "marks a return to the positive characteristics of the Real Man of yesteryear (strong, resolute, fair)," the authors write. "We chose 'uber' as the descriptor because of its connotations of being the greatest, the best. In our view, these men are the most attractive (not just physically), most dynamic, and most compelling men of their generations."

The German prefix *uber* lives an extravagant lifestyle in English. In German, *uber* generally just means "over," "above," or "across." The phrase *uber die Strasse*, for example, means "across the street," and the word *Uberblick* means "overview."

But *uber* has a history of rising above its humble status as a mere grammatical marker. Philosopher Frederick Nietzsche coined the word *Ubermensch*—literally "over man"—in the 19th century, to describe an exceptional man who rises above organized religion to determine his own moral code. George Bernard Shaw translated the word as "superman," and later the Superman comic book character picked up the term and gave "super"—and, by extension, *uber*—the sense of "heroic."

Now *uber* has taken on a life of its own in English, though in English coinages, the word is usually written without the umlaut—the two dots over the "U" that denote the German pronunciation of the vowel—and pronounced in an un-German-like way, "oo-ber." (Some insist the German prefix should be spelled "ueber" if the umlaut is not written.)

The New Oxford American Dictionary defines "uber" as "denoting an outstanding or supreme example of a particular kind of person or thing," giving the examples "uberbabe" and "uber-regulator." Google turns up words such as "uber geek" and "uber scholar." When ESPN unveiled its new online fantasy sports contest, which compiles contestants' scores from each of their fantasy sports teams, it named the game "Uber."

The Future of Men may continue to turn "uber" from a prefix into an adjective, just as "super" can now stand alone (as in, "That's super!"). "I think it will," Salzman says by phone. "I've been doing it myself, saying, 'They're not metro; they're uber.'"

If so, it will mark a transformation of "uber" from its German meaning and usage, says David Smith, professor of German at Calvin College in Grand Rapids, Michigan, and editor of the *Journal of Christianity and Foreign Languages*.

"Foreign words have an aura of mystique and deeper meaning, even if they're more mundane in their original language," Smith says. "They tend to get used in ways that make them sound a little more out of the ordinary than English words."

"Maybe American English is running out of superlatives," adds Smith, a British native. "In England, we tend to understate. Americans tend to overstate."

um and uh

WE LOOK down on "um," "uh," and other speech malfunctions, but they're integral parts of language, says Michael Erard in his 2007 book *Um . . . : Slips, Stumbles, Verbal Blunders, and What They Mean* (Knopf).

"Our ordinary speech is notoriously fragmented, and all sorts of verbal blunders swim through our sentences like bubbles in champagne," Erard writes. His term "verbal blunders" covers both "slips of the tongue," when we flub a word that we know, and "speech disfluencies," when "uh" and "um" invade our sentences and stop them in their tracks.

244   Verbal blunders happen as often as once every 10 spoken

words, by some measurements, for a total of more than 1,000 per person, per day. Erard said media coverage of George W. Bush's flubs during the 2000 presidential campaign launched him into the field of study he calls "applied blunderology."

Blunderology may have begun with Sigmund Freud, whose psychoanalysis gave us the idea of the "Freudian slip"—saying a wrong word that supposedly reveals what you're really thinking about, like saying "had sex" instead of "had success." But Erard tells the story of linguist Ruldolf Meringer, a contemporary and critic of Freud's, who insisted that slips were mostly sound mix-ups, not psychological revelations. Meringer said sound slips can be "forward errors," when we insert a sound too early, like "fish those shingles" instead of "fix those shingles" (anticipating the "sh" sound), or "backward errors," when we repeat a sound from an earlier word, like "phone flan" instead of "phone plan" (repeating the "ph" sound).

Today, scientists tend to agree with Meringer's views that slips are mere malfunctions, but the idea of the Freudian slip as a revelation lives on.

While slips of the tongue are the most famous kind of verbal blunders, disfluencies such as "um" are more common—and, Erard says, more interesting. "They happen because talking is an activity that takes place in time, and disfluencies are signs of the inevitable friction between thinking and speaking," Erard writes. He says that selecting and speaking from the thousands of words in our vocabularies at lightning speed is a feat that's almost impossible to execute flawlessly.

"Grabbing these words, one every four hundred milliseconds on average, and arranging them in sequences that are edited and reviewed [by us] for grammar and appropriateness before they're spoken requires a symphony of neurons working quickly and precisely," Erard writes.

And so Erard argues that we should see "um" and "uh" as natural byproducts of the complicated process of speaking—not necessarily signs of low intelligence, anxiety or deception. (Disfluencies may mark anxiety or deception only when their rate increases in a person's speech, not merely by showing up in a

245

person's speech, Erard says.) "In general, anyone who thinks or acts at the same time as they speak, especially under pressure, will blunder," Erard concludes. "They are, in the term of the actuarial tables, 'normal accidents.'"

Still, Erard says, studying verbal blunders has made him more careful in his own speech. "Now, I speak slowly, in a way that some would call saturnine," he writes. "I make my points, but I take my time getting there.

unnecessary quotation marks

BETHANY KEELEY, the blogger behind *The "Blog" of "Unnecessary" Quotation Marks* (quotation-marks.blogspot.com), says she isn't a member of the punctuation police and doesn't want to be.

"The grammar police want to claim me for themselves, but they're never going to get me on board," Keeley says by phone. That's because her punctuation spying is purely for fun, not anger management, says Keeley, a doctoral student in rhetoric at the University of Georgia.

Keeley collects pictures of signs that use quotation marks in questionable places, and posts them on her blog. She finds it entertaining to pretend that quotation marks that are used for emphasis instead indicate insincerity, sarcasm, or euphemism.

For example, when a reader submitted a photo of a hotel sign telling guests, **Please "Do Not Remove" our guest towels**, Keeley imagined the quotation marks made the phrase sarcastic. "Maybe they say 'Do Not Remove' because they really mean 'go ahead and take them, so we can charge you outrageous prices for them,'" she wrote.

A reader in Milwaukee sent in a picture of a sign that read, **Floor Space For Rent: "Reasonable"—Inquire Within**, with the quotation marks making you wonder how reasonable the rates really are. A sign at a Super 8 in Sioux Falls, S.D., told customers Your cooperation is "sincerely appreciated," but the quotation marks made the sign seem anything but sincere.

A recent wave of attention in 2007 boosted traffic to Keeley's blog and made Keeley—whom I know from Calvin College in Grand Rapids, Michigan, which we both attended—an unlikely blogger celebrity. In the span of one month, Keeley's blog was the Pick of the Day at *Yahoo!* (picks.yahoo.com), and was featured in an Associated Press report that appeared on the websites of *The New York Times* and *The Washington Post*.

The AP headline read, "Blogger 'Exposes' Annoying Quote Abuse," but Keeley says she isn't annoyed and doesn't consider questionable quotes a matter of abuse. She's uneasy about being celebrated by supporters of Lynne Truss, the acerbic author of the best-selling screed *Eats, Shoots and Leaves*, who cheekily threatens bodily harm to punctuation perps. "In most cases I'm intentionally misinterpreting people," Keeley says. "What they mean to say is clear. I'm mostly just trying to have a little fun with language."

Even before he knew about Keeley's blog, linguist John McWhorter wrote an opinion article in the *New York Sun* arguing that quotation marks can be considered legitimate indications of emphasis in non-standard English (especially on hand-written signs, where bold and italics are difficult to use).

"Call it the new boldface," McWhorter wrote. "It is an understandable mistake. Quotations set off something, and it's a short step from setting something off to emphasizing it."

I asked McWhorter if it's still reasonable to chuckle at emphatic quotation marks, even if the usage is understandable. "It's a little snobbish, but we're all human," McWhorter says by phone.

"If I see a sign that says, quote, 'Fine Food,' I can't help but laugh at that," he said. "But I also can laugh while knowing it does not make [the writers of the sign] stupid—they consider themselves to be applying an alternate rule."

usage

The American Heritage Guide to Contemporary Usage and Style (Houghton Mifflin), by the editors of the American Heritage Dictionaries, is more than an authority on language usage: It's more than 100 authorities on language usage.

The advice in the guide—which is a significantly expanded and updated version of the 1996 *American Heritage Book of English Usage*—comes in part from a 2005 survey of the 175-member

American Heritage Dictionary Usage Panel, an assortment of novelists, poets, journalists, politicians, scholars and other arbiters of Standard English.

The book has more than 1,000 alphabetized entries of words and phrases, from "a/an" to "zoology." Many entries cover what the guide calls "controversies and conundrums" in English usage.

The panel, originally formed in the 1960s, now includes authors such as Harold Bloom and Anne Tyler, poets such as Diane Ackerman and Robert Pinsky, humorists such as Garrison Keillor and David Sedaris, and political figures such as former U.S. Senator Bill Bradley and current U. S. Supreme Court Justice Antonin Scalia.

UNTRANSLATABILITY INTO ENGLISH

The meaning of *tingo*, in the Pascuense language of Easter Island, is "to borrow things from a friend's house, one by one, until there's nothing left," according to Adam Jacot de Boinod in his 2006 book *The Meaning of Tingo and Other Extraordinary Words From Around the World* (Penguin Press).

A researcher for a BBC quiz show, de Boinod says he got hooked on foreign dictionaries, especially when he found an Albanian dictionary that listed 27 different words for "eyebrow." Since then, de Boinod writes, he has thumbed through hundreds of foreign dictionaries and millions of words to collect his favorite foreign words that have no simple equivalent in English.

In the tradition of Howard Rheingold's 1988 book *They Have a Word for It: A Lighthearted Lexicon of Untranslatable Words and Phrases*, (Severn House Publishers), de Boinod's *Meaning of Tingo* is even more whimsical, with comical illustrations (and some off-color categories). English has borrowed so many words from other languages, de Boinod writes, that it's amazing we didn't borrow these words too.

aimerpok: Inuit for visiting and expecting food.

alamnaka: Ulwa (a language in Nicaragua) for meeting a soulmate.

"There really is a kind of information you can get from these people that you can't get anywhere else," says Geoffrey Nunberg, a linguist who teaches at the Berkeley School of Information and chairs the usage panel. "These panelists have a long history of fretfulness over these questions. . . . They represent an educated opinion among people whose business it is to use the language."

The panel provides expert advice, but some cases still end up far from closed. In 1987, the usage panel split 50-50 on the question of whether to emphasize the first or second syllable of the word "harass." In a more recent survey, 70 percent favored the stress on the second syllable, but you're still in distinguished company if you stress the first.

ataoso: Central American Spanish for a person who always finds fault.

berhane: Turkish for an impractically large house.

berlenggang: Indonesian for walking gracefully by swinging your hands or hips.

bettschwere: German for lacking the energy to get out of bed.

biras: Malay for how the spouses of two siblings are related.

blart: Ullans (a language in Northern Ireland) for falling in the mud.

buchipluma: Caribbean Spanish for someone who promises but doesn't follow through.

cavoli riscaldati: Italian for "reheated cabbage," meaning to try to revive a former love affair.

curglaff: A Scottish dialect word for the shock of cold water when you first jump in.

dialogue des sourds: French for "dialogue of the deaf," meaning a conversation in which people are talking past each other.

gumusservi: Turkish for the reflection of moonlight on water.

When the panel's responses change over time, it often shows that English itself is changing. In 1967, for instance, 93 percent of the panel disapproved of the use of the word "enormity" to mean "large in size," saying the word should only mean "morally objectionable in its extremes" (as in "the enormity of Pol Pot's oppression"). Now that the broader sense of "enormity" has become more common, only 59 percent of the panel objects to "enormity" used in that way. "It can be interesting to look at how judgments do change," Nunberg says. "When you hand these questions to the panel, it gives you a quantitative sense of how strong the objection is, and whether educated users agree."

When members of the panel disagree, both the majority and minority views are significant. The majority tells you what

harawata o tatsu: Japanese for "to sever one's intestines," meaning to break the heart of a lover.

iktsuarpok: Inuit for repeatedly going outside to check for a visitor.

kummerspeck: German for "grief bacon," meaning the weight you gain from overeating out of sadness.

lagom: Swedish for a desirable lack of extremes, a happy medium.

lledorweddle: Welsh for lying down and propping yourself up on an elbow.

nedovtipa: Czech for someone who doesn't take a hint.

neko-neko: Indonesian for someone whose creative solution ends up making the situation worse.

nggregeli: Indonesian for dropping something out of nervousness.

presezeny: Czech for stiffness from sitting in the same position for too long.

an educated English speaker will most likely expect you to say or write. But the minority shows that even experts can validate a change or an exception to a rule. The introduction to the guide points out that English has always had "conflict between ongoing language change and the conventions of publishing," because the uses and meanings of words are constantly evolving.

In some cases, the editors of the guide take issue with the panel. For instance, the guide observes that the original meaning of "disinterested" was "not interested"—before the word developed its now preferred sense of "unbiased." "Despite this history, the 'not interested' usage has never had many fans on the usage panel," the guide says. In four surveys over 35 years, nearly 90 percent of the panel has disapproved of the older sense of "disin-

---

pulir hebillas: Central American Spanish for "to polish belt buckles," meaning to dance closely.

razblyuto: Russian for the feeling toward someone you no longer love.

sausade: Portuguese for longing for what might have been, or used to be.

torschlusspanik: German for "gate-closing panic," meaning the fear of vanishing opportunities while getting older.

utsura-utsura: Japanese for drifting between being awake and being half-asleep.

viajou na maionese: Portuguese for "to travel in the mayonnaise," meaning to live in a dream world.

waal: Afrikaans for the back of the knee.

waham: Arabic for the specific food craving of a pregnant woman.

yerdengh-nga: Wagiman (an Australian language) for leaving without telling anyone where you're going.

terested" every time. And so, while using "disinterested" to mean "not interested" is historically justified, the guide warns that this is "likely to be viewed as a sign of ignorance of the traditional use of the word."

The case of "hopefully" as a so-called "sentence adverb" (as in, "Hopefully, they'll go soon") brings up another disagreement between the guide's editors and their panel's verdict. Picky purists insist that "hopefully" should only mean "full of hope," and that "We hope" or "It is to be hoped that" should be used in other cases. Opposition to this use of "hopefully" has risen among the panel over the years.

The guide points out that nobody seems to mind when "mercifully" or "frankly" are used as sentence adverbs (as in, "Frankly, he bothers me"). In fact, the same panel that frowns on "hopefully" approves, by a vast majority, the similar use of "mercifully." The guide says there's no good grammatical reason to reject one and accept the other. "It would seem, then, that it is not the use of 'hopefully' as a sentence adverb per se that bothers the panel," the guide concludes. "Rather, 'hopefully' seems to have taken on a life of its own as a sign that the writer is unaware of the canons of usage."

Nunberg says that while the panel has generally grown more lenient on many usage questions over the years, some words such as "hopefully" are stigmatized as telltale signs of oblivion or indifference to standards of formal English. "They become social *faux pas*, like showing up in a brown suit," Nunberg says. But he adds that everyone has pet peeves when it comes to English usage. "Even the most comprehensive usage book can have [only] 1,000 entries," Nunberg says. "The number of possible English infelicities is infinite. . . . Everyone has their bugbears and points they don't like."

See also **correctness**; **grammar, descriptive**; **National Grammar Day**; **pedantry**; and **prepositions, ending sentences with.**

Verbatim

WHEN DICTIONARY editor Erin McKean got a phone call inviting her to become editor of *Verbatim*, a quarterly journal on language written for a general audience, she thought it was too good to be true. In fact, she almost hung up the phone.

"I got a phone call out of the blue, and there was this very distinctive voice saying, 'I'd like you to edit *Verbatim*,'" McKean recalls. "I thought it was a practical joke. This is where being a polite Southerner helped me. Otherwise I would have just hung up on him."

It was no hoax. McKean, a North Carolina native, has edited *Verbatim*—a delectable, unpredictable, consistently interesting language magazine—from her brownstone on Chicago's North Side ever since. *Verbatim* celebrated its 30th volume in 2005, beginning with its belated spring and summer 2005 issues.

These issues provided a juicy taste of what *Verbatim* serves. Etymologist Dave Wilton wrote about the slang of the Hollywood trade magazine *Variety* ("'King' Nips Ship With 11 Noms," Wilton says, translates as "'Return of the King' beats out 'Master and Commander' with 11 Academy Award nominations").

In a cover article on the sizable linguistic contributions of *The Simpsons*, etymologist Mark Peters rounded up words invented on the show, and analyzes Homer Simpson's use of what linguists call "infixes"—insertions in the middle of a word, such as Homer's "edu-ma-cation." "[Some] infixes work mostly as intensifiers, but the purpose of some infixes is a little less clear," Peters wrote. In Homer's case, "they do add a certain flavor or connotation—a Homerish buffoon flavor." And yes, Peters includes three paragraphs on "Flandersisms," the idiolect of Homer's neighbor, Ned Flanders.

Elsewhere, authors tackled subjects such as corporate English, language loss, the slang of fan fiction, the coinage of bird names, euphemisms for death, "Family Expressions Deserving Wider Recognition" and "How to Tawk Like a New Yawker." One of the briefest and most entertaining features of the magazine is "Sic! Sic! Sic!," an ongoing collection of typos and malapropisms spotted by readers, such as a recent headline at Google News about a "runaway bridge" (instead of "runaway bride").

"*Verbatim* is old enough to know better, yet young enough to take risks," McKean wrote in the spring 2005 issue. "*Verbatim* certainly realizes that there is plenty it doesn't know, but still energetic enough to muster some enthusiasm for finding out. *Verbatim* is settled in its habits, but not set in its ways, and is very much in the prime of its life."

Verbatim (www.verbatimmag.com) began as a newsletter for publishing companies. Founder Laurence Urdang distributed the newsletter with a cover letter promoting the services of his dictionary editing company. He also founded Verbatim Books (www.verbatimbooks.com), publisher of language reference books.

"I thought I should prepare a newsletter on all aspects of language," Urdang says by phone from his home in Old Lyme, Connecticut. Urdang said he envisioned a publication "that would not be a technical journal like *Language* or *American Speech*, but something that would cater to the interests of people who were interested in language certainly above the level of [*New York Times* "On Language" columnist] William Safire, but not at the level of the Linguistics Society of America." Urdang edited *Verbatim* for 23 years, while McKean was becoming an avid reader.

"I always loved the magazine. I started reading it while in high school, procrastinating in the Wake Forest library, not writing papers in European history," McKean said in an interview at *Verbatim* headquarters in her brownstone basement. There, amid shelves, crates and stacks of boxes jammed with reference books, folders and back issues of *Verbatim*, McKean carries on her dual lexicographical roles: *Verbatim* editor and editor in chief of U.S. dictionaries for Oxford University Press. "Oxford takes 110 percent of my time, but the other 40 percent is *Verbatim* time," McKean explains.

Verbatim has nearly 1,500 subscribers in the U.S. and about 300 overseas, McKean says. A U.S. subscription for four 30-plus-page issues per year costs $25. The magazine is printed on light beige paper with handsome brown type.

McKean says the magazine has succeeded by targeting a general audience but not watering down its subject matter. "It's geared toward laypeople, but I belong to the Council of Editors of Learned Journals," McKean says. "It's not literary, not scholarly—it's kind of a no-man's-land." And yet, the magazine has found its niche as a serious general interest magazine on language, McKean says: "It's a good place to be. Once people find us, they hold on with both hands."

After the first two 30th-volume issues shipped, McKean said she was looking forward to a new milestone. "I would love to see *Verbatim*'s centennial," she says. "That's a good reason to live to 103."

McKean muses about what the centennial issue might contain. "Robot slang. Martian English. How will skull-phone texting change lunar English? Idioms of the methane beings of Titan. I can see us doing that."

wait on vs. wait for

When I was in junior high school in the 1950s, I had a teacher who distinguished between "wait on" and "wait for." He said "Waitresses wait on people. You wait for your friend." Has language evolved away from this distinction or was my teacher incorrect in his teaching?

—*Diane Spanier, Northbrook, Illinois*

THE AMERICAN Heritage Dictionary of Phrasal Verbs (Houghton Mifflin) gives this as its second definition for "wait on": "to await someone or something: 'They're waiting on my decision.'"

In 1996, the *American Heritage Book of English Usage* wrote that language critics "have grumbled about this for more than 100 years," but added that saying "wait on" to mean "wait for" is in "widespread use . . . among educated speakers and writers."

In its infancy, the word "wait" appeared by itself and could mean either "await" or "serve," often with ominous undertones. According to *The Oxford English Dictionary*, John Leslie's *History of Scotland*, published in the 16th century, read: "He therefore appointed certain cutthroats to wait them as . . . they returned." Two centuries earlier, Chaucer wrote, "Certainly it would be [treason] to wait him villainy." Today, if your waiter is ever villainous, you can withhold the tip.

WASP

> Why, nowadays, when I see the word "WASP" used to refer to a certain social-racial-religious lineage, the word is written as "Wasp"? Shouldn't acronyms always be all-caps, to reflect that each letter stands for a word? Do you think, as I do, that younger readers perhaps think that the word means "stinging" or "mean" rather than "White Anglo-Saxon Protestant?"
>
> —*Marie Tuohy, Libertyville, Illinois*

SOME ACRONYMS become so common that they take on all-lowercase forms. The words "scuba," "radar," and "laser" all began as acronyms and became words. "WASP" isn't there yet, but it may be on its way.

The New Oxford American Dictionary is the only major dictionary to list "Wasp" (with "W" as the only capital letter) as the primary form of this word, with "WASP" (all capital letters) as the alternate form. *The American Heritage Dictionary* has "Wasp" as the alternate form. Most other major dictionaries only recognize this word with all capital letters.

Webster, Noah

PEOPLE OFTEN introduce a definition of a word by saying, "Webster says . . . "

The truth is, Noah Webster himself—the founder of American lexicography, or dictionary-making—hasn't actually "said" anything since his death in 1843. The fact that so many people speak of Webster in the present tense while knowing next to nothing about the man sets up an apparent contradiction: Noah Webster is a little-known household name.

"He is probably one of the least known of the Founding Fathers," says John Morse, president and publisher of Merriam-Webster Inc., by phone. "His fame as a dictionary-maker overshadows a lot of his other accomplishments." Morse spent 2006 trying to reintroduce America to one of its most influential historical figures. He went on a speaking tour to commemorate the 200th anniversary of Noah Webster's very first dictionary, *A*

Compendious Dictionary of the English Language.

"Noah was one of the most influential political thinkers going into the Constitutional Convention. Just about every delegate had read his tract *Sketches of American Policy* and was influenced by it," Morse said, noting that George Washington and James Madison picked Webster's brain about how to set up a government.

Webster's political involvement has contributed to popular confusion over two famous Websters of the era—lexicographer Noah and New England lawyer and statesman Daniel Webster, one of the great orators of his day. (The two may have been distantly related; biographers disagree.)

Though Noah Webster might have preferred to go down in history as a political philosopher rather than a dictionary-maker, those two jobs were closely related, Morse says. "The dictionary is the quintessential democratic document," Morse said. "The question I'm always asked is, 'Who determines what words get in the dictionary?' Well, we the English-speaking people collectively determine it."

Webster loathed linguistic elitism, which struck him as being too British. To Webster, the dictionary was never a book to tell people how to use language, but a book to tell them how they already were using it. So it's ironic when purists today appeal to a dictionary to try to prove that someone is saying or writing something "wrong," Morse said.

"[Webster] believed that the true determiner of correctness is the usage of the large body of people in a society—not edicts from an individual or the habits of a privileged social class," Morse said.

Webster's 1806 *Compendious Dictionary of the English Language* was not his magnum opus. His 1783 *American Spelling Book* (popularly known as the "Blue-backed Speller") was by far his biggest commercial success, while his 70,000-entry *American Dictionary of the English Language* in 1828 sealed his legacy in lexicography. But it was the *Compendious Dictionary* that struck a balance between Webster's bold ideas for spelling and vocabulary, and his pragmatic concessions to tradition.

The 1806 dictionary also introduced some of Webster's biggest imprints on the language. Webster was the first English lexicographer to recognize "J" and "V" as separate letters of the alphabet rather than as alternate forms of "I" and "U." Before Webster, English dictionaries commonly interspersed "J" words throughout the "I" section—the entry for "ice" came after "jangle"; "jealous" followed "idiot" and so forth—while "V' words appeared under "U."

Webster added words to reflect the new influences of Native American and political terms on English being spoken in the former colonies—"hickory," "skunk," "wigwam," "presidential" and "lengthy," to name just a few. He also simplified some spellings that broke from British norms: "honor" instead of "honour," "music" rather than "musick," center" and not "centre," "racket" for "racquet," and "ax" for "axe."

Webster actually had much more ambitious spelling reforms in mind, many of which eventually failed—his 1828 dictionary still insisted on "tung" for "tongue" and "aker" for "acre." In his early years, Webster wrote that when it comes to simplifying our spelling, "there iz no alternativ."

Morse has both patriotic and commercial reasons to spread the word about Noah Webster's life and legacy. There has been a wrestling match over use of the Webster name on reference books ever since the lexicographer's death. After Noah Webster died, Springfield, Massachusetts, publishers George and Charles Merriam purchased the rights to Noah Webster's dictionaries, but not—in the opinion of later court rulings—the rights to Webster's name.

"The name has always been a problem," Morse said. "Merriam-Webster publishes the works that are based on Noah Webster, but does not have exclusive rights to the name 'Webster.' Anybody can write a dictionary and call it 'Webster,' and there's nothing we can really do about it."

Morse says the strategy of his company, which is still based in Springfield, is to emphasize the "Merriam" part of its name, and to use cover design to set its products apart. (Merriam-Webster also owns and uses the Web address www.webster.com.)

"Reinforcing the notion of 'Merriam-Webster dictionaries' has been a very important project for us," Morse said. "I think it still is the case that a large portion of the population thinks that all those 'Webster's' dictionaries somehow come from the same company. It's crucial because while some of the other 'Webster's' dictionaries are perfectly fine dictionaries, there are also some terrible dictionaries out on the market called 'Webster's.'"

Windy City

"THEY DON'T call it the Windy City for nothing," said an ESPN announcer during a 2006 Northwestern football game, as the camera showed the wind whipping the flags atop Ryan Field.

But why *do* they call it the "Windy City"? Consult most tour books or talk to city history buffs, and they'll gleefully point out that the nickname "Windy City" originally referred not to lake breezes but to Chicago's long-winded politicians.

The Chicago Public Library supports this definition. "In the early part of the nineteenth century, Chicago promoters went up and down the East Coast loudly promoting Chicago as an excellent place to invest. Detractors claimed they were full of wind," the library says on its website.

"Later, Chicago and New York were competing to hold the 1893 World's Columbian Exposition. Charles A. Dana, editor of the *New York Sun*, wrote an editorial advising against the 'nonsensical claims of that windy city. Its people could not hold a world's fair even if they won it.' This editorial is widely credited with popularizing the 'Windy City' nickname."

The Chicago Historical Society's website agrees that Dana "dubbed" Chicago the "Windy City." So do at least three pictorial guides to Chicago displayed at area bookstores, as well as Joel Greenberg's *A Natural History of the Chicago Region* (University of Chicago Press) and Erik Larson's bestseller set in Chicago at the time of the Columbian Exhibition, *The Devil in the White City* (Crown). The Dana explanation has been printed over and over in the *Chicago Tribune*, the *Chicago Sun-Times*, and *The New York Times*.

There's just one problem. The Dana editorial is nowhere to be found, and no one can prove it was ever written. Etymologists say it's just a myth.

In his 2006 book *Word Myths: Debunking Linguistic Urban Legends* (Oxford University Press), etymologist Dave Wilton takes the city of Chicago—and, yes, the *Tribune*—to task for buying into the Charles Dana story.

"It illustrates a very important point about urban legends: If they are repeated enough, they become accepted unconditionally as truth," Wilton writes.

Wilton points out that no one has ever provided a date for the supposed editorial or supplied any other convincing evidence that Dana coined the nickname. Wilton adds that Mitford M. Mathews' *Dictionary of Americanisms on Historical Principles*, (University of Chicago Press, 1951) cited a "Windy City" reference to Chicago in the *Louisville Courier-Journal* from 1887, before the lobbying for the Columbian Exposition began. *The Oxford English Dictionary* cites the same article. Neither mentions Charles Dana.

Tim Samuelson, Chicago's cultural historian, has doubts about Dana's role too. Though he hasn't specifically investigated the term, Samuelson says he has come across uses of the nickname "Windy City" for Chicago as early as the 1880s.

"Based on things I've seen in the course of other research, the concept predates Dana," he says.

Erik Larson says he knows there are various theories on where "Windy City" got its start, but he supports the idea of editor Dana's influence during the rancorous exchanges between New York and Chicago over the world's fair.

"Even if you're finding a reference from 1886 to 'Windy City,' you have to think, when did it become the name that everybody knew?" Larson says. "It's not just when something first became a name that people heard, but when it became a name that stuck."

Donald Miller, author of the landmark 1996 book *City of the Century: The Epic of Chicago and the Making of America* (Simon & Schuster), says he deliberately avoided getting tangled up in the nickname debate.

"I stayed away from this business because I could find no proof for the Dana story," he says. "I checked it out and found nothing I could go with as a reliable source."

In response to my inquiry, the librarians at the Chicago Public Library compiled a stack of *Tribune* articles, letters and editorials that mention Dana and the "Windy City" nickname. Several *Tribune* news clippings from the 1890s discuss Dana's bellyaching about Chicago's bid to host the fair. But there's no direct link between Dana and the nickname until a June 11, 1933, article in the *Tribune* titled "Chicago Dubbed 'Windy' In Fight For Fair of '93."

That 1933 article says Dana "fixed on us" the label by writing "day in and day out in his *New York Sun*" about "'the nonsensical claims of that windy city,'" but there is no specific text or date for the fabled Dana editorial coining the nickname.

The Library's file shows numerous *Tribune* responses in the 1890s to Dana's regular disparagement of the city. But none of those responses say Dana used the term "Windy City" for Chicago.

Still, the Chicago Public Library stands by the assertion on its website that Dana popularized the term "Windy City," even if he didn't coin it.

"A lot of these articles indicate that Dana was a ringleader in questioning Chicago's ability to host the fair," says Margaret Killackey, the library's press secretary. "'Windy City' didn't become a household name until after the Dana references. There had been isolated references to the Windy City, but a flurry of references in print show it was used repeatedly in many parts of the country around the time of the world's fair."

Killackey adds, "Should something new be unearthed, we would look at that information. As of now, we feel confident that the phrase was popularized after the Dana editorial."

The Encyclopedia of Chicago, published in October 2006, isn't so sure Dana should get even that much credit. Its entry for "Windy City" was written by Jonathan Boyd, an independent historian and lifelong Chicagoan. Boyd says the term had currency before Dana wrote his tirades.

"Chicago's exposed location between the Great Plains and the Great Lakes—and the wind swirling amid the city's early skyscrapers—lend credence to the literal application" of the nickname, even though the city "is not distinctively windy," the entry reads. It goes on to say that the city's bloviating boosters of the 19th century have historically given "metaphorical . . . power" to the name "Windy City."

The encyclopedia includes a picture of a newspaper clipping from the September 19, 1885, edition of the *Cleveland Gazette*, provided by the Ohio Historical Society, in which a roundup of news briefs from Chicago is introduced by the headline "From The Windy City."

Boyd says he was trying to capture the cultural significance of the term, rather than settle the nearly impossible question of who coined it and when. But he says the 1885 article was the earliest available example of its use when the encyclopedia went to press.

The closest anyone has gotten to the truth about the "Windy City" nickname seems to be the research of etymologist Barry Popik. He says the earliest examples of the moniker for Chicago meant both wind and windbags, and that Charles Dana had nothing to do with it. And he's sick of people who can't get it straight.

Popik, a consultant to *The Oxford English Dictionary*, spends his days working as a judge in New York City's bureau of parking violations. He spends his nights in libraries looking at old newspapers, microfiche and digital databases, hunting for early examples of famous nicknames and slang. Then he embarks on vigorous letter-writing campaigns to let everyone know what he has found.

In the mid-1990s, Popik set his sights on "Windy City," and started scanning hundreds of editions of the *New York Sun*—which was published from 1833 to 1950 (a new New York newspaper calling itself *The Sun* launched in 2002)—in the New York Public Library.

Popik couldn't find a single instance of Dana using the name "Windy City."

Then Popik started looking further back, and in other newspapers, traveling to the Library of Congress to search through them. He found a *Louisville Courier-Journal* reference to "Windy City" in 1886—one year before *The Oxford English Dictionary's* first citing. He found the 1885 article from the *Cleveland Gazette*, the same one used by Boyd in *The Encyclopedia of Chicago*.

Then Popik came across several examples from the early 1880s, in newspapers such as the *Fort Wayne Daily Gazette*, the *Indiana Progress* and the *Decatur Daily Republican*. Finally, Popik isolated a single source. "Windy City," he says, may have been coined by—drum roll, please—Cincinnati.

Popik found numerous references to Chicago as the "Windy City" in the *Cincinnati Enquirer* in the late 1870s and early 1880s. The oldest instance Popik has found is in the May 9, 1876, edition of the *Enquirer*, in a report about a tornado that hit Chicago on May 6. The headline read, "That Windy City." The Cincinnati Historical Society confirms his findings.

Popik says the *Enquirer* headline had a double meaning in its era of civic name-calling—when Chicago, Cincinnati, and St. Louis all vociferously claimed the right to be called the greatest city of the Midwest.

"The *Cincinnati Enquirer's* use is clearly double-edged," Popik says. "They used the term for windy speakers who were full of wind, and there was a wind-storm in Chicago. It's both at once."

The May 6 tornado may have provided a physical reason to use a figurative analogy. In its first report about the tornado on May 8, the *Enquirer* tastelessly quipped that the twister failed to damage the buildings in Chicago that "were so heavily weighed down with mortgages that no whirlwind could affect them." (Popik says the *Enquirer* also printed several jokes that said Chicago women had big feet; if you don't find that hilarious, maybe you had to be there).

"The regional cities in the period leading up to the Civil War and afterward are constantly poking each other in the eye," says Boyd of *The Encyclopedia of Chicago*. "They need to build themselves up and tear others down. Boosterism is the rhetorical mode of rivalry. It's trash talk."

Popik's findings have been available for years, posted at the

American Dialect Society and his website (www.barrypopik.com), published in the journal *Comments on Etymology*, and reported by the "Straight Dope" column of the *Chicago Reader*. Yet, to Popik's exasperation, the myth that Charles Dana coined the name "Windy City" circa 1890 goes on and on.

"These stories, you have to kill them," Popik says. "Not only kill them, but put a stake in their heart. You have to go to each individual source and say, 'That's not true.'"

Popik says if he were a history professor instead of a parking ticket judge, he would be taken more seriously, and the "Windy City" myth might have been settled by now. But a few authoritative sources back him up.

"He's completely right. There's no question about it," says Jesse Sheidlower, North American editor of *The Oxford English Dictionary*.

"Mr. Popik's references solidly establish that 'Windy City' was a Chicago nickname that preceded Dana and the fight to secure the world's fair," says Samuelson, Chicago's cultural historian.

"I wouldn't be surprised if the Dana quote does indeed exist," Samuelson says, but he adds, "Even if we had a specific reference to a Dana quotation, it's questionable what kind of role it would have played in giving 'popularity' to the term, since it was already in circulation as a Chicago-related reference."

Update: As of this writing, the earliest example of "Windy City" now on record is a reference from the *Milwaukee Daily Sentinel* in 1860, found in a database of 19th century newspapers by Fred Shapiro, editor of *The Yale Book of Quotations* (Yale University Press). The reference reads, "We are proud of Milwaukee because she is not overrun with a lazy police force as is Chicago—because her morals are better, he [sic] criminals fewer, her credit better; and her taxes lighter in proportion to her valuation than Chicago, the windy city of the West." Barry Popik says he is waiting for the latest release of the America's Historical Newspapers database, which will include Cincinnati newspapers dating back to the 1830s. In the meantime, Popik is tracking the latest developments on "Windy City" at www.barrypopik.com. In the fall of 2007, Popik wrote me, "That's where we are now. The earliest 'Windy City' cites are from Cincinnati or Milwaukee, and we're still waiting for the digitization process."

Yoda's syntax

THE FINAL installment of the *Star Wars* franchise is not only the end of a cinematic era. The completion of George Lucas' second trilogy will be the last hurrah for one of the most grammatically eclectic film characters of all time: Yoda.

From the moment Yoda first appeared in *The Empire Strikes Back* in 1980—assuring Luke Skywalker, "Help you I can," and warning him, "If once you start down the dark path . . . consume you it will"—Yoda caught our attention with his unique syntax, or system of word order.

Geoffrey Pullum, linguist and co-author of *The Cambridge Grammar of the English Language* (Cambridge University Press), can explain Yoda's strange way of speaking. His analysis may bring back some bad blackboard memories, but it goes to show that anyone can learn grammar with Yoda as teacher.

Take a look at this Yoda sentence from *The Empire Strikes Back:* "Through the Force, things you will see." To hear Pullum tell it, this sentence is a galactic grammatical feat. That's because it places the object of the sentence ("things") before the subject ("you"). In English and many other languages, the more natural word order would be, "You will see things."

Even before Yoda arrived on the silver screen, Pullum was keeping an eye out for this kind of sentence structure—which linguists call "object-initial" clauses—in human languages. "Until 1977, I would have said that no human language used that as the typical order of constituents in an ordinary, unembellished clause with no special emphasis effects. In fact I did say so, in print in 1976," Pullum writes by e-mail.

Later in the decade, Pullum discovered some obscure languages in South America that appeared to regularly use object-initial clauses, but those languages are exceptions. So whether he realized it or not, George Lucas stumbled upon a grammatical

265

stroke of genius with Yoda's word order.

"The one thing you could do to make your syntax seem quite strange to almost all the six billion people on this planet, no matter which of the 6,000 languages they spoke, would be to adopt [object-initial] order as the normal order of declarative clauses," Pullum said.

Yoda is actually a syntactical switch-hitter, alternating among object-initial sentences ("Rootleaf I cook"), subject-initial sentences ("A Jedi's strength flows from the Force"), and sentence fragments ("No different! Only different in your mind.")

Sometimes you will hear Yoda start a sentence with the kind of adjective that grammar textbooks call a subject complement, as in "Strong is Vader," or he will separate helping verbs from main verbs, as in "Help you I can."

"English allows this possibility but doesn't use it very often," Pullum says. "Yoda uses it at the drop of a hat."

When English speakers use this inverted word order, it's usually for special emphasis or rhetorical effect. They might say, "One thing I know . . ." instead of "I know one thing" or "Here I am" instead of "I am here." So Yoda's syntax could be a way to make him sound sophisticated, as well as extraterrestrial, says Mark Peters, who writes about language for *Verbatim* and *The Vocabula Review* and keeps a blog on words at www.wordlust. blogspot.com.

"In addition to making him sound like Kermit the Frog crossed with a fortune cookie, these Yodaisms mirror how Luke's world is being turned upside down (at times, literally, with the help of Jedi levitation)," Peters writes by e-mail. "If a green Muppet living in a swamp can be as smart and powerful as Yoda, and a mass murderer like Darth Vader can be Luke's (eventually) redeemable daddy, then maybe subjects, verbs and objects can play musical chairs too."

Peters adds that Yoda's name is itself notable to word watchers. He says "Yoda" is entering English as, in his words, "a synonym for teacher, mentor, and all-around . . . wise person."

"On *Buffy the Vampire Slayer*, Spike the Vampire says of older vampire Angel, 'You were my Yoda!'" Peters says. "I've complimented several excellent teachers I've known by calling them 'my Yoda' too, and I don't think Spike and I are the only ones. I predict more dictionaries will get with it and include 'Yoda' in the future."

INDEX

Index

Index

Index

Index

Index